The Secret Piano

The Secret Piano was first published in 2007 by Editions Robert Laffont as
La Rivière et son secret. Translated from French by Ellen Hinsey. Published
in English by AmazonCrossing in 2012.

Published by AmazonCrossing
P.O. Box 400818
Las Vegas, NV 89140

ISBN-13: 9781611090772
ISBN-10: 1611090776
Library of Congress Control Number: 2011916330

The Secret Piano

From Mao's Labor Camps
to Bach's Goldberg Variations

Zhu Xiao-Mei
Translated by Ellen Hinsey

amazoncrossing

Table of Contents

PART TWO: THE WEST

For my mother

This book would not have been possible
without the support of Michel Mollard.

Aria

My grandmother liked to tell this story:

"The evening you were born, I looked out at the sky over Shanghai. The setting sun was breaking through the clouds. I had never seen such a beautiful sunset. I remember thinking that your life would be a resplendent tapestry, just like that palette of reds. I was sure of it."

That was a few weeks before Mao Zedong's proclamation of the People's Republic of China. "Never again will the Chinese people be enslaved," he had declared on that occasion in Tiananmen Square. Rarely has a prophecy proved so true, and at the same time so false.

* * *

I hesitated a long time before telling my story.

My father often reminds me how useless it is to speak of the past:

"What does it serve, Xiao-Mei? When you die, you shouldn't leave a trace. Even if you want to, it's not possible. Your footsteps along life's path are always erased by the sun, snow, and wind." He likes to add: "Think of wild geese—they fly high in the sky, covering long distances without landing or leaving any tracks. Take them as examples, not the sparrows, which settle on the earth. The sparrow will never understand the dream of the wild goose."

He's right. For quite some time I thought I didn't have any particular reason to write—don't I express myself through music?

I even thought that I didn't have the ethical right to do so. Among the Chinese of my generation, my suffering was not the worst, far from it.

* * *

But, as is the case in life, every being, every thing has two sides.

And I wanted to write. First, for those who had fallen victim to the Cultural Revolution. Forty years later, not much is said about this period, and I have often noticed how little is known in the West about these events.

I have had the opportunity to live in both China and the West, in three different countries. Through this, I have learned a lifelong lesson: it is critical to bring cultures together, to initiate dialogue among them. I also wanted to describe this experience, which I believe to be particularly important.

This book is made up of thirty chapters—like the thirty variations in Bach's masterwork, the Goldberg Variations. *Thirty chapters plus an opening and closing aria, bringing the work full circle like time's continuum—like the wheel of life.*

I am often asked how a Chinese woman, brought up in such a distant cultural milieu, can play Bach. My hope is that after having read this book, the reader will understand and, above all, have the desire to listen, or re-listen, to Bach. I also hope that he or she will have the desire to read or reread Laozi, the great Chinese philosopher.

For these two sages are very much alike, and their two cultures—Chinese and Western—are not so dissimilar.

PART ONE

CHINA

1

The Solemn Hour

I have witnessed many men
Silently weeping
In the night
(Tang Qi, "The Solemn Hour")

There it stands, in my parents' bedroom. The room is so small it takes up all the available space. The movers had a real struggle getting it through the door, stopping a number of times, sweat running down their faces. Out of curiosity, the neighbors file into the courtyard one after the other to peek through the window and observe what is going on. Finally, it is in place. Freed from the dirty cloths it was wrapped in, it makes its appearance.

I fearfully take refuge behind a chair. My mother draws near, circling, looking, and examining it. She opens its lid, and a name appears: *Robinson*. Its ivory keyboard gives off a pale glow that illuminates the shadowy room. For a few brief seconds, my mother lets her hand pass across the small, yellowed keys. A melody issues from the piece of furniture, rising into the room. It can talk? A smile has barely crossed my lips when my mother pulls her hand back and closes the lid. The mysterious voice falls silent.

My mother turns to us and sighs:
"How happy I am—"

* * *

I didn't know what it was, a piano. I was barely three years old, and I had never seen anything like it. I was fascinated. I wondered where it had come from, this object that spoke when you touched it.

Strangely, my mother never played the piano. But every morning, she dusted it: her first act of housework.

"Such dust! In Shanghai, there wasn't so much dust. Why did you bring me here?" she would add, turning towards my father.

She never missed an opportunity to complain about Beijing. The weather was terrible, the city was polluted, and it was difficult to eat well. Sometimes in the morning when I got up, I had the impression that she had been crying. I would ask her what was wrong.

"It's nothing, Xiao-Mei. The smoke from the stove has gotten into my eyes," she would answer.

I watched her decorate the piano with paper flowers, the way in China one adorns the *jitan*, the altar to one's ancestors. In the house we didn't have a *jitan*, but we did have a piano.

I had the impression that the piano was just for me.

I would open its lid and randomly bang on its ivory keys for the pleasure of hearing the sounds fill the room. If I went to one end of the keyboard, the piano's voice sounded like a dragon. At the other end, like a bird. Very quickly, however, I felt powerless and gave up. That certainly wasn't music.

Sometimes, when other children came to the house, I would show them how to strike the keys, and the cacophony would entertain us for a while. It was amusing for us, but not for my mother. One day, she firmly shut the lid.

"OK, that's enough, I can't stand it anymore. You're hurting it—get out!"

And the piano fell silent once again. No one touched it: neither she, nor I, nor anyone. Still, it had become a new member of our household.

* * *

Our apartment: two rooms for seven people, just over five hundred square feet within a *siheyuan*—a low square of houses built around a small central courtyard. There was one water tap and one toilet for eleven families. Badly washed diapers hung from the windows. The floor was black and eternally damp, and the noise the mice made each night gnawing in the ceiling terrified me. Still, we were not the most unfortunate. The other residents of the *siheyuan* were even worse off, like the widow whose ten children all slept in one big bed.

We had lived there since my parents moved to Beijing to be with one of my father's sisters, nicknamed "Momo," which means "aunt" in Shanghai dialect. She suggested that my parents come and work in the small shop that she and her husband owned. They accepted, because there was no longer any place for them in Shanghai.

* * *

The troubles had started in the winter of 1949. The weather had been so harsh that, in Shanghai, hundreds died from cold and hunger. Each morning, the sun rose over new groups of emaciated, frozen corpses on the sidewalks. The civil war between the Communist Party and the Guomindang was over, but it had left the country in chaos. Administrative structures had collapsed, public transportation was often either blocked or requisitioned, and many companies had either gone bankrupt or were barely functioning. My grandparents' fortune had melted away like snow in the sun.

In the eyes of the new regime, my grandparents were flawed in almost every possible way.

My father's father had been a businessman who was fascinated by the West. By turns he had been a furniture manufacturer, a farmer, a tailor, a restaurant owner, a building contractor, and the director of a dance studio and a cinema. A simple desire to create, to take risks, had led him into all sorts of professions. Introducing Western customs, organizing an evening dance in 1920s China—could there have been anything more unconventional?

Where had this fascination come from? A mystery. My father, who was only thirteen when my grandfather died, was never able to explain it.

My mother's parents, the Shengs, had made a fortune in import-export. My grandfather had not learned English at school but he spoke it fluently because of his business affairs. They were steeped in foreign culture, which mingled with our own. Because of them, starting at a young age my mother was familiar with European art—she knew about

the finest paintings in the Louvre as if she had seen them herself.

With the Shengs' support, after their marriage my parents were able to move into a duplex in an elegant building in the former French Concession. Their windows looked out on a wide avenue lined with plane trees, across from Fuxing Park. It was decorated with rosewood furniture and porcelain vases, and the scent of camphorwood chests perfumed my mother's dresses. At that time, despite the damage done by the war, Shanghai was still a little Paris, refined and bustling.

* * *

However, everything changed during that terrible winter. The clinic where my father worked lost its patients, or at least those who could pay for consultations. It was forced to close its doors.

If my father had not had family obligations, he would no doubt have gone on working for free. He was a dreamer and an idealist—he still is. This was due to his years of study with an old Chinese master, whom my father patiently assisted on his rounds visiting the sick and on expeditions in search of rare plants in the mountains. It was also the result of my father's childhood. Because his mother died shortly after his birth, his older sisters had taken on the task of raising him.

My father—Qixien—was a strange child. He was never hot, nor cold, nor hungry. He seemed so incapable of expressing himself that there were doubts about his intelligence. Absolutely nothing affected him. Perhaps he had

withdrawn into himself after his mother's death, not wanting to know anything more of the misfortune that surrounded him. My grandfather, however, saw my father's condition differently. Such wisdom, and at such a young age! The greatest philosophers spent a lifetime trying to reach such a state of detachment, and here his son had already attained it. He paid particular attention to my father—care that his son repaid in full, and for a lifetime. Later, my father confided that during the worst moments of his life, he thought of his father in order to find the strength to go on.

Thus, my father would have continued practicing medicine free of charge, but he did not have the liberty to do so. He had a wife and three daughters to feed: me and my two older sisters, Xiaoru and Xiaoyin. Since he could not practice his profession, he had to give up medicine and take whatever job he could find—as an accountant, a sales representative—anything to support his family.

Then my parents received Momo's invitation to come to Beijing and work in their little shop. They accepted, and in the summer of 1950 we left Shanghai.

* * *

Our family came very close, however, to having a different destiny altogether.

It was a few weeks after I was born. My father had received several letters from his brother, Qiwen, who had moved to Taiwan. He had found work and asked my father to join him. My parents hesitated. The offer was tempting, but did it make sense? China had a new government; its leaders had noble ideas, they were honest and sincere,

anarchy was waning, and the future looked hopeful. On the other hand, was there a place in this new future for them?

Finally, they made up their minds. They bought tickets and were ready to depart when it was suddenly announced that leaving China was strictly forbidden. Their life was turned upside down: my parents did not go to Taiwan, and for more than thirty years the regime held Qiwen's departure against my father.

* * *

A few months after we arrived in Beijing, my aunt and uncle's property was seized. The People's Liberation Army had ushered in a new era in China: the first measures were underway to give the State control over companies believed to be vital to "the nation's economy or the life of the people." My parents found themselves without anything, in a city they barely knew, with three small children.

Fortunately, my mother quickly found a job as a music teacher in an elementary school. But since my father remained unemployed, the financial burden for the family rested entirely on her shoulders. Although her upbringing had scarcely prepared her for it, she found the inner strength to take on the multiple challenges of feeding us, keeping the house clean, and making sure we were educated.

* * *

My mother, whose first name is Ruying, was born in 1918, at a time when a Chinese woman was supposed to remain cloistered, and when her prime responsibility was to be a

"useful wife" and a "wise mother." "Too much learning is a dangerous thing for a woman's virtue," so the saying went. Girls learned only what was strictly necessary for keeping house, and most marriages were arranged, very often with an older man. In line with Confucian thought, the Chinese placed more faith in the virtues of a "union of reason" than in the odd Western notion of a Prince Charming.

But Ruying had other ideas.

Not only had she gone to school, but she had always been the best student—to such an extent that, when she was older, my grandfather was in the habit of consulting her regarding his business affairs.

Therefore, he shouldn't have been surprised when his daughter did not accept the rich gentleman he had found for her in Hong Kong. Ruying was stubborn and would not back down. She wanted to marry my father, although she had a number of good reasons not to—he was less wealthy than her, he was five years younger, and furthermore, he was a distant relative. My grandfather refused, and my mother dug in her heels. Finally, one day she left home. She disappeared for several weeks and was reported as a missing person. In the end, my grandfather gave in. My mother wanted a marriage based on love, and she got it.

* * *

As Mao was launching the first of his large-scale reforms, my sisters, Xiaoyu and Xiaoyen, the last of the children, were born and became the newest residents of our shabby little *siheyuan*. Five girls! In China, during this period, to have one girl was a burden, but to have two or three was an

embarrassment. Five girls without a single boy was a real problem.

I can see my mother after her return from the maternity hospital following Xiaoyu's birth. Her brow was hidden in a scarf, as Chinese tradition dictated; her face was white with fatigue, and there were dark shadows under her eyes. She looked like a ghost. Friends and colleagues filed through the house to congratulate my parents. I slipped into their room and approached the bed where my mother was resting. She was so tired that I wasn't even allowed speak to her. I thought she was going to abandon me—that she was going to die.

"Why are you crying, Xiao-Mei?" my father asked.

"I'm afraid Mama is dying."

"Everyone dies someday, you know that. But you also know that Mama is not going to die right away!"

"If I have to die, I want to die with Mama."

Worried, my father looked at me; he wondered how I could have such ideas at my age.

* * *

Luckily, my grandmother was there. She had come to live with us after the death of her husband. She was very beautiful, and had been born into an intellectual milieu. At the time, according to Chinese tradition, if a girl wanted to find a husband, she had to have very tiny feet. This is why girls' feet were bound when they were still children, in order to stop them from growing. But my grandmother's parents could not bear to witness the suffering this practice caused;

this is how she became one of the first Chinese women to be able to walk freely, and she was proud of it.

"But then how did you find a husband?"

She answered with a burst of laughter. One thing was certain: her large feet hadn't bothered my grandfather!

She knew how to read and write a little, which was rare for her era. Her judgment was sound, and she had a strong sense of authority. She was the type of capable woman one finds in many of the great Southern and East Asian civilizations. She had always been the pillar of our family: gay, spontaneous, and generous. Each time she took us out, she gave us presents, as if money were of no concern.

I shared a bed with my grandmother, which brought us even closer. Each night, she told me a story:

"Only one, Xiao-Mei."

Each anecdote was a joy, a light-filled moment.

She also told me stories about when my mother was young.

"She wanted to get her driver's license, and she succeeded. But since she had a rather dangerous idea of how to drive, one day, inevitably, she ran into a tree."

"And then what? Was she hurt?"

"No, but your grandfather forbade her to touch the car again!"

My grandmother laughed, and I laughed with her. Together, we forgot about our new life, about the gloomy walls, the tiny apartment, and the lack of money.

* * *

Why had our life changed so much? The answer can be summed up in one name: Mao Zedong.

Even as a small child, I knew who he was. His picture was everywhere. Thanks to him, I was told, China had been liberated. Since his triumph over the capitalist and imperialist forces, the lives of the Chinese people had been transformed. The victorious Communist Party had freed them from oppression and misery. A radiant future awaited us, one in which there would be neither rich nor poor, neither mandarins nor coolies. There would only be happy, well-fed workers and peasants, like the ones we saw in pictures. We small children should revere Chairman Mao because we owed everything to him. He was a father to us all, someone we should love even more than our own fathers. It was my parents themselves who told me these things; they were convinced they were true.

2

Mother's Library

I didn't know how to read,
Mother was my library,
I read mother
One day
The world will be at peace
Man will be able to fly
Wheat will sprout in the snow
Money will have no purpose
(...)
But in the meantime
Mother says
We have to work a lot.
(Lu Yuan, *Fairy Tales*)

A storm breaks over Beijing. The sky is black, and rain runs down the panes. My mother looks out the window. The courtyard is covered in mud. No question of washing the laundry outside, as she does at the end of each day. That will have to wait until tomorrow. Our evening meal is ready; our homework is done. It is so dark I can only make out her

silhouette. My mother lights a little lantern, takes me by the hand, and says:

"Come with me, Xiao-Mei, I'm going to play something for you."

We go into her bedroom: she lifts the piano lid and begins to play. Notes fill the air with an infinitely gentle music. The first piece she plays for me is Schumann's *Reverie*. Seated next to her, I listen with my mouth agape.

An entire world opens up. I have the impression that the music immediately belongs to me. Is it my grandparents' love of Western culture that I feel rising in me? Or the message of this work, whose profound depth and unassailable human truth has rendered it genuinely universal? I don't know.

My mother finishes playing. She turns to me. We look at each other. In this moment I believe she knows what I am thinking. I have but one dream—to learn to play this friend that has joined our family.

* * *

From then on, each evening when I return from nursery school, I open the lid of the piano and feel my way along; I explore. To occupy myself I try to pick out, with one finger, the songs I've learned during the day.

"You always play the same thing, Xiao-Mei," my mother says. "It's nothing but noise, and it's driving me crazy!"

But one day, when she comes to pick me up from school, she realizes that in fact this is a tune I am reconstructing.

She allows me to continue until she can no longer stand the repetitive melodies I endlessly hammer out. Finally, she speaks the words that for weeks I have been longing to hear:

"Xiao-Mei, I'm going to teach you how to play the piano."

* * *

Day after day, my mother taught me how to read music. But not as others go about it. She had a way of making chords, progressions, and transitions clear as if by magic. Each note stood for a member of our family: instead of going from C to G, I went from Papa to Xiaoru: it was much more enjoyable. Then we tackled Czerny's simplest exercises, scales, and arpeggios. She also had me play pieces from a collection known to every beginning Chinese pianist: *Piano Music Masterpieces*, published by Albert Weir. It contains simple, well-known pieces by the great classical composers. A favorite selection is "A Maiden's Prayer" by Tekla Bądarzewska, a piece whose name won't mean much to most readers, but is quite famous in China. No doubt, even if I returned after decades of absence, they would still ask me to play it.

* * *

My mother told me the story of her piano. As a young girl in 1930s Shanghai, she wanted to play an instrument, and her father offered to pay for piano lessons. Later, she attended art school, where she studied painting—the summit of Chinese arts—while still working on her music. The piano was a wedding present from her parents.

"Along with you children, my piano is the most precious thing that I have in the world," she said. "It has always been with me, through good times and bad."

It was because of the piano that she had been able to find work in Beijing in the elementary school—she brought the instrument there with her. Later she said her piano fed us, but at the same time, it revealed my parents for what they were.

"How is it that you own a piano?" my father's colleagues asked him.

My mother understood the meaning of this question: only the bourgeoisie, the *Chushen bu hao*—people with "bad family backgrounds"—would have been able to own such an object of capitalist luxury. Little by little, my mother fell under suspicion, but the school needed her to teach children music.

Finally, they acquired a piano, and my mother was able to take back her own. This is how it ended up at our house when I was three years old.

When I listened to my mother speak, I sensed that for her, this piano was much more than an object. It was a friend, a confidant.

"You know," she told me, "the emperor Kangxi, who some two hundred years ago was the first to own a piano in China, demanded that the instrument be hailed as a dignitary during court ceremonies."[1]

I also viewed the piano as if it were a person. When music rose from under my fingers, it seemed to me that the

1 Author's note: Kangxi (1654–1722). It was actually a clavichord or a harpsichord presented to the emperor by Jesuit missionaries.

piano was singing, that it was telling me something. When I touched its keys, it responded in kind. I adored working with my mother. She never scolded me; instead she instilled in me the desire to make progress. We advanced step by step: for her, it was better not to work too much, like not eating too much. This didn't keep her, ever the astute psychologist, from urging me on:

"Xiao-Mei, my students your age already play this piece."

She encouraged me to tell stories through music, to let my imagination soar. I composed little melodies, and my mother, who was good at improvising, accompanied me. These sessions of four-handed playing were the apex of happiness: all of a sudden the piano drew together its lowest and highest voices, and I had the impression of ruling the whole world. I never wanted to stop.

In contrast, everything around me seemed darker.

* * *

This included my father. I don't understand him well, and I understood him even less during this period. He was harsh with us, sometimes even violent.

"You must obey me!" he would thunder.

For him, children should follow the teachings of his master, Confucius, for whom "filial piety and respect for one's elders is the basis of humanity." As soon as he returned home, the atmosphere changed, became tense. We no longer dared to move or to speak. He flared up at the smallest thing.

One evening, my parents gave my older sisters and me tickets for the circus. We decided to return home on foot to

spare them the cost of the bus, and we arrived home later than expected. My father was waiting for us, enormously worried. But he didn't utter a single caring word. Instead, he began to shout at us and hit us with his shoes. It was something I never forgot.

The truth was that my father was suffering terribly from his situation. He had found work, but it was far beneath his capacities and his education, and he couldn't support his family as he would have liked. Deep inside, he loved us, but he never let it show. We, his daughters, feared him above all.

It wasn't until I had started to play the piano that I ceased to be scolded. Did the sound of the instrument cause my father to imagine a better life, like the one that his parents had once enjoyed?

* * *

My father is, above all, an honest man, to such an extent that it's pathological. When he began to teach me how to write, the first ideogram he showed me was "honesty":

He drew it for me before providing an explanation:

"Xiao-Mei, the cross at the top represents the number ten. Below, there are eyes, and in the corner to the left, a person. Ten eyes are watching you. That is honesty."

My father practiced honesty every second of his life. When he did the shopping, he would return with fish that

was not fresh and unripe fruit, for fear of depriving others. One of my earliest memories was hearing my mother say to him in Shanghai dialect:

"How foolish you are!"

The next time he came back from the market, I repeated this little sentence to him:

"How foolish you are!"

Everyone around me laughed. In the end, my father was forbidden to do the shopping.

* * *

My grandmother also passed on to me what was important to her. This is why, one day, she got it into her head to introduce me to the Beijing Opera. "To broaden your musical culture," she told me. But perhaps also as a way for her to escape her daily life.

The Beijing Opera is the height of accomplishment in the Chinese theatrical arts. The performers act, sing, dance, mime, and do acrobatics amidst magical sets. They devote their lives to their career, and their talent is based on a thousand-year-old tradition dating back to the Tang dynasty.

For the occasion, my grandmother had slipped a lily into the buttonhole of her jacket. Sitting next to her, filled with anticipation, I watched as the lights dimmed. The orchestra, which was next to the stage, played a drum roll followed by a furious clashing of cymbals. The actors appeared, spectacularly made up, wearing magnificent, sparkling, multicolored costumes. They began to sing, talk, and then dance.

A few minutes passed. I was completely confused. Why were they all jumping about, and why were all the female roles played by men? I looked around me: everyone in the audience seemed so happy. They applauded the actors while eating and drinking. Peanut shells littered the floor. "For the people, food is heaven," as a Chinese proverb says.

Today I'm able to understand it, and I'm moved by this way of appreciating art, which reflects a simple, ancient tradition and a natural way of living. But that evening, I saw it differently. I turned to my grandmother:

"I'm afraid. I want to go home."

"That's impossible! You don't know how lucky we were to get tickets!"

I shut my mouth and absently observed the show. But nothing caught my attention, nothing appealed. Before I knew it, I had closed my eyes, and a few seconds later I drifted gently off to sleep, roused occasionally by cheers that erupted at critical moments in the performance.

What a strange Chinese girl I was: moved by Schumann's music and put to sleep by the Beijing Opera...

* * *

My grandmother didn't always understand me, but my mother did.

During those moments we spent playing together, she too forgot everything around her: the damp, the dust, and the fatigue. But then she had to stop, start the laundry again, scrub and mend our clothing, and count and recount the money—which kept dwindling. For some time now, she

had been forced to weigh the food she gave us, in order to keep expenses down.

Every month we went to the Dong An market, the large market for Beijing artisans. For my sisters and me, it was a real outing, a great pleasure. We didn't know where to look first. Fabric, clothing, toys: we breathed in the smells and our eyes devoured the sweets. What we didn't know was that our parents used these occasions to secretly sell my mother's jewelry, which fell in value each day, because to wear it had become suspect. You had to have been bourgeois, *Chushen bu hao*, to have acquired such things.

Then came the day when my mother had sold everything of value. One evening, I heard my father ask her:

"What are we going to do now? We have nothing left."

"There's still the piano," my mother answered.

I felt my parents exchange glances, and then my mother said:

"But we can't sell it. Xiao-Mei plays it."

* * *

"Xiao-Mei plays it." For me, in 1955, this sentence had taken on a different, less joyful meaning. Gone the nursery rhymes and playful scales, the four-handed tunes practiced while laughing. I had just turned six, and my mother wanted me to take the entrance exam for the children's music school, a preparatory program for the Conservatory. She underestimated herself; she didn't think she was competent enough to be my only teacher.

I passed the exam and in the process discovered another world.

The children's music school was run with an iron fist; the professors were very exacting, too much so for me. I hungered for music, for discovery, and they forced me to work endlessly on the same few pieces. They weren't wrong, but the consequences were not long in coming: I went to my weekly lessons with less and less pleasure, and I neglected my exercises.

So much so that my teacher came to the house to complain about me. Our neighbors, always nosy, didn't miss a trick about the visit, and rumors immediately spread through the *siheyuan*: "Did you see, Xiao-Mei's professor came because she is not applying herself at school!"

My parents were mortified.

"If you don't want to work anymore, I will close the piano, but I hope you won't regret it," my mother said to me gently.

Since I didn't answer, she carried out her threat. Over the course of three weeks, I acted as if nothing were wrong. But my mother finally opened it up again. I couldn't stand it any longer.

I went back to work.

* * *

What my mother didn't know was what I was learning at school in addition to my piano studies.

To begin with, I learned that all students were not equal. There were those, like me, who came to school in clothes that were worn and mended. There were others who always had new clothes. There were some who went for vacations

by the sea, who took airplanes. And there were others whose only world was their little *siheyuan*.

There were the "young pioneers," who could be identified by the red handkerchiefs they tied around their necks. And others who weren't allowed to join the organization, for mysterious reasons.

Little by little I discovered that the well-dressed children who took airplanes were often in the young pioneers as well, and that their parents had high-level posts in the government or in the army of the New China. Other children had parents of whom they should be ashamed. This was my case.

This was the period of the Great Leap Forward, which had been launched by Mao Zedong. The goal was to make up for the country's economic backwardness: we had to catch up to Great Britain as quickly as possible. To meet the challenge, they said, we had to pull together, forget about bourgeois individualism, and put ourselves at the service of the people. All at once, classes were canceled and we found ourselves in the streets: our task was to gather all the iron implements we could find and bring them to foundries. In this way, even ten-year-old children could contribute to the collective effort of industrialization. Our lives revolved around the word *collectivism*. Each day we learned that it was paramount, even more important than family.

In order for collectivism to advance and for individualism to recede—and to put the spirit of Communism into our little heads—every Saturday morning we attended a session of self-criticism and denunciation. The principle was simple: our thoughts did not belong only to us, but also to the Party. We had to submit them, even our most private

ones, for judgment, because only the Party knew what was good or bad, right or wrong. In this way it could eliminate "contradictions among the people."

For us, it meant you had to report on who had behaved well during the week, and who had not. A name was read out. You gave your opinion: had he truly worked on behalf of the collective? Was he a good revolutionary? Those who were not in agreement spoke up: no, he is not a good revolutionary because he was lazy, he cheated in class.

These sessions were presented as a way to help us make progress. But we were so young. Mostly, we wanted to be accepted or we were afraid of being rejected. If our schoolmates criticized us, we felt ashamed, and we no longer dared look at them; we lost our friends.

The more time passed, the more we dreaded being seen as bad revolutionaries. And progressively, like all children, we were ready to do whatever was necessary to be loved and admired.

* * *

It was even more difficult for me than for the others. I was well aware that my parents were different from those of my schoolmates. My father and mother did not resemble the good revolutionaries found in books and on posters, or the ones our teachers endlessly described. I wanted to be proud of my father, but something held me back. He wasn't like other fathers. And yet, he had finally found a stable job as a university administrator. It was a good position, and the president of the university, Lao Xue, trusted him entirely. He even made it possible for my father to exercise his

original profession by allowing him to oversee the university medical service.

Nevertheless, a doubt remained in my mind. He had to be guilty of something if my teachers distrusted him. Moreover, he said it himself: my mother and he were ashamed of what they had been before the Liberation. They knew that they were *Chushen bu hao*—of "bad family background"—and that they should make amends.

Of course, if my parents were guilty, then I was as well. And then there was the piano. It also had a bad family background.

* * *

And yet, this same piano, which singled me out as guilty, allowed me to be admired. I was only eight years old, and I was being asked to give concerts. One day for the radio, another day on television, which had recently been invented. It was fun: spotlights shone on the piano, warming my hands. Technicians bustled around everywhere. They were nervous while I, entirely innocent, felt unafraid; I wanted only one thing: to please the public by playing "Red May" for them.

One time I was asked to play at the Imperial Palace in Beijing. I wasn't scared, but a single question obsessed me. What was I going to wear? This time I wasn't going to be playing for machines, microphones, and cameras but in front of an audience, more than a thousand people. I couldn't show up in my patched clothes. The knees and elbows of my clothing were mended with pieces of fabric cut from my mother's dresses.

I knew I was poorly dressed. Not long before, when we were rehearsing a play at school, the teacher had said to me:

"Xiao-Mei, you take the role of the beggar-woman. You won't need a costume."

I didn't say anything, but I returned home in tears. My parents tried to convince me that he was only joking, but I didn't believe them.

I didn't want to go to the Imperial Palace dressed like a beggar-woman. When I asked my mother to find me something nice to wear, she answered that she couldn't buy anything, that I was fine the way I was. But I kept pestering her until finally, with a heavy heart, she gave in and approached one of her students, a diplomat's daughter: could she borrow something for me? I tried on the clothes. The skirt was red, and the white blouse with puffy sleeves was made out of such fine fabric that it was practically transparent. When I went on stage that night I had only one thought: that I looked like a butterfly. I don't even remember what I played.

* * *

My mother didn't criticize me, but after the concert, when I was in bed, my grandmother spoke to me about the red skirt:

"You've upset your mother, Xiao-Mei. It's so hard for her to keep you dressed correctly. She spends whole evenings mending your clothes."

There was a brief moment of silence, and then she began again:

"I'm going to tell you an old Chinese story that will help you to understand. It's about a king who had a very old stable master. This stable master always knew how to choose the best horses for the king. One day, he said, 'My lord, I would like to stop working. I am too old, and I am no longer able to care for your horses.'

"'Do you know anyone who might replace you?' the king answered.

"'My lord, I have heard of a remarkable young stable master, but I have never met him. Perhaps we could ask him to choose a horse for you and in this way see if he is worthy to serve you?'

"The king accepted and commanded the young stable master to find him a new steed. Three months later, the young stable master presented himself at the king's court: 'My lord, I have found a marvelous horse. It is a thoroughbred, calm and light, and it parts the air without a sound.' The young stable master indicated where it could be found, and hesitated before adding, 'It is bay-colored, I think.'

"'Someone bring this horse to me!' the king proclaimed.

"His servants left and returned two days later, stammering:

"'My lord, we couldn't find the bay-colored horse. There was a horse, but it was black.'

"The king turned to his old stable master and said:

"'You are mocking me! How could your young stable master work for me? He can't even remember a horse's color!'

"The old stable master reflected for a few instants, then said to the king:

"'Now I know for certain that this young stable master is even more talented than I am. He perceives only what is most essential, and forgets all that is secondary.'"

3

First Teacher

To see the smallest thing, this is clairvoyance.
To remain gentle, this is the soul's strength.
(Laozi)

In the spring of 1960, I was admitted to the Beijing Conservatory. As it was a boarding school, I would only see my parents once a week and during vacations, but this did not worry me. Although I was only eleven, I sensed that a gap had opened up between us.

Nineteen sixty was the year that Chairman Mao's Great Leap Forward, which had been launched three years earlier, went terribly wrong. When implementing it, Mao had stated that the Chinese people were "poor and blank [...] but on a blank sheet of paper the freshest and most beautiful pictures can be painted." Instead of beautiful pictures, there was famine: twenty million Chinese starved to death in the years that followed. Officially, the cause was drought in the north and floods in the south—certainly not Mao's madness.

But I was not really aware of all this.

When I first saw the Conservatory that September, I had the impression that I was in heaven: its traditional

Chinese-style gate, its central courtyard, its majestic trees and fountains, and its five red brick buildings, which were so much larger and more beautiful than our *siheyuan*. The classrooms and practice rooms were located in these low, three-story buildings, as were the library and housing for both professors and students. An annex, an old printing office that had been converted into classrooms, was ten minutes away on foot.

* * *

Once the happiness and emotion of the start of the school year were over, I became disillusioned. The workload was exhausting. In addition to intensive music courses, there were general education classes. These were indispensable in case we failed our musical careers and had to return to the regular school system. And then, of course, there were the sessions of denunciation and self-criticism, which had become routine.

We worked at the piano like galley slaves, in little, closed rooms whose doors were fitted with a small, round window. Absorbed in my practicing, I would suddenly feel a presence at my back. When I turned, two eyes behind a pair of glasses would watch me for a moment before disappearing. A monitor.

The school's leaders also encouraged rivalry between students. The best pupils not only had the right to more classes, but also to better food. Only wind instrumentalists automatically qualified for such meals—it was thought that they needed extra energy to be able to work.

At night, forty of us slept in the same dormitory. Bunk beds were placed one next to the other, leaving just enough space to move around the room. The atmosphere was suffocating. One of the students who suffered most was Aizhen, which means "gentle truth" in Chinese. She was a quiet and somewhat solitary girl, poorly dressed, to whom no one paid much attention. A country girl. Since her parents lived far away in the north of China, she almost never went back to see them. One day, we learned that Aizhen had been taken to the hospital because of respiratory problems. She returned covered in lice, scratching her head from morning to night. After that, no one went near her.

* * *

Luckily, there was Mama Zheng. Since the founding of the Conservatory, this old man had looked after the students' health problems and the daily running of the school. Mama Zheng gave us his all; he never seemed to have time to eat or sleep. You could always see his little round figure bustling about. He had so many appointments during the day that there was a long wait to speak with him. But when you were finally with him, Mama Zheng knew how to be comforting and helpful. "Hot water is the best medicine," he never tired of saying. This made us laugh, but we all adored him. He was so devoted that, after the infirmary had closed for the day, he continued to give consultations in his little room, which contained only a single bed.

When I went to see him for the first time, I couldn't keep from exclaiming:

"But, Mama Zheng, where do you eat? You don't even have a table!"

One evening, when I was standing in line in front of the infirmary, I finally dared to ask one of my classmates:

"Do you know why is he nicknamed 'Mama'?"

I was told his story.

A long time ago, Mama Zheng had lived in Indonesia and was very wealthy. When Japan invaded China, he left everything in order to serve his native land. The Conservatory was in the process of being established. He donated his entire fortune to it, and then oversaw the first student orchestra—in which the youngest member was only five years old. Everything was in short supply, and he took care of the orchestra as he would have looked after his own children. He caught fish and scoured ponds for lotus roots to feed the students. He sheltered them from all sorts of harm. This is why, in affectionate acknowledgement of what he had done, the Conservatory's first pupils nicknamed him "Mama," and it stuck.

As soon as I could, I went to see Mama Zheng. I confided my eleven-year-old fears to him: I was worried that my hands were too small, and that I wouldn't be admitted to the program's second year. In addition, my wrists constantly ached. Playing the piano was a torment. He listened to me, massaged my hands, and reassured me.

* * *

It was the day of the final examination. With my wrists bandaged, I played my program, and when I was finished,

I turned to face the jury. Silence. Stern faces. The atmosphere in the Conservatory's auditorium was suffocating.

Then the remarks began: all of them unpleasant, disapproving. I stood facing the jury, waiting for it to be over, the sooner the better. Just then a professor, who had been silent up until then, asked to speak. He was a very young man with an athletic build and a thick southern Chinese accent. He gave the impression of someone who was there by mistake.

"Dear colleagues, excuse me, but I do not agree with you," he said. "I think she plays very well, and more importantly, there is something behind those notes. Let's talk it over."

I left the room so they could deliberate.

* * *

This professor, who had saved me by taking me into his class, was Pan Yiming. He had just turned twenty-five and a few months earlier had earned his diploma from the Beijing Conservatory. Inspired by some of his professors, he was drawn to the Russian school of piano playing. When you looked at him, you had to ask: was he really a piano professor? He didn't wear glasses, his hair was not white, and it was said that he was an excellent ice skater. Was it really possible to study seriously with someone like that?

During our first lesson, Professor Pan talked to me about my hands:

"You know, Zhu Xiao-Mei, there are two sides to everything, a positive side and a negative side. Of course, you have small hands, and that's not going to make it easy to play certain works. But small hands are the swiftest. This

works wonders with certain repertoires. You'll see, the negative can become a positive, just as the positive can also become a negative. I have known a lot of students who, because they had large hands, didn't bother to practice. To their detriment."

Was Professor Pan aware that he was opening up an entire world to me? He had shown me that a weakness can be turned into an advantage, and had given me back my confidence. That was the most important thing.

Right away, he diagnosed another of my weak points: I was completely tense.

"Which is the finger that controls all the others?" he asked me.

"I don't know."

"It's your thumb. If it is tense, all the other fingers will be tense, too. If it's relaxed, the others will follow."

Then he added:

"Stroke the keyboard, never strike it. It's not hard, as you seem to think. You don't have to fight it. In reality, the keyboard is soft and supple. Search out that softness, that flexibility, at the end of your fingers. Try to draw energy from the keyboard, not just transmit energy to it. Imagine you are kneading dough. Ask your mother to knead some, to give you a better idea. It's the same movement of the hands and wrists. You'll see, this will entirely change your relationship to the instrument."

Then he asked me:

"Where do you think the energy comes from when you play?"

"From the shoulders?"

"No."

"From the whole body?"

"No. It comes from the breath, the place from which life and the spirit originate. Try to breathe correctly, and take care that your feet are placed solidly on the ground and that your diaphragm is steady. You'll see that you are much less tense. If you are more flexible, in reality you will be stronger."

Professor Pan had just given me a lesson for life.

* * *

After that first encounter, Professor Pan decided to give me a two-hour lesson twice a week, instead of just once, as originally planned. Deep inside, he was opposed to Communist ideas of egalitarianism, according to which everything must be shared.

That was the beginning of two happy years for me, two years that made me forget all the rest: the organized competitions between students, the sessions of self-criticism and denunciation, everything. I lived for Professor Pan's courses; all week, I thought only of them.

What is more, his teaching went well beyond those four weekly hours of class. According to him, it wasn't enough to teach one's students; one also had to live with them. He took us to the mountains, invited us to dinner, gave us books, had us listen to records, and encouraged us to grow beyond the limits of music.

"To become a good musician, Zhu Xiao-Mei, one needs a great deal of culture, sensitivity, and a lot of imagination. I can teach you to play the piano, but I can't give you every-

thing. Read a lot; experience all you can. You'll see: it's essential."

I immediately began to read everything I could get my hands on: Tolstoy, Chekhov, Dostoyevsky, Balzac, Flaubert, Zola, and others.

In return, we, his students, did our best to respond to his magnanimity and to give him our best: our own generosity and our own high standards. He gave us the desire to play, to be artists, a desire that subsequently allowed each person, in his or her own way, to solve technical problems and to move mountains. I can't count the number of times that, after leaving his course, I worked six to eight hours without stopping, carried away by enthusiasm.

Professor Pan tried to develop the positive points he detected in my playing. This was the exact opposite of so many professors, who doggedly attempt to change everything about the way their students play, or who seek to mold students in their own image out of sheer egotism. He defined a few essential points that needed improvement, and focused on them. He chose composers who corresponded to my sensibilities and my technique. His philosophy of life, which was as simple as it was true, was based on the principle that one cannot change everything and ask the world of someone all at once.

"During a difficult passage where you must play fast and loud, first play slowly and loud, then fast and softly, make sure you are at ease, and then finally play it fast and loud."

He also took care never to block a student, again in contrast to so many professors. When I would play an excerpt, he never stopped me.

"Can you start over and play it through again?" is the most he would ask at the end.

I would stop in the middle of a piece, having missed a difficult passage:

"Keep going to the end," he would say. "It's not important, keep going. You have the responsibility to go right to the end. Think about your listeners. Be generous!"

Professor Pan had a rare virtue: he told the truth directly but didn't offend you in the process. His natural sensitivity allowed him to understand completely the meaning of a word or gesture.

* * *

When it came to pure technique, Professor Pan was mercilessly demanding.

"You know, Zhu Xiao-Mei," he told me during one of our first lessons, "the Chinese have a wonderful advantage: they are flexible by nature. This is essential for excellent piano technique and good tone. You must cultivate this asset."

The work he gave me was unrelenting. I reviewed all the basics of technique with him, playing the *Hanon* in every key, as well as the main volumes of Czerny, Cramer, Moszkowski, and Brahms. He also gave me Bach's *Inventions* and *The Well-Tempered Clavier* to work on.

"I want you to play all of this by heart. From now on, for each lesson, you must play a piece by Bach and two etudes from memory and with no mistakes. Try to memorize each of them from the very first time that you sight-read them."

Easy for him to say! At the very beginning, in the three days he gave me, I had great difficulty memorizing the

pieces, particularly Bach's *Inventions*. At night, after lights out, I would shut myself up in the toilets, the only place where there was still light after ten o'clock, and stay there until my eyes started to close. Essentially, Professor Pan was right: if you don't work your memory early, afterwards it will be too late. But it was a real challenge.

"If you are not attentive," he said, "you cannot learn how to focus. To help with this, you will write a short summary of each of my classes. You will show it to me, and then we will be able to evaluate if you were listening closely to everything."

Another day, he told me:

"You know, unfortunately I only have a few records. If I could, I would play opera for you, because to play the piano is to *say* something. That is something that a singer could make you understand better than anyone else. Instead, go and listen to the older children: observe how they play and take notes."

I followed his recommendations, and one week later I returned with several pages of comments concerning a dozen pupils who were entering international competitions. During the following class, he spoke the words that I will never forget:

"I read your notes and what you said about the need to have a sound, a presence, an engagement. Deep inside, you know what you like and what you want to hear. This will help you a great deal…You'll see, you are going to succeed."

It was also Professor Pan who, to help me concentrate, made me play with my eyes closed, which I still do today in concert.

The first time we spoke about it, we were working on Mozart's Piano Concerto No. 23 in A Major. When Professor

Pan announced that we were going to tackle this miraculous piece, I lit up with pride and happiness. I was the only student to whom he had proposed this. It was summertime, and the windows of the classroom were open. Below, my girlfriends listened to us: they would have done anything to take my place. That day, we rehearsed the beginning of the first measure of the slow movement for two hours: C sharp–D–C sharp, in dotted rhythm for the right hand, a small tonic chord for the left. All the desolation of the world in a few notes. Too fast. Too slow. Too loud. Too soft. Professor Pan was still not satisfied:

"That's not the right color."

Why was he talking about color? As far as I knew, the hammers of the piano hit the strings, and always in the same place. One could play louder or softer, fine, but how could the sound have a different color?

"Relax, Zhu Xiao-Mei, and close your eyes."

C sharp–D–C sharp. I sensed that it was better that time. Professor Pan said nothing. I slowly opened one eye.

"There you go," was all he said.

How many times did he tell me, "Close your eyes. You'll feel your hands better, you'll hear yourself better."

Professor Pan dreamed of scores in which differences of tone and touch were shown in different colors.

"That would be wonderful," he told me. "Imagine—the passages in B flat major would be in orange, just like I hear them."

Professor Pan also insisted on working the imagination. He often used poetic imagery. "Each note is a pearl in a velvet box." "Each note is a drop of dew on a flower at dawn."

Above all, he wanted me to always have an idea, an image, a story, or a feeling in my head while I was playing.

"Today, you aren't thinking about anything."

How could he know what was in my head? It was impossible. Was he some sort of magician?

"You can feel it, Zhu Xiao-Mei. The listener can hear it."

* * *

One day, when I played one of Bach's *Inventions* too dramatically, he burst out laughing. I wanted to please him, to thank him for everything he had done for me, and he guessed it:

"Be careful, that's not a good thing to do. You get up on stage, you want to please the public, and then you lose your way. Truth and error are very close to one another."

Seeing my disappointment, he added:

"A good pianist is like a good cook. He must have a sense of measure and proportion. Do you like dishes that are too sweet? Or too salty?"

"No, of course not."

"Do you like dishes with no seasoning at all?"

"Absolutely not!"

"You see, it's the same thing when you're at the piano. You need seasoning, but one that is neither too salty nor too sweet. Search for that balance, look for—" Here he stopped for a few seconds, as he often did when he had something important to say, and then he went on: "Look for the golden mean."

Another time, I was trying to impress him by playing a piece with particular brio, like the older students at the

Conservatory who showily lifted their arms throughout the great pieces by Liszt or Rachmaninoff. He turned to me.

"Why such drama today, Zhu Xiao-Mei? Do you think the music needs it? Do you really think you have to play the piano that way? Don't you think it's possible to play in a more sober manner?" And he added, "Do you know the story *'Hua she tian zu'*? It is the tale of a painter who drew a snake on the ground that was so lifelike that people thought it was real. By accident, a passerby stepped on the drawing. She began to shout, 'I've been bitten by a snake!' Those around ran up to see what was going on. Everyone began to laugh, and exclaimed, 'We've never seen such a well-drawn snake!' Soon everyone in the town knew about the drawing and the artist. The painter began to wonder how he could make his drawing even better. He decided to add feet. But when the passersby discovered the footed snake, they made fun of it: 'What a ridiculous animal!' And the painter fell back into oblivion."

I absorbed the lesson so completely that now, whenever I walk on stage, I am always worried that someone might think I'm putting on a show. I am reminded of the wonderful remark by Pascal: "The unfortunate thing is that he who would act the angel, acts the beast."

Those years spent studying with Professor Pan were happy times. Today, when I give my classes, I often think of him. He was a marvelous professor who stood at the crossroads of two schools of piano playing. On the one hand, there was the Chinese school, which favored flexibility, lightness, fluidity, and a calligraphic sense of the melody line, but also a distance from, and a control over, emotion. Then there was the Russian school, with its grand

gestures, Romanticism, powerful imagination, feeling, and generosity.

* * *

One day in the spring of 1963, when I was approaching my fourteenth birthday, Professor Pan said to me, smiling:

"Zhu Xiao-Mei, we must now start preparing for your first recital."

There was a rule at the Conservatory that one must regularly play in public, particularly during the end-of-semester examinations. But this was not enough for Professor Pan.

"In order to have a real feeling for the stage, you have to stay up there for at least an hour. And even an hour is not that long. You know, some Japanese dancers live on stage for several days before giving a performance."

Together, we chose the program: Beethoven's *Pathétique* Sonata, Mozart's Concerto No. 23, for which he himself would play the orchestral reduction, and Chopin's Etude Op. 25, No. 3. He warned me:

"You must be two hundred percent prepared. As Sun Tzu said: 'Invincibility is in ourselves.' If one is not ready to wage war, one abandons the idea. It's the same thing for a recital. If you are not sufficiently prepared, don't play. It takes too long to undo a bad experience."

And then he added, mysteriously:

"Pay attention to yourself as well. Obey."

What did he mean? I didn't dare ask him.

* * *

One Saturday night, a few days before the concert, it was very hot, and the dormitory was even more stifling than usual. I suddenly needed to get some air, to walk around the Conservatory. Three classmates went with me. We wandered around outside and along the corridors for a while, and then we decided for fun to secretly climb onto the roof of one of the buildings. It was pitch black. We neared the edge of the roof and, jokingly, I said:

"And what if I jumped?"

A few moments later, overcome by fatigue, we returned to get some sleep, unaware of the storm that was about to break.

Our little outing had been observed. The watchman had heard our voices on the roof. The next day, he investigated and uncovered the guilty party:

"It was Zhu Xiao-Mei. She wants to commit suicide."

I had been denounced by a classmate. Typical.

But I could never have imagined how far the affair would go. I didn't yet know that, in a totalitarian regime, suicide is the worse of sins, an act of rebellion that says: *No, I am not happy in your system; it is so harmful that I would prefer to die.* For the Conservatory hierarchy and that of the Party, the danger was clear: I might pollute the minds of my classmates. An example had to be made of me; every shred of individualism had to be rooted out of my small person.

In the hours that followed, the director summoned me, my three classmates, and the main professor for our class.

"What is their background?" she asked.

Two of my classmates were *Chushen hao,* "those of good family backgrounds." The third—whose father in 1957 had been viewed as an opponent to the government—and I

were in the category of *Chushen bu hao*, those of "bad family backgrounds."

"This explains everything," the director concluded.

Her daughter stood at her side. She had brought her in to show her the meaning of class struggle.

I attempted to defend myself: it was just idle talk, I had absolutely no desire to kill myself, I was very happy at the Conservatory and proud to be studying there. Nothing worked. Finally, it was discovered that I had written about *Anna Karenina* in my diary. About her suicide, the little red bag, the first carriage, and then the second…One evening, I had written, "This woman is magnificent. She is so different from the others in her way of being, and so courageous. If playing the piano doesn't work out, if my recital is not a success, I, too, will kill myself!" My case was a serious one.

* * *

It was decided that I should be isolated from the other students. I was led to a small office furnished with only a table and a chair, and I was locked in. From now on, this was where I would take my meals to avoid all contact with my classmates while my case was being decided. During this time, the students were asked to comment on my attitude. What did it mean? How should they understand it?

As the hours passed, my future began to look bleak. Not only was I a *Chushen bu hao*, I was also guilty of harboring bad thoughts. Professor Pan would refuse to work with me, I would be expelled, I would never play the piano again, I would be a political outcast, I would be exiled to the countryside, and my family and parents would be criticized.

Hadn't I proved myself unworthy of the trust Chairman Mao had placed in us?

Finally, I was summoned by the Conservatory's administration, and the verdict was pronounced:

"You must write and present your self-criticism. You will remain locked in until it is completed."

4

Downfall

Would you sacrifice the child that is before you
to put a revolutionary plan into practice?
(Dostoyevsky, *The Brothers Karamazov*)

Dear professors and students,
 I am very sad because I have betrayed your trust and disap-
pointed you. I have also betrayed Mao Zedong, our great leader,
and the Communist Party, which has given me the chance to study
in one of the best schools in China.
 On the evening of May 27, I committed an error. I did not
abide by Conservatory regulations. After lights out, at 10:30 p.m.,
I left the dormitory with three students. We climbed onto the roof of
the Conservatory without permission. Worse, once I was up there, I
said to them, "And what if I jumped?"
 With your help, professors and students, I understand that
what I did was a very serious error. For me, it is now clear that the
wish to commit suicide is a wish to protest against the government,
to oppose it, to not place one's trust in it. I am ashamed that I had
this thought.
 Everyone in China—soldiers, workers, and peasants—works
hard for the victory of Communism. The soldiers protect us from
capitalism. The workers and peasants work for us and feed us. As

for me, I think only of myself and my piano. I am egotistical and individualistic.

Thanks to you, however, professors and students, I understand why.

It is the fault of my bourgeois and capitalist family, which has always exploited the people. As Marx said, existence determines consciousness. The proletariat has a proletarian vision of the world. The bourgeoisie has a bourgeois vision. If we wish to change the bourgeoisie's consciousness, we must change its existence.

It was also the fault of my reading.

For a long time, I have read bourgeois literature uncritically: Tolstoy, Chekhov, Dostoyevsky, Pushkin, Romain Rolland, Balzac, Flaubert, and Zola. I was corrupted by the individualist example of Marie Curie.

In particular, I want to tell you that two novels, Tolstoy's Anna Karenina *and Romain Rolland's* Jean-Christophe, *have had a bad influence on me. With insufficient reflection, I committed the error of taking two individualist and petit-bourgeois heroes as role models. Capitalists seek to ensure their long-term survival, to shape the minds of their successors, by turning out such works of petit-bourgeois literature. Communists do not need to read them: it is enough for them to imitate soldiers, peasants, and workers.*

It was also the fault of Western music.

I lost contact with the proletariat and its struggles. I placed art and literature above the revolutionary ideal. I profoundly regret my mistake.

But today, I have decided to distance myself from my family and to fight these bad influences in order to profoundly change myself. I want to follow Mao Zedong, I want to follow the Communist Party and become a true musician of the proletariat. I ask forgiveness from Mao Zedong and the Communist Party. I ask for your

forgiveness. I am also counting on you to continue to criticize me and to help me change.

Zhu Xiao-Mei

I had just put the finishing touches on my self-criticism. The director of the Conservatory came into the small office where I was confined. Over the past three days, she had come to see me several times. "You should speak more about your family." "List the books that you have read." She read my text over one last time.

"That's fine. Now, we must all talk about it in a meeting, and you'll have to make your self-criticism in front of the others. The meeting will be held tomorrow at four in the auditorium. Because of you, all classes are canceled."

The auditorium! A few days earlier, I was preparing to give my first recital there: Beethoven, Mozart, and Chopin. Now I was being asked to give a very different performance.

That evening, I was given permission to leave my little office for the first time. It was the Conservatory's annual party. The students sang and danced around a big bonfire that they had lit in the middle of the sports field. Since I had been forbidden to take part in the festivities, I watched them from afar, alone in the dark. I didn't know what to do. I went back inside and tried to play the piano. But my mind was elsewhere, and my hands had been drained of their strength.

The next day, my heart in my throat, I walked to the auditorium. I wanted to get started right away, but at the same time I was terrified. I saw a hundred students coming from the Conservatory annex: they marched in step, in tight rows, singing a hymn to the glory of Mao. Everyone was there. On their faces I read incredulity, mistrust, and fear as

well. *She seemed so wise, Zhu Xiao-Mei, with whom Pan Yiming had rehearsed Mozart's Concerto No. 23. How had this happened to her?* Their looks were as sharp as daggers. I felt ill.

* * *

The session began.

"Zhu Xiao-Mei, we are listening. What do you have to say to us?"

Standing alone on stage, I stammered a few sentences right out of the self-criticism I had written. In front of me, sitting in the first row, I saw Professor Pan with a vacant look on his face. What was he thinking?

The Conservatory administration questioned me. Yes, I understood the seriousness of my error. Yes, existence determines consciousness. Yes, Anna Karenina is a dangerous bourgeois figure.

After an hour of this, the director joined me on stage and asked those present:

"Who would like to speak?"

There was total silence in the hall. No one uttered a word, as if none of my classmates had understood what I had just said. The director spoke again:

"Professors, workers, and students, Zhu Xiao-Mei now understands that she has committed a very serious error. But she wishes to change, and we will help her."

The worst was yet to come. As the hall was emptying, Professor Pan came up to me.

"You cannot play the piano well if, deep inside, you are hostile to the regime," he said. "I do not want to teach you

anymore. Self-criticism will be more useful to you than piano lessons."

What could I say? I broke down in tears and left the auditorium, defiled and crushed by the enormity of my shame. I had only one thought: to go and hide. In one week, everything had been destroyed. I had fallen from first place to last.

* * *

I wandered alone through the corridors, thinking of what would become of me. I had committed a serious error, that much I knew. How could I redeem myself? How could I renew my connection with Professor Pan, with my professors, and with my classmates? I was lost, alone in the face of a situation that was beyond me.

A group of students were joking in the courtyard; as I approached them, they stopped laughing. I wanted to join their conversation, but they scattered. According to a popular expression at the time, the regime "kills the chicken to frighten the monkeys." Unfortunately, this time the chicken was me.

As I didn't want to see anyone, I didn't go to the dining hall. I grew weaker and weaker. It had been two days, and I had eaten almost nothing. I watched the door of the dining hall from afar, waiting for everyone to leave. Then I would slip in, looking for a few scraps of food: there was nothing left. I began to feel faint.

I forced myself to return to the general education classes, avoiding people's gazes. It was then that I found a bit of food on my desk. Who had put it there? I didn't

touch it; it wasn't for me, there must be some mistake. But my neighbor to the right leaned towards me:

"You should eat," she whispered.

I looked. It was Aizhen, the girl who had caught lice in the hospital.

I asked her why she had taken such a serious risk.

"I don't understand why they did that to you," she answered.

Deep inside, I felt a rush of warm emotion. At least I had a friend.

* * *

The roof affair was not over, however. It would start up all over again. During sessions of self-criticism and denunciation, I endlessly went over my error. I had to listen to my classmates discuss it, comment on it, analyze it, and say how much they had learned from my bad example.

And that wasn't the end of it.

A particularly zealous student decided to write to Chairman Mao. She was from a family of government dignitaries, and wanted to explain to him what was happening at the Conservatory. She told him about the students who had made disparaging remarks about workers and peasants; how they judged them to be incapable of appreciating Western classical music. She informed him that there was a boy who styled his hair like Beethoven. That another listened to classical music on a stereo system. That yet another prostrated himself listening to Tchaikovsky's *Pathétique* Symphony. Finally, and worst of all, she revealed that a student had been on the verge of killing herself because of Western music.

The letter could have been lost among the many letters that Mao received every day. But it was returned, annotated in his handwriting:

This letter is very well written. We must solve this problem. Western culture must be put to the service of our country. We must develop our own culture.

Mao Zedong

The author was going to be received by Madame Mao herself, Jiang Qing. What we didn't know was that Jiang Qing was just then entering the political scene: it was the beginning of a career that would be remembered with fear.

As for me, I only knew one thing: Chairman Mao had judged my actions and my words—me, barely fourteen years old. How was this possible? How, amidst seven hundred million Chinese, could he have taken an interest in me?

In short, my plans collapsed; it was a life sentence. Every door would be closed to me forever. There was no question of attending university, finding a normal job or any sort of future life. Many Chinese in similar situations preferred to die. In my own circle, the guilty owner of the stereo system was the first victim. He left the Conservatory, moved to the country, and joined the army before committing suicide, overwhelmed by the weight of what he considered to be a grave error.

* * *

Actually, Mao's answer was part of a vast movement that, in 1963, heralded the arrival of the Cultural Revolution.

The first reports and instructions began to circulate about changes that should be made to art and literature to ensure that they served the Revolution properly. Soon, on the orders of Zhou Enlai, the Conservatory would be divided into two parts, with a department of Chinese music on one hand and a department of Western music on the other.

In reality, Mao—whom the disaster of the Great Leap Forward had forced, in his own words, "to withdraw from the front"—was waiting in the wings, and took advantage of the economy's relative recovery to attempt to regain power. To do so, he understood that he had to isolate his political enemies and dismantle the Chinese state apparatus. He did so by calling directly on the people, in particular on the young, for whom he was a living god.

In the midst of these political struggles, I was only a tiny pawn, easily manipulated. Why me? Because of my bad family background, or because I had been arbitrarily chosen—something characteristic of all totalitarian regimes? Whatever the case, I had little idea of the consequences.

5

From Mozart to Mao

If our writers and artists who come from the intelligentsia
want their works to be well received by the masses,
they must change and remold their thinking and their feelings.
Without such a change, without such remolding,
they can do nothing well and will be misfits.

(Mao, "Talks at the Yenan Forum on Literature and Art")

The trucks into which the professors and students had been packed rolled along the dusty highway. All we could see were fields stretching to the horizon.

It was the beginning of the *Shang shan xia xiang* movement. Its goal was to send students into the countryside in order to radically change their way of thinking.

"Over this summer vacation, we will have the chance to help the peasants with their work, and to practice our art in their service," announced the Conservatory's director.

As we bounced along the road, everyone was enthusiastic, especially me. I saw this as a way to redeem myself, to reclaim my place in the group, to win back people's trust…I promised myself that I would behave in an exemplary manner. I couldn't stand being an outsider anymore.

Finally we arrived at the little village where we would live. We drove past a large drawing of Mao, next to a blackboard on which a maxim from the Great Helmsman had been written in chalk. The portrait, which had to have been done by one of the locals, was not particularly skillful—its subject was barely recognizable. Then the trucks turned onto the village's main street, which consisted of a large group of *siheyuan*. The peasants were dressed in rags, and their children went unclothed. Chickens cackled everywhere. I had never seen such filth and misery.

For most of us, this was our first experience in the fields, and the shock was enormous. And yet, compared with other intellectuals who had been sent to the countryside to follow the rule of *san tong*—i.e., the "three withs," to "eat with, live with, and work with the peasants"—we received special treatment. Starting at dawn, we helped the peasants in the fields all day, and we slept in their houses on huge, flea-infested straw mattresses, but we took our meals separately. The work was hard. The more time passed, the more my admiration grew for these people who had devoted their entire lives to the earth.

At night, among ourselves, during our sessions of denunciation and self-criticism, we drew on these experiences. We commented on "Talks at the Yenan Forum on Literature and Art," a famous text by Mao from 1942, and on one passage in particular, in which he declared:

> *But after I became a revolutionary and lived with workers and peasants and with soldiers of the revolutionary army, I gradually came to know them well, and they gradually came to know me well, too. It was then, and only then, that I fundamentally*

changed the bourgeois and petit-bourgeois feelings implanted in me in the bourgeois schools. I came to feel that compared with the workers and peasants the unremolded intellectuals were not clean and that, in the last analysis, the workers and peasants were the cleanest people and, even though their hands were soiled and their feet smeared with cow dung, they were really cleaner than the bourgeois and petit-bourgeois intellectuals.

Inspired by these lines that we knew by heart, we discussed the best way to definitively join the proletariat, and to create an art that truly served workers, peasants, and soldiers.

Towards the end of our stay, a session of *Yi ku si tian* was organized for us: a peasant joined us in order to "remember the sufferings of the past and to evoke today's happiness." This meeting, which was followed by many others, would remain forever imprinted on my memory.

There were about sixty of us, gathered around a rickety table in a small room lit by dirty neon bulbs. An old woman came in. Her face was deeply lined, her hands calloused, and she had tiny feet. She smiled at us—she had lost nearly all of her teeth. One by one, we greeted her. She had a kind word for each of us, and a smile that was full of humanity. She was curious about all the new things that we had brought with us. "What do you have there?" she asked me, pointing to my little transistor radio.

And then we sat down to eat. While we shared her meal—a completely inedible gruel—she told us her story.

She had been born seventy years ago. From a very young age, she worked for a landowner from morning to night for

no wages. He gave her a bit of bran for food. In winter, to keep warm, she had no choice but to plunge her hands and feet in cow dung. One day, her mother fell ill; nevertheless, the landowner demanded that she continue to work in the fields. She saw her mother collapse: she ran over—her mother was dead. One of her little brothers starved to death before the age of ten. She was married at sixteen, and lived with her husband in such poverty that they had to sell off one of their daughters as a domestic servant.

At this point in her story, the old woman began to weep. She could not go on. No one dared say a word. We were moved to tears. How could such things have happened? How could they have existed? We did what we could to comfort her. Had her situation improved? Yes, she said, thanks to Chairman Mao, her life was better today. She was no longer exploited; she had recovered her dignity. She owed everything to the Great Helmsman and the Communist Party. She stopped crying and stood up, proclaiming in a voice that quivered with emotion:

"Long live Mao!"

The next day, we discussed at length the lessons we could glean from the previous evening. The old woman's story had touched us deeply. It was unacceptable that a human being could be so exploited; no one could deny that her condition had improved.

* * *

As the date of our departure drew near, we prepared a little concert for our hosts. The news spread, and spontaneously, processions of peasants came from dozens of miles around

to hear us. The village was crowded with people, and the audience, hungry for music, applauded wildly.

* * *

As we took our leave, we were all convinced that we had been transformed by our stay. The peasants cried when they saw us climbing onto the trucks that would take us back to Beijing. We were also in tears, convinced that what we had just experienced would help change the world and make it a better place.

In the truck on the way back, I thought about what I had learned in the course of this month of *Shang shan xia xiang*, and during the evening of *Yi ku si tian*. I thought about how hard it was to work the fields, and how essential it was for feeding China. About the generosity of the peasants. I was overwhelmed. I told myself that I was not living in the real world. I only thought about playing classical music, but it meant nothing to these peasants. The proof? During our farewell concert, the only classical work we played was a short piece by Grieg. The rest of the program consisted of popular works.

* * *

A few weeks later, the school year started, and I resumed my studies at the Conservatory. Thankfully, the memory of my errors had begun to fade. The summer holidays and our stay in the countryside helped; no new catastrophe had occurred. Also, I had behaved in an exemplary manner.

But the start of this school year was not like those in the past. Individual classes were replaced by group courses

in which all students, regardless of level, had to study the same works. My new professor, a Party member chosen by the Conservatory's administration, gave us mostly Chinese music to practice.

During the sessions of denunciation and self-criticism, the discussions became increasingly animated. We were pre-occupied—even obsessed—by two main questions. Should we perform music that really served the masses, or class-oriented music? Should we try to educate people by bringing them classical music or play music that they spontaneously enjoyed?

* * *

Over time, my outlook changed and altered. I understood better what was expected of us, and I was becoming a better revolutionary. I could feel it.

And the more I felt it, the more ill at ease I was with my family. I clearly saw that my parents could never become good revolutionaries. And I hated them for it. I hated them for their bad family backgrounds, which were the source of all my troubles. My father became increasingly self-effacing, saying nothing. After my self-criticism, his only reaction was to forbid me to read, on the recommendation of the Conservatory's director. I couldn't keep from expressing my hostility, even my contempt. When I came home on Sundays, I never smiled. My mother cooked my favorite dishes; I never thanked her. One day she came to the Conservatory to invite me to go to the theater with her. I refused. And yet, as I watched her walk away, I felt a pang. What had I done? How could I cause her such sorrow? But

I was doing just what was expected of me. The new China would never be built unless the children of bad family backgrounds disowned their parents.

* * *

In 1964, everything changed.

We returned from our winter holidays. This time, we had spent them with workers in a steel mill, and it had reinforced our belief that we were serving the wrong cause with our music. We resumed our discussions about our role in society with a vengeance. Yes, Western classical music was for the elite. And what was more, who among the peasants, workers, and soldiers really liked it? A tiny minority. Yes, we had to play music, popular songs, ones that the people appreciated and understood. This would be our contribution to serving the revolutionary ideal. Our talks became impassioned. We took turns speaking:

"Classical music is bourgeois. It was not written for the people!"

"Beethoven was an egoist."

"All his life Bach wrote for the Church. Do you believe in the story of Mary, the mother of Christ? No? Well, he wrote works about her!"

"Chopin was nothing but a sentimentalist."

"And Debussy was an idealist."

Only Mozart escaped this bonfire of criticism. I never really understood why. No doubt this was additional proof of his genius.

A few months later, we were all convinced: from now on, we had to play genuinely proletarian music and to perform

it in the countryside, in factories, and in military camps. I went a step further than the others: I wanted to change my life, stop playing the piano, and become a soldier. I wanted to be a real revolutionary! We were shown examples of young university students who had gone to live in rural areas. Among them was one of my cousins—I idolized him. Many were *Chushen bu hao* students who had severed ties with their families. One of my schoolmates had disowned his mother and had gone in search of a new one, in a factory or in the countryside.

By late spring, events had begun to accelerate.

The Little Red Book had just been published. Purges in the literary and artistic world began. We divided our summer break between a new *Shang shan xia xiang* and a few weeks of vacation before starting at the Conservatory again. On the first day of classes, the director informed us of instructions she had received from the Ministry of Culture. From now on, we would no longer play Western classical music. Only a few volumes of technical exercises would be tolerated— Czerny, Hanon—but nothing else.

Like my other schoolmates, I was neither surprised nor distressed. It was a logical decision. We were prepared for it. In the course of a year, the vast majority of the four hundred students and professors of the Beijing Conservatory had been completely turned around in their thinking. We were now convinced that we should put Bach, Mozart, and Beethoven behind us and only play authentically proletarian music. Mao could be proud: he had accomplished something that no one in history had dared to imagine.

* * *

Under such conditions, life at the Conservatory no longer resembled anything coherent. Without scores, music classes no longer had any reason to exist. Mao had invented a "Conservatory without music." The only classes that were still held were those of general education, as well as denunciation and self-criticism sessions. We discussed the new heroes that the regime provided as examples, first and foremost Lei Feng, a young soldier who had died in 1962 after a life devoted to the revolutionary cause. We read his journals with fervor, and by so doing followed Mao's slogan: "Learn from Comrade Lei Feng." Every day we asked ourselves how we could best imitate his example by attempting, in turn, to come to the aid of our family and friends. We were told that Lei Feng had drawn his strength from a close reading of Mao's writings. It was through his ceaseless study of them before taking any action that he had been able to attain such a level of perfection. I was captivated: Lei Feng dominated my life.

New forms of interpersonal control were put in place. The regime sensed that the relative idleness of several hundred musicians, most of them from bourgeois backgrounds, was a dangerous thing. Each one of us was therefore obliged to be part of a two-person "red team," where each person criticized the other in order to help him or her progress. The composition of these teams was carefully worked out to match good revolutionaries with those who were less so. To avoid any collusion, the teams changed frequently.

* * *

However, the situation created by the ban on Western music soon became untenable. In the autumn, the professors decided to collectively write a certain number of compositions. At least that way we would have something to play. The works that emerged a few weeks later were inspired by scenes from the life of peasants, workers, and soldiers. The titles included *The Little Shepherd, Return from Shooting Practice,* and *The Wheat Dance.* The most cheerful of them all was *Return from Shooting Practice.*

The scores were dreadfully difficult: using a pentatonic scale, they forced us to rework whole areas of our technique. For months, the "Conservatory without music" resounded with this handful of works that hundreds of students played at the same time.

Concurrently, the administration decided to teach us to dance and to train us in the performing arts. This was so we could participate in the staging of the *Yangbanxi,* the "model works" that Madame Mao—whose political role continued to expand—had decided to commission to compensate for the enormous gap left by the ban on the great Western works. The *Yangbanxi* dominated the programs of every concert given in China, no matter what the venue, whether it was a theater, soldier's camp, factory, or countryside; and the students from the Conservatory had a duty to promote them. For me, it was a form of torture: physically awkward, I was nevertheless obliged to, by turns, dance, sing, recite, and play the piano. Once again I was severely criticized: if I was incapable of dancing, it was because I didn't have a real feel for the proletariat.

It goes without saying that under these conditions, any competitive spirit and drive for success disappeared. How

one played was now of secondary importance: the only thing that mattered was one's political behavior.

At the end of 1964, intensification of the class struggle had become the battle cry. Mao demanded that we, the young people, never forget it. The term "Cultural Revolution" was heard for the first time. The whole of 1965 was spent between the monotonous life of the "Conservatory without music" and an increasing number of *Shang shan xia xiang* in the countryside, factories, and military camps. Beneath an outer calm, the storm was brewing.

6

This Piano Was Acquired by Exploiting the People

To all revolutionary intellectuals,
Now is the time to fight.
Let us unite.
(*Dazibao* of 1966)

The East is red
The sun has risen.
Mao Zedong has appeared in China.
He is devoted to the people's welfare.
He is the people's great savior.
(Anthem from the Cultural Revolution)

Early one June morning in 1966, the music that woke us was louder than usual. Jolted from sleep, I sat straight up, filled with a sense of foreboding. We were scarcely out of bed when we were instructed to assemble in the Conservatory's auditorium.

"Professors, workers, and students," our director began, as an article from that day's newspaper was being handed

out, "we have just received some very important news. Please read this immediately. We must discuss it."

The article was a reprint of a *Dazibao*[2] that had been written a few days earlier by a certain Nie Yuanzi, a philosophy professor at Beida, Beijing's largest university. In the article, Nie violently denounced the university's rector and the municipality of Beijing, accusing both of being revisionists. To defend the Cultural Revolution, she called upon the Chinese people to take up arms.

The reaction in the hall was one of astonishment. The Revolution was in danger! Discussions continued afterwards outside, and we met to examine Nie Yuanzi's article in greater depth.

Each time someone began to speak, I couldn't keep myself from trembling: someone was going to accuse me, I was sure of it. My father had hidden something about his past, and it would be revealed; I'd be thrown into the abyss. I tried to calm myself down. We had to trust in Mao, he was right, he was *by definition* right. It couldn't be otherwise.

But the target was someone much more important—the Conservatory's director. I was overlooked that day. The few students who had taken charge of the discussions insinuated that she might be a revisionist and an anti-revolutionary. The Conservatory immediately split into two groups: those defending the director and those opposing her. I joined the ranks of the supporters. The person who had made me write my self-criticism, who accompanied us on every *Shang shan xia xiang*—how could *she* be against Chairman Mao?

2 Literally, "big-character poster." During the Cultural Revolution, *Dazibaos* were one of the most frequently used means for denunciation.

This was explained to us: because of the Conservatory's leadership, we had received a bourgeois education, which had cut us off from the lifeblood of the New China—its peasants, soldiers, and workers. The sentimentalism of the works we had been taught had led us to become egotists, concerned only with elitism. We had forgotten about class struggle and had placed ourselves above the proletariat. In doing so, we had jeopardized the central goal of the revolution: to bring dignity and well-being to the oppressed. Hence, we had been trained to be enemies of the revolution and thus enemies of the people.

Wasn't this in fact true? we asked each other. I thought back to the old peasant woman who had suffered so much in her youth, and her gratitude to Chairman Mao for everything he had done for her. Under the erroneous guidance of our professors and their admiration of foreign music, we were in the process of cutting ourselves off from her, and didn't people like her matter the most?

The agitation grew. *Dazibaos,* denunciations, insults, and abuse: the extremist students progressively took over, organizing meeting after meeting, fanning the flames. Most of them were from high-ranking Communist families and had been admitted to the Conservatory based on their political merits rather than on their talent. They were excellent students when it came to general subjects, but their lackluster musical gifts put them in an uncomfortable position with the best of our music professors.

The very professors who were to be targeted next.

We were told to gather on the sports field. When I arrived, I saw our teachers on their knees on the running track, surrounded by Red Guards.[3]

"Comrades, here are the guilty ones!" yelled a Red Guard.

He turned towards them:

"You are all bourgeois intellectuals. Because of you, professors, the Conservatory is betraying the Revolution. Because of you, this place has become a temple of elitism. Because of you, a student attempted to commit suicide!"

My heart nearly stopped. I thought he was going to ask me to step out of the crowd. But no, he continued his litany of insults. I caught my breath while the Red Guards required each professor to deliver a self-criticism. They were forced to bow ever lower before us. When the oldest ones attempted to straighten up, a blow to the neck pushed them to the ground.

"That's not enough! Delve deeper! You are hiding things. Give us details!" they shouted at each person in turn.

Then the violence escalated: the Red Guards took off their belts, swung them above the kneeling professors, and struck them. The buckles scraped, cut, and dug into them.

From a distance, I could see the men and women on their knees. By now, most were bleeding. A violin instructor's head had been gashed open. He was bald, and the blood dripping from his wounds turned his head completely red. He looked close to death. I was afraid, but at the same time I was ashamed of my fear. To bolster my courage, I thought

3 Author's note: Officially, the movement was born on August 18; these are radical students who after August 18 would become Red Guards. See next chapter.

constantly of the face of the old, oppressed peasant woman. One had to choose between classes—that was the law of the Revolution. I chose to side with the oppressed over the bourgeois and the petit-bourgeois. The bloody scene horrified me, but this was the price one had to pay for New China's future.

The bloodbath went on and on. Each self-criticism ended with blows and wounds.

"He is guilty," one of the Red Guards decided.

"He is guilty," we had to reply in unison, before endlessly shouting, our fists in the air: "Long live Mao and the Revolution!"

I saw Professor Pan in the crowd. He was too young to be on the running track with the other professors, but he no doubt sensed that his time would come. The self-criticism session came to an end. The Red Guards doused each professor in ink, then flour and water, before parading them in front of us as we shouted:

"Long live Mao and the Revolution!"

* * *

In the days that followed, the violence spread. We lashed out against the teaching staff. We wrote one *Dazibao* after another, each day searching for something new to say, whether it was based on fact or not: "It is our professors' fault that we have had a bad education!" "The father of our Russian professor translated Chiang Kai-shek!"

Professor Pan was no longer spared. A number of *Dazibaos* found fault with him. "Pan Yiming has given us a bourgeois education. He invited us to his home. We ate bourgeois

food there. He took us traveling." "Pan Yiming had us work on Chopin's Ballade No. 2. He told us, without criticizing it, that the piece was inspired by a poem composed by the Polish bourgeois intellectual Adam Mickiewicz." We wrote so many *Dazibaos* that there was not enough room on the walls for them to remain posted for more than a day.

Our professors were paraded all day long in the school's courtyard or made to clean the toilets. The most senior among them were suspected of collaboration with the old order; they suffered the worst abuse. Our teachers no longer dared speak to us, and fled when they caught sight of a student. We no longer addressed them, either. When I met Professor Pan, I didn't say anything and pretended I didn't know him. Now I understood that what he had given me was nothing compared with the damage he had inflicted by educating me to be an intellectual.

* * *

Some didn't survive. Like a number of other major Chinese intellectuals, two piano teachers from the Shanghai Conservatory—Gu Shengying and Li Cuizhen—decided to take their own lives.

After having been beaten and humiliated in public, Gu Shengying killed herself, along with her mother and brother. It was rumored that she had turned on the gas, sat down at her piano, and played Chopin's Funeral March. The news of her death came as a terrible shock. She was a very beautiful, delicate woman who had performed at the very first concert I ever attended. That evening, she had interpreted Chopin's Scherzos with simplicity, fluidity, and

lightness of touch. As I listened, I had made a wish: one day I hoped to be able to play like her.

She was followed by another legendary musician: Li Cuizhen. When I was very young, people often asked: "Do you know who is the only Chinese pianist to have all of Beethoven's thirty-two sonatas and Bach's *Well-Tempered Clavier* in her repertoire?" She had dedicated her life to music, and was a role model for us all. She had put on her loveliest concert attire—in which she had given so many magnificent concerts—and ended her days.

Why would such a great artist refuse to take the path that was leading us to socialism? Why hadn't she trusted in Chairman Mao? Her choice was a sign of cowardice. Every day, at each meeting and in each self-criticism session, we were told: the Revolution is in grave danger, the class struggle must continue. If not, the traitors of the proletariat will reestablish the old order. At sixteen years old, the only thing I could do was to believe this. It was a question of survival, but also one of ideals: at that age one yearns to give oneself, body and soul, to a great cause. And wasn't the well-being of the proletariat a worthy cause?

* * *

The Conservatory had drifted into such a state of anarchy that the Central Committee decided to step in. I was on the front lines, standing at the school's entrance, when twenty soldiers arrived to reestablish order. We cheered them on, calling out our encouragement. The army had now become my role model. I admired them—the *Chushen hao*, those with "good family backgrounds"—they were courageous,

dedicated, and selfless. I was impressed by their uniforms. For me, like many others who were followers rather than leaders, the fact that the military had taken charge of the Conservatory was more than just reassuring: it was an honor. We were immediately told to assemble in the auditorium for a meeting. A soldier urged us to see reason:

"Order must be restored here! Students, you are not solely in charge of the Revolution!"

A semblance of calm was restored. Each class was placed under the authority of a soldier. To calm the extremists' enthusiasm, the army interrogated them about the details of their own activities over the "last seventeen years"—as the expression went—that is, since 1949.

But the lull in the storm was short-lived. A new rift appeared, between those who supported the soldiers and those who opposed them. The latter maintained that the army's intervention was anti-revolutionary. They wrote to Madame Mao, accusing the military of stifling the Revolution. Mao himself took the students' side, proclaiming that investigations into what they had done in the "last seventeen years" should stop; the only thing that mattered was their support for the Revolution today. A few days later, an order from the Central Committee came down: the soldiers were to vacate the premises.

One by one, I was deprived of my reference points: first the director, then the army...Clearly, I didn't understand a thing about either the Revolution or the class struggle. I was tired of always being on the wrong side, losing each battle, making a mess of everything. My friends kept repeating that Mao was always right, that the best strategy was to follow him, even if it wasn't always clear where he was leading

us. So, we followed. It was the safest way—the only way—to reassure ourselves. We had to go forward, abandon music, heed Chairman Mao's call, and seize the initiative of the Revolution.

* * *

The soldiers' departure foretold disaster.

In late July, a directive from the Ministry of Culture ordered the suspension of all classes at the Conservatory. The "Conservatory without music" became the "Conservatory without teaching."

Soon after, it was announced that Mao was going to deliver a key speech in Tiananmen Square. Before hundreds of thousands of frenzied young people brandishing *The Little Red Book*, a group of students presented Chairman Mao with an armband with "Red Guard" written on it. By accepting it he officially gave the movement his blessing. The most extremist students at the Conservatory now believed they had taken power with Mao's public and unconditional support.

The first victims were the *Chushen bu hao*. At first, I kept a low profile, but I quickly understood that I was of no interest to the Red Guards. Mama Zheng, the man who had looked after us like a mother, was much more interesting prey.

The extremist students went to the infirmary, the very place where, for so long, he had taken care of us. They forced him to his knees and shouted insults:

"What were you doing in Indonesia, you dirty dog? Why did you come to China? Why did you give your fortune to the Conservatory, you stinking bourgeois? Spy!"

The old man didn't know what to say. He wept, voicelessly,

That night, there was a thunderstorm over Beijing. We couldn't sleep because of the thunder and lighting, the wind and the rain. We lay silently awake in the dormitory listening to the storm—together, and yet so alone.

In the morning, we learned that Mama Zheng had hung himself from a tree in the courtyard, in front of the infirmary.

We didn't dare look at each other, but we remembered the storm and the sky's fury. Images of Mama Zheng came back to me—how he would rub my hands when I was eleven, his glasses of hot water that had done me so much good. I felt that something unimaginable had occurred.

And yet, at that time in my life, I could no longer separate the guilty from the innocent, the victim from the torturer. Deep in my heart I asked Mama Zheng: *Why didn't you trust Chairman Mao? Why, like Gu Shengying and Li Cuizhen, did you lack courage?*

* * *

Shortly thereafter, the Conservatory's siren went off at two in the morning. We awoke with a start and were ordered to assemble immediately in the auditorium. This time it was Cunzhi, one of my schoolmates and a wonderful bassoonist, who was on stage. He was tied up and surrounded by six Red Guards—five women and a man—who had begun to beat him with their belts even before our arrival. The Guards waited for the hall to fill up. It was absolutely silent. Then, a girl addressed the crowd:

"Comrades, something extremely serious has occurred. This worthless Cunzhi has tried to oppose the regime.

We have found a rifle and a Guomindang flag in his possession!"

At this, the Red Guards began to kick him mercilessly.

"I am innocent, I don't understand any of this! I am loyal to Chairman Mao!" Cunzhi moaned.

Each of his denials was met with another kick or blow from a belt. He could no longer speak. Finally the Red Guards dragged him by the arms out of the hall. Mercifully, Dapeng—a trombonist who was politically very well regarded—discretely intervened:

"Leave him be or he will die."

The Red Guards ordered us back to our rooms. We were rigid with fear; it was impossible to fall back to sleep. Who was guilty? Who was completely above suspicion? I could not stop thinking about my family and its past.

At dawn, I rushed to my parents' home.

* * *

"Mother, is there a rifle in the house?

My mother had no idea what I was talking about.

"Why, do you want to shoot someone?"

I persisted:

"Mother, has anything of a compromising nature been hidden in the house?"

Finally I described what had happened at the Conservatory. I was terrified that the Red Guards might have followed me. She told me that my father was being held at the university under close surveillance.

For a few seconds, we were silent, sharing the same thoughts.

"Xiao-Mei," she said, "we have nothing to feel guilty about. The only thing that could be considered dangerous for us is the piano. We have to get rid of it."

I agreed. We had to sever our connection with this symbol of the past. There was no point in holding onto it: we were not going to put ourselves in danger because of a piano.

My mother went out and flagged down the first Red Guards she met. She asked them to help her get rid of the piano immediately. They came in and took a look.

"Out of the question," they said. "We're not touching it."

A worthless thing, too heavy to move, was their assessment. There was only one thing to do: we gathered up all the old covers we could find and piled them on the piano to make it look like a cupboard. One cover, then two, then three! The more we tried to hide it, the larger it grew, or so it seemed. It was no longer visible, but its presence was more apparent than ever. As a precaution, we hung a *Dazibao* on it:

> *"This piano was acquired by exploiting the people,*
> *through their sweat and blood*
> *We want to return it to the people."*

A few days later, at the end of August 1966, the violence reached a new height. The *People's Daily* appealed to the Red Guards: "One by one, drive out the old parasites, the bloodsuckers hiding in the shadows." This time it was quite clear: the Red Guards weren't going to come get me at the Conservatory, but rather, at home.

7

A Bonfire of Bach

A revolution is not a dinner party;
it is an act of violence by which
one class overthrows another.

(Mao Zedong)

I was at home with my mother, my grandmother, and my two younger sisters late one afternoon when we heard a noise outside. Someone began to hammer on the door. We jumped in fear, looking at each other. When I opened the door, I found myself face to face with five members of the Red Guard:

"Your father is a criminal. We are interrogating him at the university, and he has begun to confess. As of this moment, he has no rights. Are you hiding anything here?"

"No," my mother answered.

"That's a lie."

The Red Guards entered and scrutinized each of us in turn. Then, wordlessly, they began to ransack the apartment. We silently remained standing, stiff with fear, waiting.

"Are these yours?"

How could letters and family papers not belong to us? The Red Guards seized them: they would prove useful

evidence in their investigation. Emboldened by this initial success, they turned to our bankbook—and confiscated it.

"And what's this?"

One of the Guards held a small bottle in his hand. My mother had been saving this little bit of French perfume since she was a young woman, not touching it. The perfume was so old it had turned dark brown.

"I asked you what it is!" the Guard repeated.

My mother still didn't answer. The Red Guard emptied out its contents. Then he threw the tiny bottle against the wall. It completely shattered, the pieces falling to the floor, leaving behind an elegant scent.

"Do you have any books?"

"No, we don't have any." As a precaution, we had gotten rid of them, with the exception of my childhood *Piano Music Masterpieces,* which my mother had hidden in the piano bench. One of the Red Guards turned to my sister Xiaoyen:

"You, go prepare some glue! You'll need it to put this up," he said, brandishing a *Dazibao* they had brought with them. "This is about your worthless father!"

My mother was overwhelmed and fainted. Before leaving, the Guards bellowed at us:

"We'll be back tomorrow. This *Dazibao* must be posted on the wall of your building!"

That evening, my sisters and I went out and put up the defamatory poster denouncing our father. As we returned, we found our neighbors, the Guans, talking with my mother and grandmother. They were simple folk who worked as laborers in a shoe factory. They had observed the Red Guards' visit but had discreetly waited until nightfall before coming to see us.

"It is impossible that Mr. Zhu is a spy," they told my mother. They then turned to the rest of us, incredulous: "Your father is a good man. How could anyone accuse him of such things?"

The conversation continued into the night. After they left, I sensed how much their visit had helped my mother. From then on, the Guans stopped by each day to see her, to offer a few words and smiles that kept her from despair. Without them, I now know, it is entirely possible that my mother could have ended up like Mama Zheng.

* * *

The following morning began shamefully for us. From our window, throughout the day, we saw little groups gather in front of our *siheyuan* to read the *Dazibao* we had pasted up. People glanced at our windows; sometimes they would point at them and then move on. We didn't dare go out. In the middle of the afternoon, when my sisters and I were deep in discussion about how we could get rid of the *Dazibao*, there was once again noise outside the apartment. The Red Guards were back. This time they wanted to speak to my grandmother:

"You, what is your background?"

"Bourgeois," she replied calmly.

"Where are you from?"

"Shanghai."

"You must go back there. *Chushen bu hao* are not permitted to stay in Beijing. They are a danger to Chairman Mao. We don't want to see you here tomorrow morning!"

I tried to intervene, using every possible argument: I explained that we had no money for a train ticket since the Red Guards had confiscated our bankbook.

"You're on your own! We'll be back tomorrow. She'd better not be here."

After the door closed, we sat for a long time in silence. Then my grandmother spoke:

"The best thing is for me to leave. I will return to Shanghai, and I'll come back later on. If not, tomorrow will be a terrible day. Xiao-Mei, Xiaoyin, try to find me a train ticket."

A ticket for Shanghai cost twelve yuan. I spent most of the evening on my bicycle with Xiaoyin, going from friend to friend, trying to borrow enough to pay for it. Finally, the student from the Conservatory who had written to Mao about me loaned me the money, on one condition:

"You must trust in Mao. We are too young to know if your grandmother or your family are guilty, but he knows."

I got back around midnight; my father was there. He had been released that evening. Unable to speak, he uttered only a few words:

"There is nothing to be done."

* * *

The next morning when I awoke, I saw that my grandmother had carefully done her hair and had put on her best clothes. She caught my astonished gaze. For three months, like a good revolutionary, I had hardly washed, I wore an old jacket and pair of pants, and I used bad language that, most of the time, I didn't understand.

"You know, Xiao-Mei," my grandmother began with a little smile, "even if people don't respect me, I have self-respect." Then she added, "Don't worry about me. Look,

they didn't beat me or forbid me to travel. I'm fortunate. I know a lot of people in Shanghai. I won't be alone. It will be easy for me. Rest assured, we'll see each other again."

I accompanied her to the train station. Her strength of character was impressive. Next to her, I felt weak, unable to protect her. When we were on the platform, she smiled at me:

"I've lived well. I've had a good life. It's really you that I'm worried about."

Then she climbed aboard the packed train. In China, people don't embrace one another, and even in life's most painful moments, one tries not to show any emotion. We simply said good-bye. The train pulled out of the station, and I watched it disappear into the distance.

Back at the house, I noticed that the *Dazibao* had disappeared. In our apartment, I found the Guans talking with my mother. They had devised a scheme to get rid of the poster, and had kept it a surprise. A six-year-old boy, whom they knew well, went and tore it down, as simple as that. Because of his age, no one could hold it against him. Plus, if he were hauled in, we didn't know him, and no one would put two and two together. The next day, my mother was already feeling calmer.

* * *

In Beijing, violence reigned. The Red Guards attacked anyone who represented the old order, even remotely. The least little former shopkeeper was labeled a "capitalist bloodsucker." Whole families were sent back to where they had come from. Others were forced to wear signs around their

necks stating that they had bad family backgrounds. Still others had half their heads shaved, as a mark of shame. Some women were beaten, not by the Red Guards, but by their own sons, who were forced to comply. But the worst was yet to come.[4]

I had barely arrived at the Conservatory at the start of the school year in September 1966 when we received an order from the Red Guards:

"Bring your records and musical scores. Everything you have left."

One of my classmates asked what they were going to do with them.

"They're going to be burned."

I suddenly remembered that I had left some things in the Conservatory's annex, a print shop that had been converted into classrooms. I hastened to get them, but as I crossed the threshold, I ran into Dapeng, my trombonist friend. He stopped me:

"What are you doing? Don't you know what's going on? Over the last week, dead bodies have been brought here."

At that exact moment, the stench hit me. It was so strong, I felt ill. I turned to him, completely speechless.

4 Author's note: The Cultural Revolution was responsible for millions of deaths (although the precise figure has not yet been established). Events similar to those that occurred in Beijing took place throughout China, orchestrated behind the scenes by Mao Zedong. Mao feared losing control to his two political rivals, Liu Shaoqi (the "Chinese Khrushchev") and Deng Xiaoping, who accused him of being responsible for the catastrophic outcome of the Great Leap Forward and the resulting famine, which claimed the lives of between twenty and thirty million people. See: John Fairbank, *The Great Chinese Revolution, 1880–1985* (New York: Harper & Row, 1986). See also: Simon Leys, *Essais sur la Chine*, Robert Lafont, Paris, 1998.

"If you don't believe me, go see for yourself," he said.

I stood there, frozen with fear.

Dapeng explained to me that the practice rooms were full of corpses. Since the crematorium only functioned on Tuesdays, and due to the large number of dead people in Beijing, the Red Guards had turned the Conservatory's annex into a vast morgue.

"There are even people in there who aren't yet dead, who are still suffering," he added. "The Red Guards forced others to wear their fur coats before shooting them. That's why it smells so terribly."

This was more than I could stand. I fled.

Everything was burning. Today it was the bodies; tomorrow it would be the spirit.

I imagined the bonfire where the Red Guards were melting down our records and burning our scores…a thin veil of smoke lifted towards the sky. Bach, Mozart, and Beethoven vanished into the air.

But in the end, the Red Guards were right: it had to be done. As Mao said: "The Revolution is not a dinner party. It is an act of violence by which one class overthrows another."

8

A Revolutionary

We must carry out not only those instructions we understand,
but also those we fail to understand for the moment,
and we must try to understand them
in the course of carrying them out.

(Lin Biao)

Confusion. Emptiness. Oblivion. At the end of 1966, courses at the "Conservatory without music" were replaced with political action. Exhaustive study of *The Little Red Book*, discussions between various student factions: everyone wanted to show that he or she was better at interpreting Mao's thought than anyone else. A disquieting sort of order reigned: on the one hand, the school was tidier than ever before, thanks to our professors, who were now cleaning people. On the other hand, any sort of education had been utterly abandoned; there was no more homework, no more books, no other goal but to tear down the old order.

The regime chose this moment to set in motion the *Da Chuanlian* movement, which means "mass exchange." The idea was to spread the Cultural Revolution across the entire country through inter-city and inter-university exchanges between Red Guards and students. The best candidates

from the Conservatory were asked to take an active role. Because of my background, I was not among them, but during the autumn of 1966, I was allowed to go to Beida University, where the Cultural Revolution had begun. I took it as a harbinger of a possible rehabilitation: it was still possible for me to become a real revolutionary.

Studying the thought of Mao Zedong was now mandatory for the entire population, for both the young and the old. When you wanted to board a bus, the Red Guards would step up and ask you, "In *The Little Red Book*, where does this passage come from? Or this one?" If you couldn't answer, you weren't allowed to get on the bus. It was no surprise that elderly people, whose memories were poorer, were ruthlessly pushed aside by the Guards.

Scenes of public confessions multiplied. Even today, I am haunted by images from one session I witnessed. It took place in a stadium in Beijing, before eight thousand people. The victim was a twenty-seven-year-old man who had dared to put forward the idea that you could be a good revolutionary even if your parents weren't. He considered himself to be one, even though he came from a bad family background. Despite our revolutionary convictions, I had difficulty repressing my bourgeois instinct, which caused me to admire the courage of this young man who had not denounced his parents. Over the course of an hour, he held up under the blows and humiliations to which he was subjected. When the session was over, they hauled him through the city on public display. Then he was executed. "Reactionary father, bastard son" was a popular slogan.

* * *

Early in 1967, I finally received permission to leave Beijing and participate in "mass exchange" visits to the countryside. I was warned that these trips were serious business, and that I wasn't to use them to visit family. I was accompanied by a comrade, because I wasn't yet allowed to travel by myself. Nevertheless, I took it as an encouraging sign.

My first trip was to Shanghai. But besides this official business in my native city, I had something to look into, a mystery to solve. Was there any truth to the claim that my father was a spy, or not? Had he really been in the pay of imperialists? If the Red Guards were right, would I have the courage to denounce him? If I did, I would feel less torn between my revolutionary faith and my attachment to my family—less crushed by the weight of my bad background. Forty years later, I see myself as I was that year—how I had been shaped to be: a brainless being fashioned for a single purpose—to be just like everyone else.

In Shanghai, political meetings were supposed to keep me fully occupied, but that wasn't the case. I had a great deal of time on my hands, which fit my plans perfectly.

I couldn't help myself. Contrary to what I had been told, I had to go see my grandmother. She was living on a squalid street on the edge of town. The inhabitants had turned it into a narrow lane by erecting all kinds of structures on either side: kitchens, garages, anything to increase the size of their living spaces. My grandmother lived in a 160-square-foot former kitchen, without electricity, furnished only with a bed, a table, and a slop pail in the corner.

"Xiao-Mei? What are you doing here? What's happened?"

She spoke softly with a weak voice and coughed incessantly. I gazed at her, so small and frail; she looked like a flickering candle. I explained why I was in Shanghai. I also told her about my resolve: to become a good revolutionary. This time I had a good chance of succeeding, but for it to work, my behavior had to be exemplary. My grandmother asked me for news of our family. I glimpsed our family photographs in the corner of her room.

"I look at them," she said, "and I read the letters your mother sends me, over and over."

I realized that I had come without a gift; I could have brought her favorite brioches from the Chenghuang Miao temple district in Shanghai, and I suddenly felt guilty. As I prepared to leave, I could read the disappointment on her face. My grandmother, who had said she knew all sorts of people in Shanghai, was clearly very alone. To fraternize with someone who had fallen out of favor with the regime was dangerous for one's friends.

She insisted that I stay.

"I can't, I am not allowed to. I'm afraid they'll find me here."

"Then try and come back before you leave. How long will you be here? Come and have lunch with me. I can't cook, but I can ask the neighbors to prepare bamboo shoots with tofu."

She knew it was my favorite dish. But I wasn't going to return. Out of fear and revolutionary commitment. Besides, I had important research to do.

To start, I paid a visit to my father's older sister:

"You know, Xiao-Mei, your father is a good man. For years, without your mother knowing it, he sent us money. Without him, we wouldn't have had enough to eat."

She wasn't about to tell me the truth about my father's activities as a spy.

Next I went to see the place where I was born. I looked at the bourgeois building, Fuxing Park, the wide avenue— how could I not feel guilty?

I questioned old friends of my father. They couldn't even understand my questions:

"Don't you understand? Your father is honesty itself! He was never a spy!"

But one of them took care to add:

"If you don't understand what the Party has against your father, trust in the Party. You'll understand later."

This was a paraphrase of something we heard incessantly repeated: "We must carry out not only those instructions we understand, but also those we fail to understand for the moment, and we must try to understand them in the course of carrying them out."

I returned to Beijing both satisfied and frustrated. Satisfied because I had passed my first test of being a good revolutionary, but frustrated because I hadn't uncovered the truth about my father. I would have to continue living with uncertainty.

In the meantime, my mother had received a letter from my grandmother.

"You know, she was so sad that you didn't go back and see her again," was all my mother said.

The image of my grandmother belonged to the world of my childhood. I needed to look forward, to the shining future of Communist China.

After Shanghai, I was given the chance to go on a pilgrimage that was dear to every Chinese person's heart: a trip to Shaoshan, Mao Zedong's birthplace. Two thousand one hundred miles in packed trains—but a great joy. I had never even seen Mao, but he had finally allowed me to get closer to him, to gather strength from his path.

Shaoshan is a mountain village of a few hundred inhabitants, some thirty miles from the main town of the district. Mao's birthplace, with its gray-tiled roof, was much larger and more beautiful than those of its neighbors. Starting in 1949, it had been transformed into a sort of shrine. We had to stand in line for a good two hours before being allowed in. I also visited the little village school where Chairman Mao studied. I was most moved, however, by his bedroom. How had this man risen to become the country's leader? Someone from a humble background, living in a tiny village in the farthest reaches of China, who never went to university. How could one not admire his intelligence, his courage, and his willpower? I wandered around the village for hours, turning these questions over in my mind. By the end of the day, the purpose of the trip had been achieved. My devotion was close to elation.

* * *

Upon returning to Beijing, I was allowed to go on a new trip, this time to Chengdu in Sichuan Province. I was told that the situation there was particularly serious. There were violent clashes between different student factions, and every

day brought a new death toll. Before leaving, I wrote a note to my parents:

> *I am leaving for Chengdu where the Revolution is in danger. If I should die, you must not be sad. I will have given my life for Mao. What I am undertaking is the most meaningful thing that I could do in life.*
>
> Xiao-Mei

A few months before, the regime had decided to make train travel free in order to facilitate the mass exchange of the *Da Chuanlian*. The train I got on was so overcrowded that I had to travel in the toilets most of the way.

The next day, when we arrived in Chengdu, I headed for the university, to the office that was responsible for orienting visitors.

"We have come from Beijing."

The woman who greeted us was impressed; she imagined that Mao himself had sent us! This was obviously naive of her, but I was secretly pleased. At last, I was free from people's criticism; I was admired and respected. This was simplistic on my part, of course.

She filled us in on the situation:

"It's total chaos. The university is divided into two main groups, within which there are also factions. On one side there is the 'Movement of August 26,' and on the other side there is the 'Red Chengdu Movement.' Be careful; there have been many deaths. The students have guns."

In the days that followed, I listened carefully to the arguments of the various factions. We had to figure out which side to support. Who upheld the Revolution better? Today,

forty years on, I wouldn't be able to tell you, nor could I describe why the factions were on opposing sides. But at the time, my mind was made up: I sided with the Medical School.

My first task was to write *Dazibaos*, with the aim of criticizing the opponent and summing up our beliefs. Everything was turned into slogans, meticulously written on posters that we put up all over town. I took part in all sorts of debates, interrupted by exchanges of gunfire between various buildings on campus.

At the end of a particularly bloody day, the faction that I had been supporting had seen a dozen deaths. A meeting was called to decide what action should be taken following this massacre. These comrades had not given their lives in vain! Why not lay out the corpses as a way to convince those still undecided of the correctness of our cause? Preparations for this took several days. The bodies had to be embalmed and then displayed in such a way as to have the maximum impact. This was easier for medical students than it would have been for others. Furthermore, photos of the deceased had to be located, so that each corpse would have, just like in a museum, its own information label. Appropriate music should be used to prepare visitors. We decided on the Funeral March from Beethoven's Symphony No. 3—the *Eroica*—which, for the occasion, was not censored.

These were the first dead bodies I had seen close up.

A few days later, the government finally decided to put an end to the slaughter. They confiscated all weapons and issued a new slogan: "Fight with words, not with guns." I reached Beijing only to leave again immediately. I wanted

to use my right to travel to "make mass contacts and fan the flames of the Revolution."

Marx distinguishes between three types of slaves: those who obey, those who wish to become masters, and revolutionaries who want to change the lot of the slave. I leaned in the second direction: I, too, wanted to give orders. It didn't matter to whom.

* * *

In the fall of 1968, the Chinese government continued to rein in a situation that had gotten completely out of hand. Chairman Mao himself addressed the issue by publishing a directive: "Continue the Revolution, but return to the classroom" and "Further the Revolution through teaching" were the latest slogans. A certain number of courses were reestablished.

But it was impossible to reopen an institution like the Beijing Conservatory just like that. There were no longer any musical scores, no textbooks. The only thing for sale in the bookstores was *The Little Red Book*—you could buy it in any number of editions: hardcover and paperback, and in small, medium, and large formats. Apart from that, everything had disappeared, even dictionaries.

The only musical scores left were the *Yangbanxi*, the "model works" composed under the aegis of Madame Mao, and a bit of Albanian music, the result of friendly Chinese-Albanian relations.

By the end of 1968, eight *Yangbanxi* had been written: four operas, including *The Red Lantern* and *Taking Tiger Mountain by Strategy*; two ballets, including *The Red*

Detachment of Women; an orchestral piece, the *Yellow River Piano Concerto*; and a play, the *Rent Collection Courtyard*. The works were not without merit, having been written by artists with solid musical backgrounds. Amusingly, however, some of them lifted entire passages from masterpieces of Western classical music, which had been roundly condemned. For example, the *Yellow River Piano Concerto* included the central passage from Chopin's *Heroic* Polonaise in A-flat major!

Since there was so much demand across the country for *Yangbanxi*, a pianist-protégé of Madame Mao's—who had a coterie of musicians around her—had the idea to transcribe them for piano, to make them more accessible. In particular, he transcribed eight sections of *The Red Lantern*. This gave me an idea. I remembered having met people from Beida University who wanted to organize touring theater shows. I went to see them and asked if they were still interested—which they were. I returned to practicing the piano. The transcriptions were extremely demanding; I worked on them tirelessly but with great pleasure, because they were well done. Adding them to my repertoire meant that I might be able to perform them throughout China.

The first concerts took place in the fall. We performed at military camps, factories, universities, administrative buildings, and in country villages. In just a few months, I took part in sixty concerts with my selections from *The Red Lantern*, sometimes playing two concerts in a day.

Other than selections from *The Red Lantern*, my musical horizons were reduced to the Red Army Choir—which I had the opportunity to hear at Yu Kuan's house. He was a professor at the Conservatory. We were both in the same political group, and I liked him a great deal. He was a renowned

musicologist whose specialty was Russian music, and he had been in the Conservatory's first graduating class. When the famous violinist David Oistrakh came to give concerts in China, Yu Kuan's knowledge of Russian allowed him to serve as an interpreter. Like everyone else, during the first days of the Cultural Revolution, he had given all his records to the Red Guards, who had zealously melted them down. Everything except a recording of the Red Army Choir, which we listened to endlessly for lack of anything else.

* * *

It was at the end of 1968, while I was touring with my *Yangbanxi,* that Mao decided to curtail the Cultural Revolution and revive the *Shang shan xia xiang* movement. Millions of city dwellers—"educated youths" as well as adults—were sent to the countryside, primarily to *Laogaichang,* or "reform through labor" camps.

It is estimated that some seventeen million Chinese were exiled to these camps. In the course of a few months, the seven members of my family would find themselves scattered to the farthest reaches of China.

9

Departures

I am not afraid, because I have crossed through storms and deserts.
I am not afraid, because I must cross through storms and deserts.

<div align="right">(Yi Men, Be Not Afraid)</div>

My sister Xiaoyin was the first to leave.

This was a completely voluntary decision on her part. As she had excellent calligraphy skills, she had been chosen to imitate Chairman Mao's handwriting on the armband— inscribed with the magic words "Red Guard"—which had been presented to him during the grand ceremony at Tiananmen Square on August 18, 1966. Despite this, she had not been given permission to attend the celebration because of her *Chushen bu hao,* her "bad family background." She later told me how, after the ceremony, all her comrades had hurried over to shake the hand of the young girl who had been lucky enough to give my sister's armband to Chairman Mao. This girl was a friend—or rather, she had once been a friend. Now Xiaoyin felt as though a glass wall separated her from her friends. Another consequence of her "bad" background.

This is why she was one of the first to voluntarily leave for a *Shang shan xia xiang.* The initial location she chose

was close to the Russian border, but she was immediately suspected of wanting to escape. Thus she opted for Inner Mongolia.

Although my father was still under close surveillance at the university, he believed in the ideas of *Shang shan xia xiang*. He thought that the movement was beneficial for his daughters, that they should travel widely, "explore the high seas," as he put it, in order to grow and change. My sisters and I shared his views.

On the other hand, I was worried for my mother. She had just received the news that my grandmother had died in Shanghai. The neighbors hadn't found her body until two days after her death. My mother was deeply affected by the news. I was as well. Despite my efforts to erase all petit-bourgeois family feelings, I was consumed with remorse when I thought about my visit, and how I had run away.

Xiaoyin's departure was another painful blow for my mother. My sister left our house and headed up the little street where we lived without turning back to wave good-bye. No doubt she was afraid of crying, but it only intensified the pain my mother felt.

* * *

At the end of 1968, it was my sister Xiaoyu's turn to leave. Her destination: far-off Yunnan Province, known for its bar-baric customs. One heard stories of how men would kidnap young girls, rolling them up in blankets like animals. This was yet another shock. I now saw my little sister in a new light: before, I had looked down on her, as can happen sometimes with older siblings. I wasn't particularly concerned with her,

and thought of her as the least talented member of the family. Suddenly, she became a real person to me.

We waited anxiously for news from her. With every passing day, I watched my mother's anxiety grow. She was sure something had happened. Finally a letter arrived. Xiaoyu explained that it had taken ten days and nights—half by train, half by bus—to reach her destination. She was exhausted. Her legs were so stiff that she could hardly walk. But at least she was alive.

* * *

The night before Chinese New Year, we heard a knock on the door. My mother went to open it:

"Xiaoyin!"

My sister stood there—dirty, thin, barely recognizable.

"I wanted to see you," was all she said.

After a few months spent in Inner Mongolia, Xiaoyin couldn't take it anymore. She and three friends hatched a crazy plan: they would return to Beijing to see their families. They crossed the barren steppes, alone, without a map or provisions, living on food provided by the astonished natives. They took every conceivable means of transport, including carts and trucks. Their journey lasted eighteen days.

Xiaoyin spent a month with us before voluntarily returning to Inner Mongolia. Before she left, she asked my mother to find an accordion for her, because she was suffering from a total lack of music. She had no idea that, this time, she would be gone for twenty-one years. After Mao's death, she moved often, living in a number of China's provinces. She married a

worker—as much out of political conviction as for love—with whom she remained, starting her own family far from home.

* * *

Xiaoyin was still with us when my father was forced to leave for the camps.

One day, I returned home to find him packing his bags. The Red Guards had found an entry in his personal file that dated to the last months of our life in Shanghai. To them, it was unshakable proof that he was a spy. My father had been approached by a shady character who had offered him work. "Don't contact us, we'll get in touch with you," the person had said as he had left. My father was disturbed by the encounter and reported it to the authorities, which he wasn't obliged to do. This incident, along with my uncle's departure for Taiwan, had cost our family dearly. It was the reason my two older sisters had been forbidden to enroll in university. Now it was the allegation behind sending my father to a camp. As a young revolutionary, this was a painful lesson for me: if you wanted to survive in this country, you'd best not be honest.

As he left, my father thought about my sister Xiaoru. She was married, and would soon give birth to her first child.

"Write and tell me if it is a boy or a girl," he said to my mother.

* * *

It was a girl, but it wasn't possible to tell my father. At that moment he was in transit, waiting in a prison somewhere outside of Beijing to be sent to a camp. Then the prison

administration asked us to bring him a change of clothes. My sister Xiaoyin and I took on the task: four hours by bicycle to get there and four hours back.

As soon as my father entered the prison visiting area, he asked us urgently:

"Is it a girl or a boy?"

My sister immediately broke down in tears. She thought about my father, who had been waiting so expectantly for the birth, and who couldn't even see his grandchild. But he interpreted her tears in another way, thinking that the baby had been a stillborn. He began crying himself, and simply repeated:

"Was it a girl or a boy?"

Disturbed by the noise, a guard jumped up, stared at him, and yelled:

"Why are you crying? Do you think you're some kind of victim? Return to your cell and your work!"

I spoke to my father:

"You should confess whatever it is that you have committed against your county. You should be brave! You will understand later. Think about it!"

But the visit was over. It had not even lasted five minutes. We were in the process of being herded towards the exit when I heard my father shout:

"If I die, know that I am innocent! I'm going to write to Chairman Mao. He will see that justice is done!"

On the way home, biking into an icy wind, my sister and I pedaled in silence, unable to exchange a single word. Our father's voice and his declaration echoed inside us. They remained engraved on our memories.

* * *

This was at the beginning of 1969. Three members of my family were in camps when my older sister Xiaoru received an order: she was to remain in Beijing. Why? We don't know. We never knew why some were forced to leave while others remained.

Then it was my turn. The order came down from Madame Mao that all students from Beijing's art schools should leave for the camps. I was instructed to leave for Zhangjiakou in the northern part of Hebei Province. It was close to Mongolia: until the creation of the People's Republic of China, the Zhangjiakou region was part of Chahar Province and therefore belonged to Inner Mongolia. I felt lucky: unlike the others, I was being sent to a military camp and not one in the countryside. I thought I'd be gone a year, two at the most, and that it would be a valuable experience. March 16 was my departure date.

On that sad late winter morning, the two of us—my mother and I—were in the apartment. I watched as she finished packing my bag, filling it with various objects, a flashlight, toilet paper, and so on.

"You may need them. I'd prefer it if you took them with you."

In just a short while, we'd have to separate. After I left, my mother would be alone with my sister Xiaoyen. How would the two of them manage? Could they hold up? One day, they would also be forced to leave.

The moment had come. My mother handed me my bag, and we both went down to the street. The sky was gray, and

a freezing wind blew through Beijing. As is the custom with all Chinese people, we didn't say good-bye.

"It's time to go, Mama. I'm off."

I walked up the little road where we lived. When I got to the corner of the street, I turned around. I saw that my mother was pale, staring into space.

10

Camp 4619

If God does not exist, everything is permitted.

(Dostoyevsky, *The Brothers Karamazov*)

The streets of Beijing were deserted, emptied out after the departure of the city's inhabitants. This contrasted sharply with the packed railway station plastered with banners glorifying the Revolution.

I pushed my way through the dense crowd, trying to get my bearings. Finally, I found the platform where we had been told to assemble. My future comrades slowly began to arrive. Every art school in Beijing was there—the Conservatory, the Fine Arts Academy, the Film Academy, the Dance Academy, and the Opera School. A soldier checked off each new arrival and assigned us to a section. Two cars had been reserved for us on a passenger train headed for Zhangjiakou.

As I waited to leave, I glanced around me. Families were separating: couples exchanged last, tender words, grandparents whispered good-byes to their children. People gazed at each other, some thinking they would never see each other again. At a distance, I could see young mothers handing their babies over to their families. I felt ill at the sight, and

my courage flagged. Then I pulled myself together; this was ridiculous. A real revolutionary rejects all sentimentalism.

We were about a hundred people altogether. The soldiers ordered us to board the train cars. After an initial jolt, the train set off. Slowly and quietly, the Beijing station receded. Shortly after our departure, our *jiji fenzi*—the activist assigned to our section—encouraged us to break into revolutionary songs to the glory of Chairman Mao, and to read aloud selections from *The Little Red Book*. Halfway through our trip, the sky darkened. I looked out the window; the clouds were so threatening, one had the impression it was already night. The landscape was no longer visible; a few lights appeared here and there.

At the end of the day, we arrived in Zhangjiakou. The soldiers directed us to get off the train. After lining us up in front of the station, they packed us into two open military trucks, fifty students in each. Our destination: camp 4619 in Yaozhanpu.

We crossed the city of Zhangjiakou. We were a mere three hundred miles from Beijing, but it felt like the end of the earth. The unpaved streets were empty; the only sound came from our trucks. I looked at the modern, ugly buildings. Any invasion by the Soviets would pass directly through Zhangjiakou. This was no doubt why the city had been left in its present state, more of a big village than a city. It was hard to imagine that it had once enjoyed a Golden Age in the seventeenth century under the Qing Dynasty. It had been the center of tea and opium trading between China and Russia. Today everything exuded an air of poverty and gloom.

We left the city and turned onto a road full of potholes. Two hours later, we finally reached our destination, our faces covered in dust. We no longer resembled human beings; it was difficult to recognize one another. A harbinger of the years to come.

* * *

The Yaozhanpu camp was up in the hills. It was composed of three low, military-style buildings made out of red brick, positioned around a large square.

"Line up!"

We stood at attention in the dark and cold.

"Students, you will be divided up into sections. Then you will go to your quarters."

Along with the rest of my section, I entered the room that had been assigned to us. Ten straw mattresses lay directly on the floor of a two-hundred-square-foot room. They were so narrow I wondered how we were ever going to sleep. I placed my things down on mine; it was covered with cockroaches. At that moment a soldier entered.

"Students, report to the mess hall!"

At the entrance to the hall, we were each handed an old, filthy mess kit. It looked as though it had served as a chamber pot, rather than a bowl. My stomach tightened, and I couldn't eat a single thing.

That first night, I was unable to sleep. I thought about the cockroaches. I was sure they were going to crawl into my ears and puncture my eardrums. The girl next to me, Ouyan, was also a pianist. Each time she shifted, I woke up.

We finally decided to lie head to foot, so we could get some rest.

* * *

The next morning at six, we were awoken by a soldier, and soon we were assembled on the square in front of our barracks. A fifty-year-old man with compassionate eyes approached us. He was Tian, the camp commander. He observed us at length, then addressed us in a serious voice:

"Among you there are tigers and dragons (a Chinese expression meaning "remarkable individuals"), but your minds remain bourgeois. This is why you must be re-educated."

After Tian's short speech, other soldiers explained our schedule and informed us about the rules of the camp. Everything was regulated, down to the smallest detail: only black, blue, and gray clothing was allowed; hair must be short; everyone was to wear the same cap; for the women, no skirts were allowed.

In a very short time, my hope of learning and transforming myself into a real revolutionary collapsed. The goal of camp life was not to educate us—it was to break us. Every day was the same, structured around the same hard labor. I didn't know it at the time, but it would last five years.

Every morning, we were awoken at six.

"On your feet!" shouted the soldier in charge of our room, switching on the light.

The day began with running and marching exercises. Then we studied Mao's *Little Red Book* for an hour, and always the same passages. We focused on two fundamental essays,

"On Practice" and "On Contradiction," and on two texts: "Serve the People," a speech given in memory of Chang Se-di, a soldier who had given his life for the people, and "The Foolish Old Man Who Removed the Mountains," the story of an old man who decided to use a hoe to remove two high mountains that were blocking the way to his house. His neighbor made fun of him, but not Heaven, who finally sent down two angels to carry the mountains away on their backs. For Mao, the two mountains were imperialism and feudalism.

At eight o'clock, having finished our study of *The Little Red Book*, we left for the fields. Our mission was to cultivate rice, in an area of China that was highly unsuitable for rice growing. Dry, sterile stretches of land lay battered by glacial winds and hemmed in by ominous yellow and black hills. Our first task was to dig irrigation ditches, using shovels that were for the most part broken. After that, we brought excrement from the camp latrines to spread on the fields. Then we carried water, which we poured into the ditches.

After a few minutes standing in freezing water, I no longer had any sensation in my feet. I often ran a fever, which caused me to sweat. My periods stopped, and I suffered from stomach pains, but there was neither a doctor nor a nurse in the camp. A few workmates knew the basics of acupuncture, which somewhat lessened my pain. In the summer, we were covered in insect bites, and leeches clung to our legs. I tried hard to reason with myself, but my courage failed me.

To spur us on, our *jiji fenzi*—with the help of the soldiers—organized competitions among us. How quickly could we dig this ditch? Who could fetch water the fastest?

Who could haul back the largest amount of excrement from the latrines? Our *jiji fenzi* set an example by working faster than we did. I tried my best, anxious about criticism that might await me during that evening's public denunciation session. Given my small build, however, I never had the slightest hope of winning.

We ate our midday meal right there in the fields. One of us was given the task of fetching hot water and food, generally potatoes, which we cut up each day in a different manner—in little cubes, in strips, in slices—or mixed with a bit of cabbage and carrots, just for a change. Occasionally we were allowed to have pork.

The afternoons were endless, even worse than the mornings, and I looked at my watch every five minutes. We worked until sundown. Then we returned to the camp. After sweating all day while standing in water, we were unimaginably filthy. Before we were allowed to wash, however, we had to go immediately to a self-criticism and denunciation session. This was not an arbitrary rule, and it played a role in our "re-education": not allowing us to wash was just one way among many to deprive us of our dignity.

In small groups of ten, we were put under the authority of a soldier who had been trained in the art of pitting us against one another. I was well acquainted with self-criticism sessions, but this godforsaken place gave them a very particular cast. We quickly understood what was at stake, although it was never explicitly stated: those who demonstrated the best behavior would be allowed to leave first. The battle had begun, and the prize was our freedom.

When existence is reduced to a series of deadening tasks, when no higher consciousness, either cultural or religious,

is there to guide one's instincts, the only way to defend one-self is to attack. "Zhang didn't work enough," a comrade would exclaim. "He spent twenty minutes in the latrine!" Zhang would then respond in kind: "I heard Li complaining twice about camp conditions!" We left these sessions exhausted. Conversation was impossible. We couldn't even look each other in the eye. And yet, we had to continue to live together.

* * *

We returned to the dormitory, where we ate dinner seated on our straw mats: potatoes with cabbage, accompanied by small yellow rice. It wasn't until dinner was over that we finally had the right to clean ourselves up. Bent over a hole dug in the corner of the room, we splashed ourselves with a bit of water. In front of the others. Here, there was no room for any sort of privacy. The very notion implied a bourgeois attitude.

After washing, we finally had the courage to look at each other and exchange a few words. But the only place that we could speak freely was a little adjoining room where we went to get hot water.

Guo Baochang, an exceptional individual, held forth there. One day, he would become one of China's greatest filmmakers. He was older than the rest of us, and the minute he arrived in camp he was considered to be a serious opponent to the Revolution. For this reason, he was given the task of heating water for the camp. Every day he carried large amounts of water and coal, going from the freezing cold outside to the sweaty heat of the boiler. Despite this, he was always in a good mood.

He had recently fallen in love with one of us, a very pretty singer from the Conservatory. In order to declare his undying affection in the traditional Chinese manner, he asked someone to deliver a love letter. His choice of messenger was, he thought, a cautious one: a young student from the Beijing Opera with so little schooling that he had trouble writing his own self-criticisms. Guo Baochang believed he was safe. Unfortunately, the young artist was not only uneducated, he was also nosy. He opened the letter, and discovered a text so difficult that he couldn't even decipher it with a dictionary. So he asked a few of his comrades for help, and before the message had even reached the beloved, the whole camp knew about it!

* * *

And so the day ended. But our trials weren't over yet. Often, we were awoken in the middle of the night, and had to carry out emergency drills in preparation for a Soviet invasion. We would hear the wail of the siren and then an order for us to assemble.

"Alert! Alert!"

We had to quickly leave camp wearing our packs. The first challenge—gathering up our things in the pitch-black room—was so daunting that, for safety's sake, I began sleeping fully dressed. Then we had to run for hours in the mountains in the middle of the night. We would return to camp at dawn, not having been allowed to sleep.

Sometimes, it was not an alert that woke us in the night, but a voice. A mysterious voice, arising it seemed from nowhere, singing the praises of the Revolution. Our *jiji fenzi*

talked in her sleep. At first, we were impressed: such faith-fulness, such devotion, even when asleep! How admirable! Little by little, however, we became suspicious. *Every* night—wasn't that a bit much? And each morning she worried that she had disturbed us: wasn't that a way of making sure we had heard her confession of loyalty? We decided on a strat-egy: each time she apologized, we assured her:

"Oh no, you didn't disturb us. We didn't hear a thing."

* * *

Sunday was laundry day. As we washed our sheets, we looked to the sky, hoping for just a little sun to help them dry. Quite often, not even an hour later, a sandstorm would roll in, and our sheets would be gray and yellow, just like the landscape, and dirtier than before.

Sometimes on Sundays we were shown films, usually Albanian ones. Their artistic merit was questionable, but we never missed one—the few kisses they portrayed would have been inconceivable in a Chinese film from that period. Each time a torrid love scene approached, the soldier in charge of the evening would race to the screen to try and hide the unthinkable. Often though, to our very great pleas-ure, he would get there too late. Need I add that we were all between eighteen and thirty years old?

In the midst of this daily deprivation, the arrival of the mail provided a ray of sunshine—that is, when the letter hadn't been censured, or the recipient was not obliged to read it aloud. This happened to a friend in another camp: she was forced to read the contents of her fiancé's letters to her assembled comrades.

I corresponded regularly with my mother, who was still living in Beijing with Xiaoyen. Shortly afterwards, my youngest sister, who was by then fifteen years old, was sent to Beidahuang Anlun, in the rugged northern region of Manchuria, where she continued to write to me.

Her first letters were horrifying. During the harvest, she had to work from two in the morning until eleven at night. At lunchtime, one had to sprint to the end of the field, where the food had been set out. The first to arrive ate as much as they could. Since she was the youngest in the camp, she couldn't run as fast as the others, and often there was nothing left.

Among other tasks, she was responsible for a deer farm—in China, deer are raised for their horns, which are used to make medicine. One day, chasing after an animal that had escaped, she nearly drowned in a swamp. Another time, while she was using a scythe, she saw her best friend electrocuted after the girl touched a cable that had fallen to the ground. Xiaoyen was ordered to stand guard over the body until the girl's parents arrived. One night, however, she nodded off and awoke to the sight of her friend's body being eaten by rats. The young girl's father went mad and died shortly thereafter.

What answer could I give to Xiaoyen's letters? The only thing to do was to try and keep her spirits up. Later, as a gesture of support, I sent her a copy of Marx's *The Communist Manifesto.*

One day I received a letter from my mother. She was also now in a camp.

11

A Piglet and Five Kittens

The night is well along,
Give me a match...
(Lu Yuan, *Melancholy*)

After a few months, the camp regimen had taken a toll on my health. I became very weak and suffered from endless bouts of diarrhea, which meant I had to drag myself to the latrines ten times a day. They were at the far end of the camp, and I almost didn't have the strength to return. On the way back from the fields, I would collapse, get to my feet, and stagger on towards the dormitory.

When I had lost over twenty pounds, a decision was made to move me to Zhangjiakou Hospital. There, I was reunited with a friend, Like, a wonderful cellist. I had known Like since we had attended the Children's Music School together, where he had studied piano. For a long time, we shared the same music stand at the Beijing Conservatory. He had a keen, direct look in his eyes, generous and very human. He was tall with a solid constitution, which hadn't kept him from contracting acute septicemia. Not surprisingly, I had been diagnosed with the same thing. The water we drank was cloudy, and by the time we walked several

hundred yards to get to our midday meal—which had been deposited in a corner of the field—the wind had covered it with a film of dirty sand.

As I lay on my hospital bed, I felt completely alone. *What was I doing here*, I wondered. *How had I ended up in this sad, filthy room?* I was going to die, I felt it, far from my parents and abandoned by everyone. My death would be meaningless, as my life had been. I thought about my family and the memories we had shared. It was all over. I would never see them again, and I would never know freedom. In my troubled dreams, my father appeared, working in the fields. Suddenly, he fell to the ground, crushed beneath a load that his weak back couldn't support. Was he dead?

For several days, I was delirious, hovering between life and death. The doctors never uttered a single word to me. But my time had not yet come. One day, I felt better. The fever broke. Little by little, I began to recover. I was sent back to camp to convalesce.

* * *

One afternoon shortly after my return, as I lay on my mattress, I heard the far-off sound of music. I listened attentively. Who could be playing music in camp in the middle of the day? I held my breath so as to hear better: it was the sound of an accordion. I went outside to see what was happening. Tian, the camp commander, stood in a corner of the courtyard, surrounded by musicians.

"Everything is ready. Until tonight, then—" he told them.

One would have thought he was Hamlet, welcoming the players to Elsinore with the line: "You are welcome, masters; welcome, all."

Tian had once been a teacher, and he was an intellectual at heart. He had decided to take advantage of the presence of the Beijing art students to organize concerts in camps near Zhangjiakou. For this, he had chosen a handful of singers, dancers, and musicians. He would pay dearly for this later on: he was denounced by certain people, myself included, for not being enough of a revolutionary, and was forced to leave his post.

The next day, while everyone was in the fields, I wandered around the camp. From afar, I spotted the accordion that had been played at the concert the night before, lying on a table. I went up to it: it was old, its keys were dirty, and its strap was worn. But this instrument, left here in these grim surroundings, was a sign from on high: I had to heed it.

I looked around me. I was alone. I snatched up the instrument and tried to produce a few notes. Nothing came out. What would happen if I tried to play a real piece of music? After my sickness, after all the frustrations, I was overcome with desire. But which piece? It would have to be one written mainly for the right hand. I ran through the scores I knew, and thought of one: Chopin's Etude Op. 10, No. 2. It is an etude for the right hand, and fairly easy for the left: thus it was perfect for the accordion, even though the octaves were missing. I played it endlessly most of the afternoon and in the days that followed, until the artists left. I had forgotten the power of music: but it hadn't forgotten me.

* * *

We left the camp in early autumn. We were transferred to Qingshuihe, about thirty miles from Yaozhanpu. The official reason was that the buildings we were occupying had to be turned back over to the military. It was true that Yaozhanpu, situated high in the hills, was an excellent observation post, while Qingshuihe, located on the plains by a river, was not of equal strategic importance. The real reason was no doubt that the soldiers didn't want to keep us too long in the same place for fear that we would develop relationships with the local population.

Life at Qingshuihe was even harder than it had been at Yaozhanpu. There were only two dormitories, one for men and the other for women. Cui, the camp commander, was strict, rigid, and ill at ease: for him, rule following was serious business, and he never once smiled.

Soon after our arrival, we were asked to contemplate the example of a professor at a nearby camp who had shown exceptional loyalty to Mao. Two successive telegrams arrived stating that her young son was gravely ill and that she should return immediately to Beijing. Both times, she answered that she had to look after a piglet that was also sick, and for which she was responsible. A third telegram arrived informing her of her son's death. She didn't shed a tear. A few days later, the piglet died. She broke down and wept.

We were confused. Was it *really* necessary to go that far to be loyal to the thought of Chairman Mao? But once our initial astonishment had passed, we got used to the idea. Soon, most of us considered this woman laudable: a pig feeds the collective while one's attachment to a child is an individualist and bourgeois sentiment. The young mothers among us voiced a few reservations, but ended up agreeing.

Were they really convinced? It would take me five more years until I was capable of asking myself this question with any clarity. Five long years in camp before I could make a space for doubt, before I could allow something that resembled lucidity to arise in me.

* * *

Winter arrived. The landscape was covered in snow, and the temperature dropped to freezing. As we could no longer work in the fields, we were assigned to huge barns and given the task of extracting corn kernels from stalks. The year 1970 began. And then spring returned. We lived our lives in rhythm with the seasons. The months went by, and nothing changed. The hard physical labor of the fieldwork, the inhospitableness of the surrounding landscape, living in close quarters with the same group of people...Add to this the boredom, the monotony of our days counted out in minutes—and the absence of any future prospects. I progressively lost sense of the meaning of my captivity; I asked myself why I was there.

The time came when some of us were given permission to leave. People returned home, while others remained. For the first time since I had arrived in the camps, I experienced a feeling of rebellion. The injustice was too glaring. I couldn't forget that accordion, and how a selection had been made among us as to who would go and play music for the soldiers. Why had some been granted this privilege and others not? I was aware that I was harboring a grudge that wouldn't go away.

Then something happened that changed everything. One of my companions, a newlywed, decided to escape—he

wanted to see his wife at all costs. He was quickly recaptured and subjected to a lengthy public self-criticism session. In the end, however, this didn't clear him of his misdeed. Later, at the moment of his *Fenpai*—his "posting" after leaving camp—he paid dearly for it.

Escape?—this gave me pause. A public session of self-criticism? I was used to that. One session more or less didn't really matter. But trouble with my posting after I left camp? This was more serious. But it all seemed so far away, so abstract. Who was talking about freedom at that stage? And my mother had just written to me that she was back in Beijing: her health was too poor to handle camp life, and the authorities had decided to send her home.

I talked with two comrades whom I knew shared my feelings. I figured out an escape route: the latrines were roofless and adjoined the outer wall. I asked them if they wanted to go with me on my adventure. Yes? All right then, the following week, after we had had time to work out the final details of our plan, we would leave.

On the chosen day, at five in the morning, we slipped into the latrines. There was no one around. We gave each other a leg up, scaled the wall, and ran to the train station. A few hours later, on the train to Beijing, we relished our first moments of freedom in more than a year.

As the landscape rolled by, we discussed our big plan: we would write to Madame Mao, who had sent us to the re-education camps, and inform her about the real conditions at Zhangjiakou. The departures, the injustice, the dishonest compromises, the lack of any true revolutionary spirit—she couldn't know about any of that, and we were sure she wouldn't accept it. The whole thing

had been corrupted by incompetent underlings, and she needed to step in. Like Solzhenitsyn's *zeks* in the wilds of Siberia, who were convinced that Stalin knew nothing of what was happening in the Gulag, we trusted in Madame Mao completely. We agreed to meet the very next day to write her a letter that would open her eyes to the actual situation.

* * *

After crossing Beijing, which was even more deserted than when I had left it, I arrived at our little street. Nothing had changed.

"Xiao-Mei, what are you doing here?"

My mother was thin, weak, and covered in bandages that were supposed to ease her stomach pains. As a vegetarian, she had been unable to eat the pork fat that was the prisoners' staple food. One morning, she collapsed from fatigue in the field where she had been working. She lay there all day, unconscious, until someone came to get her. It was then that they decided to send her back.

She fell silent. She never said another word about it, and I didn't talk about my camp experiences either. It was our neighbors the Guans—whom I called *Shushu* and *Dama* (uncle and aunt)—who filled me in. They told me about a little cat that my mother had found in her camp. Its five newborn kittens had been taken away from it. Each night, the cat sought my mother out after she returned from the fields. She rubbed up against my mother and allowed herself to be petted as she meowed the loss of her five newborns. My mother cried also, thinking about her own five

children. The cat didn't understand my mother's sadness—
but my mother understood the cat's.

* * *

As the days passed and no one came looking for me, I ven-
tured a trip to the Conservatory. The first person I ran
into was a violin professor. He was one of the few teachers
who had been considered unfit to be sent to the camps. We
struck up a conversation, then all of a sudden, an idea came
to me.

"Do you know where I could find any scores?"

I couldn't help it: I was aware of the danger, but that
old accordion in Yaozhanpu had awoken in me a desire for
music that I thought had been definitively buried under my
new personality as a good revolutionary.

He looked surprised, and cautiously scrutinized my face
to judge my degree of sincerity—I knew he was worried that
I was trying to trap him. After a few seconds of hesitation,
he said in a low voice:

"I know of a little room on the third floor that's filled
with scores. At the beginning of the Cultural Revolution,
the teachers hid all they could there. Since then, I don't
think anyone has dared to go in. I think you'll find what
you're looking for."

He glanced around him to make sure that no one was
listening, and added:

"If you like, we could try and go there this evening.
Come back around ten o'clock. We'll be alone."

I thanked him. Once night had fallen, I went to meet
him. The buildings were empty and strangely silent, the final

stage of the school's metamorphosis: the "Conservatory without music" had become a "Conservatory without students."

The violin professor grabbed a flashlight, and we went up to the third floor of one of the buildings. When we got to the room with the scores, he shined his light at the transom over the door.

"I'll give you a leg up. You can climb in there."

Flashlight in hand, I wiggled my way into the treasure room. It was indeed filled with scores. I rummaged around near me; I picked one up, flipped through its pages, and then took another, and another...

"Well? Have you found what you were looking for?"

I didn't respond right away. On the other side of the door, the violin professor started to lose patience:

"Can't you hear me? What have you found?"

What had I found? Cuban scores. Nothing but Cuban scores! We had taken all those risks for dance music! I crawled back out through the transom with a few works under my arm. I wasn't about to leave empty-handed.

When I got back to the house, I dug the piano out from under the covers that had hidden it through the years.

"My poor piano, this is all I can offer you to celebrate our reunion."

I'm not sure how much the piano appreciated it, but from morning to night our apartment resounded with Cuban music. Fearful that this would draw the neighbors' attention, my mother kept watch in the cold in front of the house. She waited there every afternoon, ready to sound the alarm at the least sign of trouble.

* * *

A few days later, we saw two soldiers from the window. My mother took a deep breath and opened the door.

"We are looking for the student Zhu Xiao-Mei. Is she here?"

"She's here."

They questioned my mother and me about the reasons for my escape. I explained that I understood that I had been in error, but that I had wanted to see my mother again. They pretended to understand. If I left with them, I had their word that I wouldn't be punished.

Thus ended my escapade. When I returned to Qingshuihe, I had to undergo my self-criticism session. No big surprise. I was prepared for it. Afterwards, when I was with my comrades, they asked me questions, and I described my time in Beijing. Some of them remained silent, but others approved, and envied me. Things were changing— slowly, but they were changing. I headed back to the fields.

* * *

That summer, we moved to our third camp. On this occasion we were stationed in a peasant village, Quijiazhuang. The camp consisted of a few sodden stables. These had been requisitioned from the villagers, who earned just enough to clothe and feed themselves. Their meals consisted of a bit of rice thinned down with a lot of water. Their rice rations were determined by a point system based on their productivity in the fields. The more they produced, the more points they earned.

Our food was mediocre, but abundant. We began asking the soldiers for twice as much food as we could eat, so

that we could give the extra to the villagers. The soldiers let it happen: some because they couldn't see why not, others because they were in agreement. For the most part, they were very young and sons of poor peasants; they felt a spontaneous solidarity with the inhabitants of Quijiazhuang.

The living conditions were a bit better and the pace of work somewhat more flexible. Suddenly we had more free time, and the range of authorized texts had increased. After all those years with only *The Little Red Book*, we now had two other authors at our disposal: Lenin and Marx! *Capital* became our Bible, but due to my lack of education, there were many ideas and even words that I didn't understand. Karl Marx talked about someone named Napoleon—I had never heard of him. Nevertheless, my hunger to learn was immense, and I plunged into it.

A friend offered to help me. Her father, Zho Henli, worked for the Bank of China in Hong Kong. Since he was a good Communist and was respected by the regime for his competence and loyalty, he had more leeway and education to express what was going on around us. My friend assured me that he would be able to explain the more obscure points of Marx. Thus, I began an odd correspondence with a man I didn't know, who lived far away in Hong Kong. My letters were sometimes ten pages long, but he always wrote back, kindly and patiently.

There was yet another sign that things were becoming more flexible: the Zhangjiakou Opera asked for our help in staging a *Yangbanxi*. I was chosen as pianist, as was Huang Anlun, who was the son of an accomplished Chinese conductor and musician who had studied at Yale.

Finally, I could once again practice the piano. Sometimes several hours went by when I wasn't interrupted. It was a real joy, even if we didn't have scores. Oddly, I found that I could play from memory pieces I had learned as a child, but the repertoire I had worked on with Professor Pan, after so many intervening years, escaped me. Although I could pick out the major themes, I had forgotten many details. At any rate, I was overjoyed to be playing again. So overjoyed that when I had to stop and return to the fields, I missed music terribly, trapped in a feeling of frustration that was far worse than before.

* * *

Around this time, something happened that is the most painful of my camp memories to discuss. It was the final stage in the dehumanization process orchestrated by the system.

One night, as I was returning from the fields, I was summoned by the camp commander.

"We need your help. We have information that a secret society, the '516 Group,' is conspiring against the regime. The society is very active in the cultural milieu. The cellist Shaohua has been denounced as a member. We are counting on you to observe her and to encourage her to confess."

It would have been unthinkable to refuse, of course. In fact, it never even entered my mind. It was the logical outcome of the years of self-criticism sessions and denunciations. I was truly convinced that our commander would not accuse someone without just cause.

Thus, I began my unobtrusive surveillance, looking for clues, even the slightest ones. One day, because a door had been left ajar, I stumbled upon my comrade in the process of rifling through files to which she wasn't supposed to have access. In fact, she was looking for letters denouncing her. But I didn't know this. I would learn it from her later, when I once again could hear things and form an opinion. At the time, I didn't want to think about it. I simply wanted to unmask the spy, period.

I went and told a soldier about the incident, and I suggested that we take advantage of our next denunciation session to surprise Shaohua, evidence in hand: she had been caught in the act of rifling though confidential files. The soldier agreed, and the day of the session arrived. The entire camp was gathered for the occasion. Shaohua was attacked from all sides. She went pale, squared her shoulders, and categorically denied everything. Then, all of a sudden, a girl stood up and slapped her in the face. This was too much for me. I caught my breath. It was as if I had woken from a nightmare: I realized that I was responsible for this scene, whose violence I repudiated. As a result of the blows that she received that night, she was deaf for a week.

Shaohua and I would live together for another year, not speaking, like strangers, and we would be among the last to be freed. By chance or by fate, we would find ourselves on the same train heading for Beijing.

12

A Friend Arrives

Sitting alone in the dark bamboo,
I play my lute and whistle song.
Deep in the wood no one knows
the bright moon is shining on me.
(Wang Wei, "The Bamboo Grove")

At the beginning of 1971, we were transferred to our fourth camp. This time it was a real prison, called *Dayu*—which means "large prison" in Chinese. It had high walls topped with barbed wire, and one had the impression that even a bird couldn't escape from this place. A single entrance made our comings and goings particularly easy to monitor.

The days and nights passed; they were unbearably gloomy. I was haunted by a certain musical work, Rachmaninoff's Second Concerto. He had written it at the end of a deep depression; it matched the desolate, vast landscape surrounding Zhangjiakou.

I was obsessed with music. It was the outcome of my rediscoveries: Chopin played on an accordion found by chance, the Cuban music resounding in the gray light of our *siheyuan*, the Zhangjiakou Opera...all of it culminated in a desire for music that became all-consuming. I thought

about it day and night. So much so that I began to devise a crazy plan—to have my piano sent from Beijing.

I talked about it in secret with my closest friends—with Huang Anlun in particular—who also longed to have an instrument. Everyone warned me against it. It was total madness. It could result in more years in the camps. Wouldn't it prove, beyond the shadow of a doubt, that I had not been re-educated? In addition, I was running the risk that, when I was let out, I would be given a *Fenpai*—a posting—that I would regret for the rest of my life. I would be made to pay, that was sure.

I listened to them but still formulated my plans. I tried another approach: what if I explained that I had had the piano sent so I could work on the *Yangbanxi*? After all, that was music we didn't just have a right to play—we had a duty. My friends continued to try and talk me out of it, and to worry. It was too dangerous.

Despite this, one day, one of them came up with an idea. He had made friends with He, a former movie actor who lived in the vicinity of the camp in a small, isolated shed. Because of his political views in the 1950s, he had been jailed and separated from his family. Over time, the conditions of his captivity had been relaxed; he was allowed to live by himself, and was watched only from a distance. My friend let him in on the secret: he was willing to take in my piano.

I didn't think twice—I immediately wrote to my mother:

> *I really want to have my piano here in Zhangjiakou. Do*
> *you think it would be possible to send it to me? I've made all*

*the arrangements on this end. I know I can rely on you. Write
back as soon as you can!*

Xiao-Mei

* * *

In fact, I hadn't made any arrangements, and here I was,
in all innocence, asking the impossible of my mother! She
wrote back to say that she would do anything for me, but
really, this time I was going too far. I kept trying, sending
letter after letter. I really needed the piano, I had to have
it. I urged her to investigate all possible solutions. Finally,
although she was sick and alone, my mother gave in. She
went to the Beijing train station and made discreet enquir-
ies about how to send a bulky package to Zhangjiakou. If
one could pay for it, the Chinese railway was prepared to
transport any object anywhere in China. But there was no
guarantee about how long it would take, nor the condition
of the object upon arrival. How could one send a piano—
and not just any piano, but a chapter in our family's his-
tory—and run such a risk? My mother wrote and said that
she just couldn't do it. It was asking too much of her.

But I wanted the piano, I wanted to start playing again.
Once more I beseeched my mother, and she gave in. Yes, we
were taking a risk; too bad if it brought misfortune. In the
end, my mother overcame every obstacle that a project like
this presented. She enlisted four workers whom she knew,
and with their help, packed the piano up in such a way that
it was unrecognizable. The piano was used to it! They then

brought the package to the Beijing train station and handed it over to the railway employees.

* * *

The little Sha Lingzi train station was situated along the road that led from Dayu to the fields in which we worked. This was where I had asked that the package be delivered. Each day I took advantage of our walk to the fields to ask: had something come for me? No, nothing. But that was to be expected. It took time for a piano to arrive, but my hopes began to fade with the passing days. It looked as though the piano had been lost somewhere in the labyrinth of the Chinese railroad. Abandoned for eternity, it no doubt had been condemned to rot in a warehouse somewhere in Inner Mongolia, or worse. I was sick at the thought of telling my mother. Three weeks had already gone by.

Then, a miracle happened.

"Yes, something has arrived for you," a railroad employee told me. "Go look on the platform behind the station."

My heart started beating faster. My piano had arrived! In a few minutes I was going to see it again. I ran in search of the platform and found myself in a sort of wasteland, where I could see, in the distance, a small, black, shapeless, shabby object. Was that it? My piano—so small, so black...it couldn't be. I went up to it, a lump in my throat. I removed the first layer, then the second, then the others until I could see wood—it was indeed my piano! Clearly, it had traveled in the coal compartment, but it had arrived, and was in one piece.

I leaned against it, and I spoke to it softly:

"I'll never leave you again, I swear. Never!"

Alone in the midst of the wasteland, I gazed at it, circled it, caressed it. How could it be so small? It had seemed so immense that day when I first saw it, at three years old, when the movers had brought it into my parents' bedroom. I stayed there, rooted to the spot, unable to move. No matter what happened, I knew life would no longer be the same.

But now it was time to act, and fast. I had to wrap it back up and move it before anything could happen to it. I hid the instrument under its covers and returned to Dayu for help. My friends came running. A piano, here, sitting in the middle of nowhere…I removed the covers once more. It emerged, gleaming in the middle of the drab, colorless landscape of the Mongolian border. We were speechless. The sight was strange, yes, but also enchanting. It was as if it had fallen from the sky. My friends shared my feelings; for a moment, we contemplated the sight in silence.

Then, all together, we loaded it onto a horse cart used to bring supplies to camp, which a friend who worked in the kitchen let me borrow. Our destination: the movie actor He's shack. There, we unpacked it and carefully put it in place. Then I made a more detailed inspection. The wood was not cracked, but what about the works? There was an easy way to find out. I sat down in front of it. For a moment, I was so agitated that I didn't know what to play. I lamely tried to begin the slow movement of Mozart's Piano Concerto No. 23. Oddly—I no longer recognized the sound of my piano, it was as if it were sick, congested. I lifted the top of the piano. It was as I had feared: twenty or so of the strings were broken.

I wasn't about to give up at the very moment of victory: that was out of the question. I removed each wire one by one; the next morning, I took advantage of a free moment to go to Zhangjiakou and check in the stores there. *That kind of wire? You won't find it here,* I was told. My only chance was to go directly to the factories in the vicinity. I went to one after another, only to be turned down each time. Then one day, fortune smiled on me.

"That type of wire? Yes, we have it here. How much do you need?"

My supplier couldn't have been less curious, and he gave me all sorts of lengths and thicknesses for free. I returned lighthearted and carefully replaced the broken strings. The result was mediocre, and even terrible on the piano's upper register. But I was happy. Now I heard a sound where once there had only been the noise of the hammer. Even if it was wounded, my piano was here, with me. Our shared journey had begun again.

As soon as surveillance began to lessen, I snuck over to see He via the camp latrines, mostly at day's end. There, I could play the music I loved without fear.

"The peasants around here are illiterate," he assured me. "They have no idea what music you're playing; they won't denounce you."

It was true. No one denounced me, and I rekindled my friendship with my piano. It was so much more than a musical instrument, it was a friend who had come to visit. I thought about all we had been through, about Schumann's *Reverie*, the Conservatory, the *Dazibao*, the Cuban music. It brought with it a part of me I thought had disappeared forever. The

more I gazed at it, the more it comforted me. Yes, there was hope, and no, my life would not end in Zhangjiakou.

* * *

Around that time, a new camp commander arrived. We nicknamed all of the commanders, and his name was "Thousand-Drops." When he took up his duties, the first thing he did was to recount the edifying story of a peasant who had worked so tirelessly in the fields that a thousand drops of sweat formed in a pool around him.

Thousand-Drops was not an intellectual like Tian, the commander of our first camp, nor was he an underhanded thug like I had seen in the other camps. He was a simple, spontaneous man, who gave the impression of being able to guess what you were thinking. Nevertheless, the temptation was too strong. A few of us approached him with a proposal that seemed to be above suspicion:

"We would like to practice the *Yangbanxi*, but we have no instruments. Could we try to get some?"

Play the *Yangbanxi*? Thousand-Drops assented. Was this a trap, or was he really taken in? There was no way to know. Nevertheless, a few instruments began to appear at Dayu. Like was given a cello. He took it with him everywhere, and even played in the fields under the trees! Other comrades, including my friend Huang Anlun, managed to get hold of two pianos. All these goings-on intrigued the camp leaders, but they allowed it to continue. That was the important thing.

I decided to bring my instrument to Dayu. If my comrades were playing within the camp walls, why not me? I

found a small soundproof room where I thought I could work in peace. A few friends helped me to transport the instrument.

That same evening, I went to the room after supper. What a shock! The temperature was barely above freezing, and the room was more like a refrigerator than a practice studio. There was only one thing to do—find something to burn in the little stove in the corner, and quickly. I had never in my life stolen anything. But after three years of re-education, I had turned into a coal thief. When the pieces I picked up along the railway tracks weren't enough, I stocked up from the coal pile in front of the barracks. The soldiers never understood why their supplies dwindled so quickly. I concealed my spoils in a hiding place I had made under the flooring.

* * *

Officially, we were working on the *Yangbanxi*. We had also been given Beethoven's *Appassionata* Sonata; it turns out it was Lenin's favorite piece of music. But it wasn't enough. Where could we find more scores? Our previous ones had gone up in smoke in the Conservatory's courtyard.

I had an idea. I went to see my friend, the daughter of Zho Henli, who had explained *Capital* to me. Could he perhaps send us scores?

My friend wrote to him. It was incredibly risky, far more dangerous than sending commentaries on class struggle and the dictatorship of the proletariat. Western music was still forbidden, and censorship still very much in place. But Zho Henli didn't say no; what's more, he was amazingly

efficient. His strategy was to send many packages, one after another. Most of them never arrived, of course, but a few miraculously made it past the censor. For us, it was a veritable renaissance. We gathered around the scores as if they were buried treasure, gazing at them at length before hiding them again. What would happen if we were found out? We tried not to think about it.

The surviving packages that arrived contained the first book of Bach's *Well-Tempered Clavier*, Chopin's Scherzos and Ballades, Beethoven's Sonatas for Cello and Piano, Grieg's Concerto, and Tchaikovsky's Piano Concerto No. 1. And then there was Rachmaninoff's Piano Concerto No. 2, whose haunting strains had accompanied me in my darkest hours. As soon as a score arrived, I began to play it on the nearest table, singing the orchestral accompaniment where needed.

How we fought over those few scores! It was fine to organize a schedule for passing them around, but how much better it would be if each of us had the full set. This time I called upon my mother for help: I asked her to find music paper for me. Once again, she managed, I don't know how. Secretly, shaking with fear, I copied out all of the scores one by one. In order to save the precious paper, my notations were so cramped they were almost illegible. I took the greatest care with the first book of *The Well-Tempered Clavier*; I wanted each polyphonic voice to be clearly distinguishable.

This was how the camp and its surroundings came to resound with the music of Bach, Chopin, and Rachmaninoff. Some of the soldiers were skeptical. We reassured them that it was the *Yangbanxi*—and Albanian music as well! We

sensed that they had their doubts, but no one expressed outright suspicion.

Huang Anlun, for his part, had managed to get hold of the theoretical writings of Walter Piston, a student of Nadia Boulanger's who had taught at Yale for many years. His books had always held a mythical status for us. Now, thanks once again to Huang Anlun, I was able to diligently work on harmony, counterpoint, and musical analysis. I learned how to write fugues, and I compared my efforts with those in *The Well-Tempered Clavier*. One thing was entirely clear—I should immediately end my career as a composer and return to playing the piano in my refrigerator!

13

The "Villa Medici"

*When three men are walking together,
there is one who can be my teacher.*

(Confucius)

The refrigerator became my refuge. Despite the danger
and the cold, I was happy there. For the first time, I could
play what I wanted, for my pleasure alone—with no thought
of the future. My relation to the piano was simple, and my
desire to play and to learn the repertoire was insatiable. I
felt at peace, weightless. A sensation of balance and fullness
appeared, the kind that only comes with complete detach-
ment from the purpose and usefulness of what one is doing.

 I endlessly worked on my technique. At the Beijing
Conservatory, I had labored tirelessly under Professor Pan.
But the teaching there was very restrictive, and I was for-
ever being advised for or against this or that work, based
on whether it was "right" for me. Here, I was building my
own technique, devising my own solutions to the chal-
lenges in Bach, Chopin, Liszt, and Rachmaninoff. For
Liszt's Hungarian Rhapsody No. 6, with its formidable
passages in octaves, I learned to keep my hands as close
as possible to the keyboard, in order to soften the attack.

I practiced it constantly, taking it as a sort of challenge. At the Conservatory, I was always told that my hands were too small to ever play Liszt well. Now Huang Anlun and I enjoyed playing the octave passages as fast as possible. It is an incredible thing to relearn technique: to forget everything, to study it anew with an open mind, to seek out and find solutions. Arriving at a result within the limits of my physical resources, uncovering the music's clarity—in the end, an activity as natural as eating and drinking—I learned this at Zhangjiakou. Montesquieu wrote: "I have never known any distress that an hour of reading did not relieve." If one substituted the word *music* for *reading*, the exact same dictum applied to me.

Late in 1971, a few friends and I decided to give our first concert. The official program was *Yangbanxi* and Albanian music. Thousand-Drops unsuspectingly gave us permission—or so it seemed.

The night of the concert, twenty of my friends packed into the refrigerator to hear what, only a few months earlier, would have been unthinkable. Huang Anlun announced the real program: Tchaikovsky's Piano Trio, Dvorak's Cello Concerto, and piano concertos by Rachmaninoff and Tchaikovsky. A highly romantic selection, reflective of the repertoire we loved. As the last chord sounded, I glanced around me and witnessed an emotion barely held in check. On each face there were the same questions: *Why were we being denied a future? Why had we been shut up here, without the right to practice our professions?* We could neither speak nor disperse. That night we drank, using alcohol to drown a host of feelings—happiness at our rediscovery of music, anguish at our powerlessness, and despair for our lost youth. By

allowing us to glimpse something unattainable, Thousand-Drops had unwittingly kindled our fury. Our situation was now intolerable.

The next day, life returned to normal—the fieldwork was as exhausting and monotonous as ever. We planted and harvested. The passage of time was only perceptible to us by the births and deaths of the animals around us. A dog died, five pups were born. But we were still there.

We believed less and less in what we were doing. During collective study sessions of *The Little Red Book*, we pretended to read the assigned texts while studying scores hidden in our jackets. We became obsessed with freedom. No one gave a thought to *Fenpai*, the "posting" that would free us from the camp. A dog belonging to a local peasant family gave birth to two pups: we named them Fen and Pai.

From a nearby camp, the news came that someone had attempted suicide. A painter had twice tried to cut his wrists. Then Lidi, one of my roommates, became pregnant. Since sexual relations were strictly forbidden, she was forced to have an abortion, and a meeting of the entire camp was held to hear her self-criticism. But it wasn't working any-more. We were not so easily fooled. Weren't we men and women like everyone else? Human beings now old enough to form couples? After the meeting, we found Lidi in tears in a corner of the camp. The daughter of a revolutionary, she had always been a role model for us, and here she was—a poor sick girl who had been crushed and humiliated. In a clumsy attempt to console her, we pooled our money and bought her a chicken—the traditional Chinese gift for a young mother. Too late we realized how clumsy our gesture

had been. Poor Lidi. She later married the father, but they never had another child.

The departures continued sporadically, as if to heighten the misery of those left to rot in Dayu. Early in 1972, shortly after the concert we gave together, Like left the camp. He promised to plead my case in Beijing, but deep inside I sensed that I would be the last to leave.

The day after his departure, despite a mounting feeling of despondency, I forced myself to trudge to the refrigerator to practice. When I opened the door, I saw that the entire floor was covered in huge bags. Like had left me a supply of coal that he had stolen before leaving. I tried not to think too much about him, about our friendship and the works we had played together. There was only one remedy for my despair—to practice the piano incessantly.

As always, my mother supported me. Once, I wrote to her that I didn't understand the indications in foreign languages on my scores. A short time later, I received a small notebook filled with her sober, beautiful handwriting. She had somehow managed to borrow one of the rare dictionaries of musical terms that was still being clandestinely circulated in Beijing, and she copied it out—without knowing a word of Italian, German, French, or English.

In November of that year, I was suddenly told to move the piano. My new space faced directly north, and was even colder than its predecessor. This time, it was a real refrigerator! The keys felt like they were made of ice. Despite this, I tried to practice. I played powerfully and fast; that would surely keep me from freezing. After a few moments, I had to stop. I was chilled to the bone. I ran around the camp courtyard in an attempt to thaw out, but nothing worked. I

then remembered something that Professor Pan once said: "The best way to warm up your fingers is to play the fugues from *The Well-Tempered Clavier*, and to clearly bring out each of the polyphonic voices."

How in the world could a slow fugue produce that effect? But once again, my first teacher was correct. Over and over, I played the Fourth Fugue in C-Sharp Minor and the Twenty-Second in B-Flat Minor. They are the only two fugues in Book One in five voices, and the Fourth Fugue has three subjects. Here was meditative music whose polyphony achieved a sort of mineral-like density. To bring out all of its power and beauty, my hands—so often condemned to a sort of immobility—had to coax feats of poise, flexibility, independence, and phrasing out of my fingers. Very quickly, I felt the beneficial effects of this exercise: my mind became calm, energy began to circulate in each finger, and then in the rest of my body. The music gave rise to a sort of non-action; it was like Tai Chi, a martial art based on balance and concentration, and on "action without action." An inner strength slowly awakened. That day, I understood that limbering up one's fingers is more about mind than matter.

At Dayu, I did not spend all my time with musicians. I also made friends with Fu, a brilliant painter. When he arrived at our first camp at Yaozhanpu, he painted large murals to the glory of Mao and the Revolution that were so beautiful we were left speechless. He talked to me about Rembrandt and Van Gogh, and I taught him about music. He spent whole evenings listening to me play Bach and the *Appassionata* Sonata.

One evening as we stepped out of the refrigerator and crossed the courtyard, he stopped short.

"How many colors are there in the sky?"

I gazed intently, my brows knitted. I could only see one. He also looked upwards.

"I can see seven."

As I stood there, unhappily still only perceiving one color, he gave me a piece of advice that I have remembered all my life:

"Every night, glance upward and observe, and you, too, will finally see the seven colors of the sky."

I followed his advice. And for the first time in my life, I began to observe with awareness. Up to that point, everything had been relatively straightforward. People, things, and actions were either good or bad, black or white. By contemplating the sky, I began to understand that life was not like that. I discovered the meaning of nuance. Some nights I could see nothing. I was patient; the next time I was able to see what only the night before had been invisible.

And, of course, I also understood what Fu was trying to convey—the palette of the sky varied according to my mood.

Teng Wenji was another very good friend. He had been a student at the Cinema School. Like Guo Baochang, the man who stoked the boiler at Yaozhanpu, he would become one of China's greatest film directors.

He was short and incredibly animated; he was also a consummate actor. He made us laugh, even here, within these isolated prison walls. He introduced me to cinema, excitedly explaining the quarrel between Stanislavski and Meyerhold, the two giants of early twentieth-century Russian theater. Stanislavski, the founder of the Actor's Studio, advised actors to take on their characters' emotions,

in order to make the scene come alive. Meyerhold, on the other hand, preferred stylization over naturalism. Chekhov once said that he "gave free rein to his imagination to avoid imitating life: everything except reality." Teng Wenji tried to persuade me:

"How can you not side with Stanislavski? When you act, you have to be *inside* the character. *Inside!*"

He described the films he loved, such as Eisenstein's *Alexander Nevsky*. Standing before me, he acted out the famous battle scene on the ice of Lake Chudskoe. He explained framing, how the sky loomed menacingly over the warriors at the start of the sequence, about the brilliance of the montage, the epic feeling that it creates. He was so convincing that I was able to visualize the whole scene: the ice breaking beneath the Teutonic knights with their helmets pierced by narrow eye slits. Terrifying.

Teng Wenji was among those who came to hear me play. One day, he remarked:

"It's too late for me to study music. But one day we'll leave here. When I have a son, I want you to teach him."

Teng Wenji had married right before leaving. He and his wife, who was in another camp, were separated by a great distance.

In time—and against all odds—our group was transformed into a sort of Villa Medici. We were a gathering of artists in the wilds of rural China, practicing one of Confucius's precepts: "When three men are walking together, there is one who can be my teacher."

Towards the end of 1973, I received an alarming letter from my mother: her stomach troubles had taken a turn for the worse, and she was afraid she would never see us again.

I quickly made up my mind: I had escaped once, I could do it again.

One morning, I slipped out of camp by the latrines and hurried to the station to catch the train for Beijing.

It was the first time my sisters and I had seen each other in five years. But the Cultural Revolution had not changed certain things—we were no more expressive with our feelings than before. There were no reunion celebrations, no complaining, no pity. We had more important things to attend to. Mother needed an operation, and since Father was in a camp under close surveillance, we had to take matters in hand. The surgeon told us the worst—it was cancer. She had a year at most to live. We didn't know it, but she had overheard everything.

"Too bad," she told me. "I'm not going to treat it, and I don't want a drastic intervention; I just want to be left in peace. All I want is to see Shanghai again."

While my mother was resting at home before leaving for Shanghai, a milestone event occurred. At the invitation of Mao's wife, the Philadelphia Orchestra, under the baton of Eugene Ormandy, was the first American orchestra to tour China since the start of the Cultural Revolution. Madame Mao had personally chosen the program for the orchestra's three concerts, with Beethoven's *Pastoral* Symphony as the centerpiece.

It was my dream to hear the Philadelphia Orchestra. In China, it had the reputation of being the best in the world. I was eager to expand my horizons. I wanted to do more than just play music by myself: I wanted to learn from Western musicians how it should be interpreted. Naturally, the audience was drawn from the ranks of soldiers, workers,

and peasants, and there was no way to legally buy a ticket. I decided to risk going, no matter what. This was a rare opportunity.

The night of the first concert, there was an enormous crowd outside the hall. I joined the line, trying to look like a spectator who was confident about getting in. The crowd surged forward; the entrance drew nearer. I saw everyone showing their tickets, and quickly jumped out of line. Outside, I went around the entire building, trying to find another way in, but there were guards stationed at every entrance. Two hours later, the far-off thunder of applause put paid to my hopes.

I came back the next night, more determined than ever. But, like Tamino at the gates of Sarastro's temple in *The Magic Flute*, the doors remained shut a second time. When I saw the crowds leaving the hall, however, I noticed that some people discarded their used tickets. All of a sudden, I had an idea. I had a friend who was a painter: if I picked up one of these scraps, he could easily forge the next day's date on it.

When the counterfeit ticket was finished, my friend asked me once again:

"Are you sure you want to take the risk?"

"I'm dying to go; I know what I'm doing."

"OK. But if you get caught, don't say I did it!" he responded jokingly.

That evening, I returned to the concert hall, excited but anxious. My plan would only work if at least one ticketholder didn't show up! I got past the ticket check and headed immediately to the toilets—the best spot to wait. When the silence told me that the audience had all gone in, I slipped

into the hall just before the doors closed. I looked quickly around me. There was an empty seat in the last row, and I rushed to take it. Eugene Ormandy made his entrance on stage, greeted the public and raised his baton. For the first time in my life I was hearing what a real orchestra sounded like. What an impression it made on me—the tonalities, the miraculous beauty of the string and wind sections! But I was gripped by fear. I glanced discreetly around me. What if I were to be arrested? What would I tell the police? What would happen to my parents? I was so nervous that I couldn't really appreciate the concert. I left, frustrated but with the feeling that I had been given a lesson in music. What an orchestra! How splendid it was.

* * *

My stay in Beijing provided an opportunity for reunions as well. I learned that Professor Pan had been given a few days' leave before returning to his camp. I went to the Conservatory and knocked at his door. No answer. Nearby, however, the door to the collective laundry room was ajar. I stuck my head in and recognized a familiar silhouette bending over the washing:

"Professor Pan!"

The silhouette went on working; he hadn't heard me. I called his name again, louder this time. Turning, he caught sight of me—he was surprised and shocked. A split second later, his face lit up with a wide smile:

"Zhu Xiao-Mei!"

"I came to say hello."

He drew closer, searching my face.

"You know," he said slowly, "this is the first time since the beginning of the Revolution that one of my old students has come back to see me."

We spent the afternoon together. He had two children now. He spoke of his time in camp, explaining how he, too, had been accused of belonging to the "516 Group." He had been deprived of sleep until he made a confession—a false one, of course. I told him how I had managed to bring my piano to Zhangjiakou. He was concerned for me.

"I owe you a great deal," I told him. "Every time I play, I think of you."

He asked what works I was playing. As I felt I could trust him, I also talked about my self-criticism, the one I had been forced to make at the Conservatory so long ago.

"Do you remember?"

"How can I forget? I was obliged to attend, and I'm not proud of it. But at the same time, when I watched you that day, deep inside I told myself: *One day, she will become a real artist. She can do it.*"

We said our good-byes.

"Take care of yourself," he whispered as I was leaving.

My mother returned from Shanghai a new woman. A visit to her native city had calmed her spirits; there was talk that she was cured. I decided to return to the camp at Dayu. This time, no one had come looking for me, but I was worried about the future. I had been told that if my behavior was satisfactory, I might be able to leave and to get a job. I was afraid that if I didn't return on my own, I would spend the rest of my days at Zhangjiakou.

When I got back to camp, I saw that discipline had melted away like snow. In the following months, there were

more and more departures. How we related to each other also changed: we no longer felt jealous when one of us was fortunate enough to be freed. We even organized little farewell parties. And yet, seeing my friends leave one by one made me discouraged. I felt lost, my willpower deserted me, and I was increasingly alone. We had been united in struggle, and had forged deep and lasting friendships with one another. Now, every departure dismantled a little more of the structure that we had so patiently built. Finally, out of the original one hundred inmates, only ten of us were left at Dayu—and unfortunately I was one of them.

No one ever told me the reason, but I knew very well why I had spent so many years in supplementary camps: my *Chushen bu hao* status, my escape to Beijing, my comings and goings to visit the former actor. None of this had gone unnoticed, and of course, there was my attitude towards music. I had been officially given permission to play the *Yangbanxi*, but the guards had not been as gullible as we had believed.

One day in the winter of 1974, the camp administration told me that, for the start of the next school year, a position had been found for me. I would be a professor at a teacher training college in Shijiazhuang, a dreary town near Beijing. I would be responsible for teaching the piano to beginners as an elective course. Like had been appointed to the Beijing Conservatory. Huang Anlun worked at the Opera; since Madame Mao cherished this institution, he had the right to fancy clothes, better food— even brioche. But I was being offered one of the worst jobs imaginable. I tried to protest. What was I going to do in Shijiazhuang?

"We are being magnanimous to even offer you that!"
I was told. "You escaped twice. And remember: if you
refuse, your wages will be cut off and you'll get no ration
coupons."

I returned to Beijing to take care of my mother, whose
health was still poor. I asked her advice.

"Don't go," my mother told me. "I'll share my coupons
with you."

I spent three months in Beijing, then returned to
Zhangjiakou to get my things. There were still seven people
left.

That was the winter of 1974. Five years of my life had
been spent in camps.

I ought to have been happy to leave Zhangjiakou, but I
had no future. For years, I had only one goal: freedom. At
last this had been achieved, but what was I going to do? I
had no profession, no salaried position, no ration coupons.
I was dependent on my mother, whose poor health required
me to stay in Beijing.

At Zhangjiakou, we had all been on an equal footing.
Now, this was no longer the case. On the one hand, there
were those who were lucky enough to have been given an
interesting posting and to have a real position. On the other
hand, there were those whose artistic careers had been
destroyed by the camp, like the dancers whose bodies had
changed so radically they would never return to the stage.
Finally, there were those who, like me, felt as though their
country had rejected them.

Yes, I was free, but I was anxious and bitter. I looked
back and reflected on the lost years: on the music I hadn't
played and the books I hadn't read. I thought about the

love I hadn't been able to give to my family, how my grand-
mother had died alone, how I had suspected my father of
being a spy. About how my dignity had been taken from me.
About the acts I had committed.

14

From Mao to Mozart

There is only one beauty,
the beauty of truth revealing itself.
(Auguste Rodin, *Art*)

"You're not tired? Then continue playing."

I had just finished the *Appassionata* Sonata and was starting on Rachmaninoff's Second Concerto.

When I was done, Professor Pan laughingly chided me, "I know why you're not tired. It's because you're not inside the music. You aren't moved, you aren't playing with your heart. You're not working with your imagination as I taught you. Do you remember?"

I had called on my old teacher a few days earlier. He, too, had been definitively discharged from camp.

"I want to see you again," I told him, "to show you what I worked on at Zhangjiakou. May I stop by?"

So there we were, reunited, eleven years after the last time I had played for him.

"We are going to work together," Professor Pan said, "but we have to be discreet. I don't want any trouble. There's a small studio in one of the Conservatory buildings where

we won't be disturbed. I'll show you where. We can meet there for lessons—but we must keep it a secret."

Professor Pan was pleased at what I had accomplished at Zhangjiakou. He found, however, that my playing had become mechanical, that it was now louder and faster than before I had left.

"Zhu Xiao-Mei," he told me, "it's fine to play Rachmaninoff, but let's go back to pieces that are at once simpler and more challenging. Bach's *Chromatic Fantasy and Fugue*, and above all Scarlatti."

Professor Pan's tact had survived the Cultural Revolution—he still knew how to correct me without being hurtful.

What a joy it was to work with him again! I was also pleased to have my old piano back: a friend had shipped it from Zhangjiakou, and I had had it restored—as much as I could. In every other respect, daily life in Beijing was dismal. My sisters were still in exile, and so was my father, although he was allowed to return home for short monthly visits. When he was home, he barely spoke; it seemed as though life had cast him aside. Even when he was finally granted permission to live in Beijing, he remained under surveillance.

It was only thanks to my mother's ration coupons that I survived.

Nevertheless, deep inside I had resolved to work hard—every minute, every hour, every day—to make up for lost time. To absorb everything I had not learned over the past decade. I had seen too many of my classmates leave for the hinterlands and abandon their studies forever. I told myself that, by staying in the capital, even under these dreadful conditions, I at least had an opportunity to discover and explore. To learn about everything I had been deprived of,

from music theory to learning English. All I could think about was studying and preparing for a competition—if the chance ever came.

I had plenty of support in this crazy undertaking—there was Professor Pan, of course, but also my close friends: Huang Anlun, his wife Ouyan, and Like.

Ouyan, who worked at the Beijing Dance Academy, tried to find me work as an accompanist:

"Xiao-Mei," she constantly told me, "you can't continue like this, with nothing to live on."

Her lobbying skills were as keen as her musical ability, and she vouched for me. In addition, Lao Xue, the president of my father's university who had already helped my father so much, intervened on my behalf. One summer day in 1975, thanks to both of them, I was assigned to the Beijing Dance Academy. I worked as an accompanist; the job involved playing the piano for several hours at a stretch for young, preadolescent dancers. Each day, I had to compose little tunes and invent new programs that I would repeatedly play. At least I now had something to live on.

I had been working at the Academy for several months when I ran into a friend, Wei-Zhao. She had something to tell me: her brother and sister had managed to flee to Hong Kong by swimming across the straits that separate it from China. This was the first time I had heard of such a thing—I later learned that hundreds of people attempted it daily. I became obsessed with this idea. They had made it, I began to think about it. I made some discreet inquiries: it took a very practiced swimmer six hours to cross the waters between China and Hong Kong. After six hours, the tide came in, making the distance to cover even greater.

I was a poor athlete—this had been patently clear since my dance classes at the Conservatory. Perhaps though, with a lot of practice, I could do it.

It would require a great deal of preparation. Each morning at six o'clock, I would swim, take classes, do laps. I would also study English with ever greater determination. I would buy a blackboard and write on it twenty new words to learn each day. I was not about to spend my life playing the piano for children's ballet classes. I was going to leave China, one way or another.

* * *

While I was devising my escape plans, Professor Pan came up with a very different idea. One day, as we worked together, he remarked:

"Do you remember when we were preparing for your first recital at the Conservatory? It wasn't possible then, but it is now. At the Dance Academy, you have a big room and a grand piano. You could give a concert there."

I was taken aback. That recital should have taken place thirteen years earlier—if circumstances had permitted. I thought back to my original program: Beethoven's *Pathétique* Sonata; Mozart's Piano Concerto No. 23, which I had prepared with Professor Pan; and Chopin's Etude Op. 25, No. 3. Wasn't Western classical music still off-limits? Nevertheless, I put my trust in my teacher. I worked up a new program: some Scarlatti sonatas, Beethoven's Piano Sonata No. 18, Liszt Etudes, and César Franck's *Symphonic Variations*. I told my friends:

"It will take place at four o'clock, in secret. Keep it to yourselves."

* * *

That afternoon, in the spring of 1976, the studio at the Academy was packed. The "secret" had circulated quite efficiently by word of mouth. "There's going to be a concert in Beijing," those in the know said, "one of the first since the Cultural Revolution." Have I ever in my life played for a more appreciative audience?

* * *

Playing and listening to music became an obsession for me—for all of us. It was rumored that not every record had been destroyed during the Revolution. Addresses began to be passed around, one in particular: a professor at Beida University had managed to save a few musical treasures. Huang Anlun became a collector, buying up everything he could find. I spent all my savings on a record player, and I scoured Beijing seeking out the few LPs that had been saved from destruction. In particular, I was eager to find recordings by Emil Guilels, a powerful but sensitive pianist, who languished somewhat in Sviatoslav Richter's shadow.

After being forced underground for so long, the art world had begun to boil over. Is that why, on July 28, my piano woke me in the middle of the night? Or was it to warn me? It emitted a strange sound, muted and low. I got out of bed; it had moved to the middle of the room all by itself. My parents had also been awakened. A clamor arose in the streets—it was an earthquake! As we rushed outside, I thought of my piano, which I had left behind.

Thankfully, our house withstood the quake.

The Tangshan earthquake—which killed hundreds of thousands of people—seemed to augur some great event, an imminent change of dynasty. And indeed, on the afternoon of September 9, 1976, when I arrived at the Academy, an announcement was made:

"The esteemed and adored Great Leader of our Party, our army, and the peoples of all nationalities of our country, Comrade Mao Zedong, master of the international proletariat, of the oppressed peoples and nations of the earth, has died..."

When I got back to the house at day's end, I found my father in bed. He was pale, and his breathing was labored, as if he had suffered a heart attack.

"Xiao-Mei, I'm frightened. It's going to start all over again, just like before."

* * *

After Mao's death, political tensions ran high: a power struggle broke out between Hua Guofeng on the one hand and the Gang of Four—which included Madame Mao—on the other. It ended with the arrest of the Gang of Four. It was an uneasy period, but also an era of openness and reforms.

In 1977, for the first time in a very long while, the universities began to operate normally. Entrance exams were reinstated based on knowledge and aptitude, instead of on family background and political criteria. The Beijing Conservatory reopened its doors, and the first conventional entrance exams in more than a decade were announced.

I didn't waste a second—I had to go back and finish my studies! This was the moment I had been waiting for.

All of my pent-up frustrations exploded. The lack of scores at Zhangjiakou, the need to copy them out and to set up a schedule to share them among ourselves. The need for secrecy to study with Professor Pan, or to play before an audience. The absence of records and concerts—in all those years, the only concert I had ever attended was the one by the Philadelphia Orchestra, and even then under what conditions! At the Conservatory, it would be different, and the years of hardship since my return from Zhangjiakou would finally find their *raison d'être*.

I sped over to the Conservatory to pick up an application. *Impossible*, I was told: *The maximum age limit for enrollment is twenty-five*. I was crushed. All of my hard work over these past years, all of my sacrifices—sometimes even going without enough to eat. To think that I wasn't even going to be allowed to take the entrance exam. I hurried to see Professor Pan, who energetically encouraged me:

"Go to the Ministry of Culture. Be persistent: don't leave until you get what you want."

Accompanied by four other classmates who were in the same situation, I went to the ministry and we organized a sit-in. Our slogan was a simple one:

"If we are at the same level as the younger students, take them. If we are better, take us!"

We were prepared to go to any length; this became so apparent to the ministry that they ended up hearing our case. We were given permission to sit the entrance exam for upper-level classes. I breathed a sigh of relief.

I had three months to prepare. Three months to make up for lost time—a whole decade! Every age group was being tested in a grueling competition: harmony, counterpoint,

and musical analysis, as well as ancient and modern Chinese, English, and political science. I worked tirelessly.

There was a shortage of books, but the Conservatory professors, the same ones, who just a few years earlier, had been reduced to cleaning toilets, gave us all the courses we wanted for free. They moved mountains for us. I analyzed in detail all of Beethoven's sonatas with one of the only professors who had trained in Germany.

"You're going to make it," she said to me one day.

Her kind words lifted me up. At the Academy, I accompanied the young dancers while reading political science and English books. My mother brought me my lunch so that I would lose as little time as possible. Finally, one of the teachers grasped my situation and sent me home, saying:

"Go and study. We'll practice without music."

Every day, Professor Pan gave me a lesson. All my friends, most of whom had abandoned the idea of returning to their studies, supported me.

The day of the competition finally arrived, but I didn't want to tell my parents. My program included Schumann's *Fantasie* and *Prelude*, a piece composed by Huang Anlun. He had dedicated it to one of his friends, a *Chushen bu hao* who had been crushed by the Revolution. When Huang Anlun handed me the score for the first time, he said:

"It's music that describes the rebellion of a caged animal."

Including this piece in my competition program gave me a feeling of invincibility. It expressed the rage of an entire generation. I put so much energy into it that I broke one of the strings on the Conservatory's Steinway. Defying the rule that forbade any show of support, the spectators

in the upper balcony broke into applause. All of my friends were seated there; they understood the feeling that I was trying to convey, on behalf of us all.

The results were announced the following day. Four names were written on a small slip of red paper on the wall by the entrance to the Conservatory. I drew closer. My name was there, along with three others. I had succeeded. In the end, I was right not to accept the posting I had been offered upon my return from Zhangjiakou. I was right to choose destitution, refusal, and solitary endeavor. My stubbornness meant that I was going to be able to continue my studies. I ran home to break the news to my parents. They hadn't fallen for my ruse, however—they already knew. In secret, they had gone to the Conservatory themselves. My mother had prepared a feast.

"I'm very proud of you," my father said.

Finally, one of his daughters was going on to higher education, and had found an honorable place in his country. For him, it was a kind of sweet revenge.

* * *

As things slowly normalized in the educational sector, cultural and artistic circles also began to take advantage of the new spirit of openness.

Intellectuals, back from their *Shang shan xia xiang*—the labor camps—came together and published their writings, which often had double meanings. Huang Anlun introduced me to the publishing milieu, where I met Xiaoqin, a young editor, with whom I immediately became friends. She was a poet; she read her poems to me and came to hear

me play. Through her, I met intellectuals who were workin,
for democracy. At the time, she was very much in love with a
French man; she wanted to marry him and move to France.

Western books slowly began to reappear. Based on the
enthusiastic recommendation of a painter friend, I traded
two years of piano lessons for a translation of Rodin's *Art*.
Rodin's subject was the visual arts, but his writings corre-
sponded exactly to my experience of music. When I trans-
posed his meditations to the musical world, they spoke to
me: "Really beautiful drawing and style are those that you do
not even think of praising because you are so interested in
what they express. The same is true of color. There is really
no beautiful style, no beautiful drawing, no beautiful color.
There is only one beauty, the beauty of truth revealing itself."

Teng Wenji was working on his first film, *The Sounds
of Life*, a courageous look at how music had suffered cat-
astrophically under the influence of Mao's wife. We saw
each other often. He now had a son, a gentle little boy to
whom I was giving piano lessons, just as he had wanted at
Zhangjiakou. I often talked to Teng Wenji about my desire
to leave China.

"Don't go," he told me. "There is so much to accomplish
right here."

My other friends said the same thing:

"You have to love your country. Stay here."

I did love my country, but I felt like it didn't love me.

* * *

After Nixon's visit, American influence in China increased.
Of the few films that we were allowed to see, two had a

n my generation: *Love Story* and *Jonathan*
Such love and idealism. They weren't
hey allowed us to dream. The books on
were based were readily available; we saw the
films over and over, and read and reread the books. I was
especially moved by the story of Jonathan Livingstone,
the seagull who didn't want to live like everyone else, who
wanted to fly higher than all the others, to the point of risk-
ing his life. The idea of America filled me with lofty feelings
and wonderful ideas. People were indeed lucky to live there.

After the Philadelphia Orchestra, it was the Boston
Symphony Orchestra's turn to come to China, with Seiji
Ozawa as conductor. He was Japanese, of course, but the
public considered him to be Chinese because he was born
in Manchuria. He dazzled the audience by conducting con-
temporary Chinese works from memory. At the end of the
concert, he wept when a group of musicians surprised him
by playing traditional Chinese instruments in his honor.

In music, American cultural influence reached a peak
in 1979, with the visit of the celebrated violinist Isaac Stern.
He gave master classes at the Conservatory. A documentary
about his visit, entitled *From Mao to Mozart*, was a huge success
in the West. Stern was very tough on the Chinese students
who played for him; he harshly criticized their way of play-
ing Western music. He couldn't understand their interpreta-
tions and felt an oddness in their emotional responses. But
why? It was because the Cultural Revolution had destroyed
everything—as proof, only the very youngest students, who
had been spared the impact of the Revolution, escaped
criticism. When Stern himself performed one of Mozart's
violin concertos, the gulf that separated his interpretation

from that of the Chinese students was blindingly apparent. He played as though he were speaking with real emotion. Increasingly, I dreamed of studying with the great Western musicians.

Isaac Stern's visit was a turning point. It became clear to us that the few Chinese musicians who could find a sponsor would be allowed to study abroad.

I wanted to leave. To go to America, the land of liberty.

* * *

The administration at the Conservatory tried to dissuade me. I should stay, they told me, China was putting itself back together; it could not allow its newly-minted graduates to leave. I pressed my case for weeks on end, determined. In vain. I was not going to be allowed to go. Fortunately, a few children of highly placed officials had the same idea, and they were certainly not going to be refused. One day, I was given the green light, along with a group of them. The first obstacle was behind me.

Other hurdles followed, and I cleared them one after another. A cousin of my mother's who lived in Hong Kong gave me the name of her son, Chen. He was living in Los Angeles and offered to put me up. Then, I obtained the necessary sponsorship to apply for a visa: the California Institute of the Arts. I had managed to send them a recording I had made on the only tape recorder I could find. Then things got bogged down. The authorities in charge of granting me permission began dragging their feet. As the weeks passed, I became so anxious I made myself sick. Then it was the American Embassy's turn to torment me.

Everything ground to a halt, until one day I decided to risk it all.

* * *

An Australian friend managed to put me through to the American ambassador to China. Without thinking, I grabbed the receiver and stammered a few words in English:

"Please help me. I have been waiting for weeks. You have refused my visa application several times. I want to come and see you."

The next day, I was in the ambassador's office.

"You cannot imagine what my life has been like—"

He cut me off.

"I know everything," he said in impeccable Chinese. I know what has been going on in this country, and what you have suffered; you don't need to tell me. You will have your visa immediately."

When I went home that night, I was filled with an indescribable feeling of relief, a sense of victory that eclipsed everything else. Smiling broadly, I broke the news:

"Mama, I have it! I have my visa! I did it!"

But my mother didn't smile. She didn't even answer. She just turned away, wordlessly. And in a split second, I understood. I could have kicked myself—how could I have been so blind? Of course, she had encouraged me to go, she had helped me every step of the way, but the cruel truth was there all along—I had won my freedom, but she was losing her child.

Still, my mind was made up. The New Year was only a few days away, but I couldn't wait. I wanted to leave immediately, to flee. Forever.

* * *

I had my visa, but how was I going to pay for a plane ticket to Los Angeles? And what gifts would I bring my cousins? We had so little money. One evening, as we were in the midst of preparing for my departure, my mother said to me:

"I've been thinking. There's only one solution: we'll sell the piano. It's once again become valuable. Everyone wants to play music now; pianos are scarce and very much in demand."

We contacted a few people in Beijing. She was right, we found a buyer immediately.

"I'll come and pick it up next Monday evening," he told us after we had decided on a price.

At seven in the evening the following Monday, he arrived with three moving men and an envelope with the agreed-upon sum.

"No. I can't do it," my mother simply told them. Turning to me, she added, "The piano is you. If you leave and the piano goes, too, it will be as though you are leaving twice. I won't be able to bear it."

And so the piano stayed where it was. How could I ever have agreed to my mother's original offer? How could I have imagined selling my partner in captivity, the one I had promised—that day at the Zhangjiakou train station—I would never abandon? I would pay for the plane ticket by working for a few months in Hong Kong, and that was that.

The day of my departure finally arrived. My mother didn't have the strength to go with me to the train station. Right to the end, she had nourished the hope that I would spend the New Year with the family, giving her a few extra days before we parted. But I was terrified that my visa would be withdrawn. As I was about to leave the house, my father—who, up until then, hadn't said a word about my plans—told me:

"Stay in America; don't come back. There is no justice here. With you over there, at least one member of the family will have been saved."

That was all. We remained as stoic as ever: no farewells, no hugs. A friend took me to the station. We said good-bye. I climbed aboard, sat down across from a Westerner who looked American, and the train for Hong Kong pulled out.

I could feel my throat tighten and tears start to well up. "You must never cry," my mother had told me. "If you feel you can't help yourself, at least do it in private." I looked around. The train car was nearly empty, and it was as though I were alone. I knew no one, and they didn't know me. Outside the window, the outskirts of Beijing began to slip away. Suddenly, the dam broke and I was swept away. It was over. I let my tears fall without holding them back or wiping them away. I cried and cried, as I had never done as a child.

The date was February 1, 1980.

15

A Seagull in Hong Kong

Home I have none.

Flock I have none.

I am Outcast.

(Richard Bach, *Jonathan Livingstone Seagull*)

I cried so hard that it became contagious. Both the American sitting across from me and the train's young hostess tried to comfort me, but in vain, and they ended up with tears in their eyes. Between sobs, I told them a little about my life. From the expressions on their faces, I could see that they understood. I gazed at the passing landscape. It was the last time I would see it, and I had to engrave it into my memory; after that, it would be too late.

My mother had fixed me a little bag in which she had placed all of my favorite foods. It was her final act of kindness, the last thing she would ever do for me. But I couldn't eat a thing. I gave everything to my traveling companions.

I was wrapped in my thoughts, remembering what my father had told me: "Don't come back...at least one member of the family will have been saved." He encouraged me to go. But what would become of them? And, without them, what would happen to me?

Then I thought about crossing the border. What if I were turned back, arrested, thrown into prison? I was gripped by a sense of foreboding. Finally, night drew a curtain across the land, and seemed to whisper in my ear: "Look at it, it's disappearing forever."

* * *

After a full day and night of traveling, we reached the border. We had to leave the train and go through a police checkpoint before crossing the bridge that separates China from Hong Kong. I had been warned: one word too many, one gesture out of place, one suspicious move, and it's all over. It was a lottery in which your fate was decided.

I took one last look at China. I thought about the thirty years I had spent in my native land—about the Music School, the Conservatory, Zhangjiakou. In just a few moments, if all went well, everything would change. If all went well...I took a deep breath and set off in the direction of the bridge to meet the Chinese border patrol. I looked straight ahead of me, avoiding anyone's gaze. I got to where the police stood. They took my papers, and then gave them back. Not a word. Not a move. What were they thinking? Every second I stood there, and even after I continued on my way, I was convinced that they would call me back, bar my path.

But nothing happened. I was allowed through.

The hardest step was behind me. Now came the final one, which was much easier. I presented myself to the Hong Kong police.

"Would you open your backpack, please?"

I gave them my one piece of luggage, and they began to go through it.

"What's this?"

The policeman pulled out one of the gifts I had bought for my cousin Chen.

"That's a martial arts sword. It's a present."

"It's dangerous. You're not going through. Wait here."

The policeman went off to get instructions. The minutes dragged by, and no one returned. I said to one of his colleagues:

"If it's a problem, you can keep it."

He refused to listen. Three hours passed. Finally, the officer's superior came and looked at the sword...

"It's fine. You can go."

I wasted no time following his orders. But to tell the truth, once I got out, I was a bit lost. Where exactly was I? I turned to the people who were walking beside me, in the midst of a dense crowd:

"Could you tell me where the Louho Bridge is, please?"

They looked at me, taken aback:

"The bridge is back there. You're in Hong Kong. You're free."

I had left Chinese territory without even knowing it!

I ran to find a taxi and confidently told the driver the address. If you falter, my cousins said, you could go straight to prison. There were so many Chinese who swam across the bay every day.

* * *

A few minutes later, I rang my cousins' doorbell, on the fifteenth floor of a big tower. The door opened, and there

they stood, friendly and talkative. I hadn't been in their home for more than ten minutes before they handed me an ultimatum:

"Before anything else, Xiao-Mei, you've got to change your clothes and go to the hairdresser. We'll talk more later."

I quickly found myself in a bedroom trying on my first close-fitting shirt and pair of jeans. My cousin seemed relieved. She gathered up the magenta sweater I had traveled in. It was the nicest one I owned. I had picked it out especially for the trip. My mother had knitted it herself; along with the food she had prepared, and a few photos, it was the only souvenir of her I had. In a flash, my cousin had returned:

"I put it in the trash," she said. "You really can't go out wearing something like that. People will immediately know you're from China and that could lead to trouble."

The next day, I set out to explore Hong Kong. I never could have imagined such material wealth, such an abundance of opportunities. I was invited to people's homes and given advice: "Settle down here, give piano lessons and earn money to help your family." "You'll never have a career." My cousins got it into their heads to find me a husband. I was seized by doubt. What should I do? Work and send money home? Or stick to my plan and leave for the States?

While waiting to figure out the answer, I found work as an accompanist in a ballet school. I had never had a job that was so well paid, never imagined I could earn so much. I observed the life around me; it was comfortable, but also dull. I looked into teaching piano in Hong Kong; the level seemed rather low.

For the first time in my life, I was completely free to choose. And so I chose. A month after my arrival, my mind was made up. As usual, my decision was more intuitive—more unconscious—than reasonable or logical. But then, reason had never much interested me. I couldn't do what everyone else did: the impossible was much more exciting.

Life in Hong Kong was not for me. There was so little cultural life, and I had a thirst for everything—music, literature, cinema, painting. And I certainly wasn't going to spend my life giving piano lessons to pampered wealthy kids just to earn money. There were many more important things in life. It was absurd. The Communists despised money, and on this point, I had to agree with them.

No, it didn't make sense to stop here in mid-flight, without going all the way. What had life given me up to that point? Nothing. I was over thirty years old. The Cultural Revolution had robbed me, and my entire generation, of our youth. I wanted to make up for lost time, see what I was capable of and how far I could go. I knew it was too late for the international competitions, but so what? I knew that the piano was more important to me than anything else, and I was ready to sacrifice everything for the life of an artist. I was prepared to set off into the unknown, to go without, to struggle, to give up both seeing my family and starting one of my own. Perhaps I would fail. But deep inside, I believed in my lucky star. Later, I would view this decision as egotistical. But for now, the die was cast and the choice was clear—as soon as I had saved enough money for a plane ticket, I would leave for the States.

By late March 1980, everything was set. I had my ticket, and Chen was waiting for me in Los Angeles. I said my

good-byes to my cousins and the friends I had made during those two months in Hong Kong.

One morning I set off for the airport. I thought of Jonathan Livingstone, the seagull who wanted to fly higher than all the others. California was waiting. America: the land of liberty and wealth, the place where everything was possible.

PART TWO

THE WEST

16

The Land of Freedom

The best man is like water.
Water is good, it benefits all things
and does not compete with them.
It dwells in lowly places that all disdain.
This is why it is so near to Tao.

(Laozi)

"Who was Laozi?"

I confessed my ignorance to my seatmate, a quiet woman with a steady smile.

We had introduced ourselves just after takeoff. She had reassuringly told me that the red drink they'd served as an aperitif was not blood, but tomato juice. She also informed me that the little gold-paper packet emblazoned with a tiger, which I mistook for tiger balm, was actually something called butter. But our conversation really got underway after I overturned my food tray onto her dress.

"It's all right, don't worry about it," she said.

I learned that she was an American, a university professor and a Sinologist.

She tried again:

"Laotsi? Laotsu? Laosi?"

I still didn't understand, and it wasn't a question of pro-nunciation. I was the source of the problem, not her. I had simply never heard of a philosopher named Laozi.

"I understand," she said. "I'm aware of what happened during the Cultural Revolution."

So this American taught me, a Chinese woman, some-thing I didn't know.

"Laozi was one of the greatest Chinese philosophers. At least, that's my opinion. We know very little about his life. It's believed that he lived during the sixth century BCE, and that he was an archivist at the royal court of the Zhou dynasty during the Spring and Autumn Period. He yearned to become an advisor to the king, but he was unsuccessful. He then understood that renouncing all worldly desires was the path to wisdom, and he decided to go into exile. He got as far as the border; there a guard recognized him and begged him not to depart before he had shared the essence of his knowledge. Laozi acquiesced and wrote the *Dao de jing* before disappearing forever. He was a contemporary of Heraclitus, and preceded Plato by a century; and yet, he is much less well-known than the other two. I often teach him in my courses. I would like people to become more familiar with him in the West. In today's violent world, we have great need of him."

Unaware that I was even less well acquainted with Plato and Heraclitus, she rose from her seat and fished a small book out of her bag.

"I'd like to read you a passage, perhaps my favorite," she said. "'The best man is like water. Water is good, it benefits all things and does not compete with them. It dwells in lowly places that all disdain. This is why it is so near to Tao.'"

I stared at her in astonishment. For me, life was a series of struggles. Above all, the struggle for success, and I was headed to the United States with precisely that in mind. I did not understand what Laozi meant: my goal was first place, certainly not "the lowly place that all disdain." My seatmate must have intuited what I was thinking because she added, smiling:

"Think it over. One day you will see how true it is."

As we made our descent towards Los Angeles, she helped me fill out my disembarkation card for the immigration authorities, and gave me her address:

"I live quite a distance from Los Angeles, but don't hesitate to call me. And please, call collect."

* * *

The plane touched down. This way to the exit. The exit? But where was it? The airport terminal was so enormous, it was a veritable city. I had mistakenly stepped away from the flow of passengers, and now I was lost. An escalator brought me up to a cafeteria; I didn't know which way to turn. I caught sight of a Chinese man, seated in front of a large paper cup. I went up to him, already feeling better:

"Please sir, I'm sorry to bother you, but I'm lost. I took the escalator, and now I can't find the exit."

The man reluctantly stopped drinking from the straw, looked me up and down, and then said in a thick Taiwanese accent:

"Think about it: if there's an up escalator, there's bound to be another that goes down, right?"

It wasn't hard to understand why he had reacted that way. There was no way for me to hide I was from the People's Republic of China, and that didn't endear me to him. My self-confidence suddenly failed me. I had never heard of Laozi, I didn't know what tomato juice was, and now I couldn't find my way out of the airport. I wandered around for quite a while until I finally saw, far off, someone waving at me: it was my cousin Chen! He had come to meet me, accompanied by his two oldest daughters.

A few minutes later, we were driving towards Beachwood Canyon, a suburb near Hollywood, where the family lived.

"You know," he told me, "since the end of the Cultural Revolution, a lot of Chinese have immigrated to the US. Their behavior often leaves something to be desired. They want to get ahead and make a lot of money, but they don't want to work."

For a moment I thought about my father, who had worked hard his whole life with nothing to show for it. I reassured Chen.

"I won't be like them; I want to earn my own living. I'll find a way."

While we talked, I gazed at the passing houses. They all looked like palaces.

My cousin Amy, a beautiful woman, was waiting at the door, cradling her youngest child. I glanced around me. Their home was spacious and tastefully decorated. But so cluttered—I had only ever lived in spare places with bare walls, and my head started to spin. One detail stood out in particular: the floor was covered in toys. They were every-where, the majority new or almost new, but all of them seemingly abandoned. I had never had any toys. Except, of

course, the little spear decorated with a red flag that Mao had wanted in the hands of every child in China.

I presented the gifts I had brought from home, which had been so costly for my parents. Amy barely glanced at the two jade pendants that my mother had carefully picked out. And as for the sword that had nearly prevented me from crossing the border into Hong Kong, it never made it out of its wrapping during my entire visit. My cousins had other concerns.

A half hour later, when I came down from my temporary bedroom, I offered to put away the children's toys. It was as much for the pleasure of it, as out of a concern for order. I picked them up, examining each one from all sides. I took pleasure in touching them. Chen remarked good-naturedly:

"Take whatever you like. The kids have far too many."

I noticed a little bag. Chen insisted:

"Go ahead, keep that one, if you like it."

After dinner, we sat down in front of the television. President Jimmy Carter was addressing the nation: the US was in the middle of the Iran hostage crisis. I strained to grasp what he was saying, but my knowledge of English was wholly insufficient. Chen broke in and asked me:

"Did you understand what he said?"

I had to confess: I hadn't.

"He said, '*Help me.*' You couldn't make that out? It's going to be difficult for you to study if you don't even know simple words. You need to start learning English."

"How should I go about it?"

"One way is to watch television like us. We'll also give you cassettes of children's stories in English. Listen to them at night while you are sleeping. It's not difficult."

Amy added:

"Xiao-Mei, instead of studying, you should think about your parents. In order to send them money, you should give private piano lessons."

"Or come work as a nurse's aid in my clinic," Chen added. "In the US there are all sorts of opportunities for young people; but it's very hard for the elderly, who often live far from their families. There's a great demand for care providers. In fact, it pays quite well."

This was not easy to hear, particularly at the end of my first day. But I understood their perspective. We were from different worlds. Chen was a typical Hong Kong émigré. He had attended a British high school before his father sent him to an American university. He met his future wife there, a biology student from Taiwan. They married and then settled down in Los Angeles, where they joined a large diaspora. This community allowed them to remain faithful to their Chinese culture. Chen gave free acupuncture classes. At home, the family spoke Chinese and ate Chinese food. But that didn't prevent them from integrating into American life.

* * *

The next morning, after a sleepless night, I enrolled in a nearby language school that offered English classes to refugees. I found myself in the midst of Mexicans, unable to understand a single word, with no one to help me. Returning to my cousin's house, I admired the long streets lined with magnificent flowers: I had so often dreamed of this America. It was truly paradise. But I felt like such a

foreigner, and I wondered if there was a place for me here. To tell the truth, I hadn't experienced anything as difficult as this since my arrival at Zhangjiakou.

A few days later, a new student joined our class at the language school. She was a young Chinese woman—thin, pale, and frightened. We exchanged glances. I was sure I had seen her somewhere before.

"Dora?"

"Yes. Do I know you?"

Dora was the daughter of the Beijing Conservatory's director; she had come with her mother to see me the day after my alleged suicide attempt. How could I ever forget her? I had heard that she had immigrated to the US, but I never thought I'd run into her. She looked like she was at her wits' end.

"I'm having so much trouble," she said. "My cousins who are putting me up don't give me anything to eat, and I'm afraid to ask for anything. I'm so hungry. I'm completely worn out."

That evening, I explained the situation to my cousin Chen.

"Tell her to come here," he said straightaway.

And so Dora joined us until she could get her health back together. In the end, she stayed a number of months.

* * *

I wrote my first letter to my mother. We had made an agreement: once I was in the US, I wouldn't send my parents any money, as I would need it. On the other hand, we would write to each other every week. I told her that everything

was going well, but that wasn't really the case. Deep down, I felt as though I were suffocating.

After I had fulfilled this first obligation, I combed through the employment listings in the *Los Angeles Times*. Courses at the California Institute of the Arts didn't start until September, and I needed to find something to do until then. Baby-sitting and house cleaning were possibilities. My first few telephone calls, however, were disastrous.

"What did you say? Who do you want to talk to? Who are you?"

The people I dialed hung up in a matter of seconds, unable to understand my English and unwilling to try. I told myself that there was only one thing to do: ask for an interview. It would be much easier for me to explain things in person.

* * *

The first interview I set up was in a retirement home. It was located in Orange County, and I had to take a bus to get there. But the meeting didn't last much longer than my telephone conversations:

"Your English really isn't strong enough. I'm sorry, but we can't do anything for you."

I dozed off unwittingly on the bus ride home, worried sick about the future and exhausted by long sleepless nights of listening to children's stories.

"Hey! Wake up!"

"Are we there?"

"This is the end of the route. Where are you going?"

"Beachwood."

"Beachwood? We're nowhere near there! We passed that stop a long time ago!"

The driver looked very upset. And no wonder—it was just the two of us in an empty bus, it was nine o'clock, and I had completely missed my stop.

When I finally got back to my cousins' house, it was nearly midnight.

"Xiao-Mei, what happened? We were crazy with worry about you!"

I told them about my epic journey.

"Look for work in Beachwood instead. Please don't frighten us like that again."

* * *

They were right. I had to be more careful. When I heard that my cousins' neighbors were looking for a cleaning woman, I introduced myself. He was a doctor, and she was a dazzlingly beautiful woman. Both of them were the type of American who is "crazy about China."

"You don't speak English well? That doesn't matter—we love Chinese people. If you like, it's a deal. The job pays three hundred dollars a month. It's five days a week, Monday to Friday."

Three hundred dollars! My heart began to race: in China, Mao said that we should earn three hundred *yuan* per month, or about forty dollars. I pulled myself together.

"Why only five days? In China, I worked six days a week. I'd prefer to work six days a week."

"All right, if you insist. You can start tomorrow. Before that, let me show you the house."

We walked into the living room. I stopped short—there stood a magnificent Steinway, a concert grand. How much did my future employers earn per month that they were able to afford such a wonder? In China, there were probably only four or five such instruments between Beijing and Shanghai combined. Here, there was one in a living room. Perhaps, someday, would I be allowed to play it?

No such luck. My tasks left me without any free time. The house had five bathrooms, each one lined with mirrors that had to be polished. I did three loads of laundry per day, all of which had to be ironed. Each mealtime, the plates were changed four times, and it was after midnight before I finished doing the dishes. I also had to clean the pool, around which innumerable parties were held.

Following a flourish of limousines, the guests would arrive and stroll across the lawn...

"A beautiful day, isn't it?"

"Really quite lovely."

"What a magnificent house."

"What did you do last weekend?"

Everyone gave the impression that they were permanently on vacation, yet at the same time, they appeared to have nothing to say. They were oblivious to my existence, even when I held out the drinks tray to them. At moments like that, I didn't mind not understanding English. Rather, it spared me a lot of banal conversation.

And the Steinway? The best I could do was dust it. I was only able to play it two or three times: my employers were more concerned with my housekeeping abilities. And what they loved most was that I was from China.

"You know, we have a *real* Chinese woman!" they were forever telling their friends.

But they could also be generous: I was free every morning for two hours to go and practice my English at the language school for refugees.

* * *

One day, Chen and his wife took me aside.

"Xiao-Mei, you never smile. It's difficult for the children. They need happiness and cheerfulness around them. What's the matter?"

What was the matter? I was uncomfortable in America. The waste, the superficial conversations, the obsession with money. I was confronted with a plethora of choices every day, and I wasn't used to making decisions. This wasn't freedom. At any rate, it wasn't the type of freedom I was seeking. But how could I explain this?

One evening, to take my mind off things, some Chinese friends of my cousins offered to take me to Disneyland.

"It will do you good, you'll see."

The next weekend, they kept their promise. With touching insistence, they took me on every single ride—I even had to shake hands with both Mickey and Donald. Finally, dead tired, I told them that yes, re-education camp was tough, but at least we had been spared this kind of mental torture. They didn't take it badly; on the contrary, it made them even more sympathetic. I must really have been contaminated by Communism if I didn't even know how to enjoy myself. They assured me that one day I would recover, and that I would come back to Disneyland and have the time of my life.

* * *

Since the trip to Disneyland had been a failure, I decided to take matters into my own hands. I saw in the *Los Angeles Times* that the Los Angeles Philharmonic Orchestra would be performing Beethoven's Ninth Symphony at the Hollywood Bowl. I bought two five-dollar tickets and invited my cousins' cleaning lady to come with me. I had never heard the Ninth, and when the evening came, I headed to the concert in an emotional state of mind.

But there was an enormous traffic jam—and police everywhere. I was about to turn around and head back home when my companion took me firmly by the arm and steered me to our seats. I looked around me, dumbfounded. We were sitting in the stands of what looked like a vast soccer stadium, surrounded by nearly twenty thousand people picnicking and talking while they waited for the concert to begin. It felt like another type of Disneyland. That evening the Ninth only started for me with the first *fortissimo*: it was impossible to hear the initial *pianissimo*. It was drowned out by the people around me discussing their vacation plans.

I thought back to the time my grandmother took me to the Beijing Opera; there, too, the audience had eaten during the performance. But, at least, they seemed to appreciate the show and to give themselves over to what was happening on stage. Here, the most universal musical work had been turned into background music. I was shocked. Were these people aware of how fortunate they were? As someone who had always listened to music with

reverence, it was as if something sacred were being shattered before my eyes.

* * *

As time passed I began to lose patience—after all, I hadn't come to the States to clean houses. Luckily, my employers' dog came to the rescue. Brown was very old; it wasn't his fault, but I found that I was incredibly allergic to him. After a few weeks, I was covered in spots. Medicine was ineffective, and neither Chen nor my employers knew of something that would help. There was only one solution: Brown and I had to part ways.

That was when a telephone call once again changed the course of my life.

"Xiao-Mei, you can't go on like this! You have to get back to your piano playing. Come and audition in Boston; I'll look after you."

Like wouldn't take no for an answer, and he was right. Two months had passed since I had arrived in the States, and I still hadn't done anything of consequence. Babysitting, housekeeping—one day, I had to get back to my true calling. I quickly bought a plane ticket for Boston. It cost three hundred dollars, a month's wages. But I was going to Boston, a real cultural city. I remembered how impressed I had been with the concert that the Boston Symphony Orchestra had given in China, under the baton of Seiji Ozawa. Like's wife, Xiaohong, had met Mary Lou, a BSO violinist at a joint concert between the BSO and the Chinese Central Philharmonic Orchestra. Subsequently Mary Lou had helped the couple immigrate to the US. I could already

see myself at the New England Conservatory, where I was to audition. I immediately wrote to my mother, *Something amazing has happened!*

This time the letter wasn't just another attempt at concealing the realities of my life.

* * *

My audition at the New England Conservatory couldn't have gone better. I was accepted for the semester beginning in January and—wonder of wonders—I was given a scholarship. I was overjoyed. So much for Los Angeles and the California Institute of the Arts. I would be better off studying in Boston, I could feel it.

Greatly relieved, I caught the next plane back to Los Angeles to tell my cousins the good news—at last, I perhaps had a future. I was so happy that I managed to lose my luggage. My cousin was dismayed:

"How is it possible that you lost everything? What were you thinking? You don't even have a change of clothes."

Amy gave me things from her own closet; she also suggested that I stop by a neighborhood church where they had clothing for those in need.

A church? I had never been inside one, and I had only a fleeting knowledge of the Christian faith. Prior to leaving Beijing, a friend had talked to me about the Bible, which was banned in China:

"If you can, buy one and send it to me. I'd really like to read it."

The full extent of my acquaintance with the Scriptures boiled down to that brief conversation.

The priest who welcomed me was full of warmth and humanity. I explained my situation to him. After giving me some clothing, he told me about a meeting that was taking place at the same time and invited me to participate.

"It's a Bible study group," he said.

I stayed and took a seat. One of the members began to speak:

"My friends, thanks to Jesus..."

I listened carefully to him. The longer he spoke, the more memories arose in me. I felt as though I were hearing a member of the Red Guards:

"Students, thanks to Mao..."

Needless to say, the Christian faith wasn't going to come easily for me. And yet, out of curiosity and a sense of gratitude—or perhaps also weakness—I remained for a moment with the church members. I even tried to pray, to see how it felt. That first attempt was not very serious. I used a very down-to-earth method to test the existence of God:

"God, if you exist, tell me if the New England Conservatory will award me a diploma as a concert performer without my needing to ask anyone for money."

I waited for the answer. There wasn't one. Nevertheless, I was certain my prayer had been heard.

17

A Western Master

If you want to reach the infinite,
explore every aspect of the finite.

(Goethe)

It is better to deeply understand one field
than to be acquainted with ten thousand.

(Chinese proverb)

At the end of December, I bade farewell to my cousins and left Los Angeles for good. Like, Xiaohong, and Mary Lou came to pick me up at the airport in Boston. Mary Lou had even agreed to have me stay in her home, where my friends were already living. Her beautiful two-story house was more elegant than anything I had seen in Los Angeles.

At the Conservatory, I followed Mary Lou's advice and enrolled in the piano class of a very respected teacher, someone whom she admired—Gabriel Chodos. He had trained under one of the rare students of Artur Schnabel. But before I could begin my first class with him, I had to be tested on my knowledge of music theory.

The exam took place at eight in the evening. I found myself in a small classroom with other foreign students. The test papers were handed out.

"We will collect your copies in three hours."

Then disaster struck—I couldn't grasp the meaning of half of the questions. The proctor saw that I was panicked and came over.

"If you'd like, you can use a dictionary. There's one at the back of the room."

I wasted no time. Nearly an hour had passed, and I hadn't made much headway. I was blocked by a music history question: *Which composer wrote "Four minutes, thirty-three seconds of silence"?*

I anxiously leafed through the dictionary. I clearly didn't understand one of the words. *Four? Minutes? Silence?* They were all simple words, but together they didn't make any sense to me. No composer could have written a work consisting of four minutes and thirty-three seconds of silence!

The three hours were up, and I handed in a blank sheet of paper. I left the Conservatory devastated, convinced that this exam was going to cost me my scholarship, and even keep me from studying with Gabriel Chodos. It was after eleven p.m. I went down into the subway in a state of shock and rushed onto the first train that pulled in. As it left the station, I thought about the exam and the blank sheet I had submitted—about my failure. One station went by, then another. I didn't remember having seen them on my way. I got out at the third station to look at a subway map. For the life of me, I couldn't recall the name of the station near Mary Lou's house! I got back on another train and found myself at the end of the line, still unable to remember the forgotten station. The subway was about to close.

"What are you doing here?"

The driver, a tall African-American man, was making the rounds of the cars to verify that everyone had gotten off. There was no one left in the station, it was after midnight, and I was anxious.

"I'm lost. I'm staying with friends, and I've forgotten the name of the station where I'm supposed to get off."

"I'm not sure what I can do about that."

I gazed at him, distraught. He raised his voice:

"You should know where you live, right? I sure don't."

He was unnerving me, and he must have sensed it.

"Look, I'd really like to help you, but how am I supposed to know where you're staying?"

He scratched his head:

"Do you remember the first letter of your stop?"

"I think it was E."

"OK. I'm going to stop the train at every station that begins with E. You get out and see if you recognize the area."

There was no point in arguing with him. Off we went, the two of us, heading back in the other direction. It was one in the morning when I finally found the right station.

I'll never forget that man, who extended his shift just to help me. My inadequate "thank you" that night could not express all the gratitude I felt, and I could never locate him again. Perhaps, by some miracle, this book will one day find its way into his hands.

* * *

The next day at breakfast, I asked Mary Lou:

"In English what does 'four minutes, thirty-three seconds of silence' mean?"

Why do you ask?"

"It was a question on last night's exam that I couldn't understand."

She burst out laughing:

"It's a famous musical work by John Cage!"

As it turned out, my ignorance did not result in my downfall. A few days later, I was allowed to take my first lesson with Gabriel Chodos. Mary Lou had spoken about him so much; I was very excited to work with him after the months of house cleaning. Gabriel Chodos was a stocky man of about fifty. He gave off a feeling of strength that was, one felt, mixed with a certain anxiety. His hair, pushed back untidily, heightened the intelligence and depth of his melancholy, handsome gaze.

"What have you prepared?"

"Schumann's *Fantasie*."

"Please begin."

I threw myself into the work's first movement—which is a monument to passion—and flawlessly executed the challenging displacements at the end of the second movement that are every pianist's nightmare. Then I played the third movement as if in a dream. A half hour had passed, and he hadn't interrupted me. I turned towards him. His eyes were closed, and he had his head in his hands. He remained silent for a moment—which seemed like an eternity—before speaking:

"You have beautiful fingers, but you're not conveying any meaning!"

I blushed. I had withstood the shock of arriving in America by clinging to the idea that I could become a successful artist. And now, in less than a moment, I was

disgraced. As far as I was concerned, it was the end of the world, and the earth opened up beneath my feet. I had only one desire: to stop playing the piano. He let me suffer in silence for a few seconds, and then went on:

"We're going to work together."

He had an air of self-confidence about him. I thought about how tough Isaac Stern had been with the young Chinese violinists, and I started to feel hopeful again. I saw before me the road—the very long road—that I would have to travel to get where I wanted to go. I had only one choice, and that was to trust Gabriel Chodos.

I certainly didn't regret it. He is a wonderful musician, an extraordinary teacher, and an artist with very clear ideas. Working with him, I would learn a great deal.

* * *

I discovered his immense talent as a musician the first time I attended one of his concerts: it was a revelation. The program was Beethoven and Schubert, practically the only two composers he performed in public. I was immediately struck by the quality of his sound; it was deep, amber-colored, and delicate. He began with a piece by Schubert that I had never heard before, the Allegretto in C Minor. It is a short work written by Schubert late in life, but its few minutes encompass an entire world of sorrow. Gabriel Chodos's interpretation was extremely moving. And yet, the piece is remarkably simple: for the most part, both hands play in unison. How had he managed to express such a wealth of emotion from such a score? Conversely, when he played the other, much more difficult pieces in the program, his interpretation

seemed so natural and straightforward. Finding the simple in the complex and vice versa: something only a great master can teach you.

It is only now that I can take the full measure of his talent as a teacher.

The paces he put me through were merciless. Unlike Professor Pan, who was always natural and spontaneous, Professor Chodos was forbidding. With him, it was a life-or-death struggle. After every class, I wanted to quit the piano; here again, he was the exact opposite of Professor Pan. But the end justified the means.

I began by working on the Prelude and Fugue in B Minor from the end of the first book of *The Well-Tempered Clavier*. In this piece, which is one of the high points of the book, all twelve tones of the chromatic scale appear in the subject of the fugue, reminiscent of twentieth-century serialism. This was a piece I had copied in secret in Zhangjiakou, and had gone over for years. I thought I knew it intimately, better than anyone. We worked on it for six months together.

Gabriel Chodos's working method had one prerequisite: total respect for the score.

"The only way to be faithful to the composer," he would continually say, "is to explore the score in depth."

Anyone who turned up for a lesson without the correct edition was summarily turned away. A student who played a *rallentando* or a *diminuendo* that was not indicated was immediately set straight. He wanted me to study the score with a magnifying glass—literally. I bought one and scrutinized the work to be sure that I wasn't giving an incorrect interpretation to this or that *staccato*.

Once this was accomplished, Professor Chodos focused on what he considered to be the twin foundations of musical interpretation: phrasing and complete engagement.

For him, the attention one paid to the musical phrase was paramount. For each line, he would ask: "Where is the phrase? Beyond the bar lines and slurs, where exactly does the phrase begin and end? Where does it peak? Why is it that way?" He refused to let us count the tempo.

"It makes the piece ten times heavier," he would say. "Speak through the musical phrase instead."

He made me stop at the end of each phrase and lift my hands from the keyboard.

"It's like breathing," he told me. "You have to let some air into the music."

Playing Bach's Prelude and Fugue in B Minor—both of which are so sustained—was agony for me. I couldn't manage to lift my hands from the keyboard in the way he directed without breaking the flow of the music. But I knew he was right. No other music is more *constructed*, more *composed* than that of Bach; the beginnings and ends of its phrases are distinct, as are its sequences and links. In this, it is like a great poem, although—more than any other piece of music—it leaves its listeners with the impression that it is one uninterrupted flow of music.

When it came to engagement, Gabriel Chodos agreed with Professor Pan, although they had arrived at the same conclusion via different paths. From the very start of a piece, you had to be completely *inside* the work—more than you thought possible—and to give your utmost.

"Generosity," he would say, "is the greatest quality a musician can possess."

When we began working together, he thought that my sound was not dense enough. Too Chinese, perhaps? Over and over, he worked to help me achieve a more orchestral tone. One day he remarked:

"Draw your energy from your stomach."

I looked at him. Nearly twenty years before, Professor Pan had told me the same thing. To tell the truth, I was only partly taken aback: I knew that Gabriel Chodos was married to a Japanese woman. For both the Japanese and Chinese, the stomach is a sacred organ; many Asian people wrap their midsection in bandages to keep it warm.

To stimulate my sense of engagement, Professor Chodos sent me to study jazz with another professor at the Conservatory. Nothing could be further from Chinese culture than this type of music. I found myself attempting to improvise in a room that the professor kept in semidarkness, in order to create a jazzlike atmosphere. I was a mediocre jazz player, but I learned a series of lessons from those around me: the ability to be free within limits, the capacity to give one's all during a concert, and the ability to create a mood. These were lessons that I wouldn't forget.

* * *

After Bach, Gabriel Chodos had me work on two pieces, and two pieces only: Schumann's *Davidsbündlertänze* and Beethoven's Sonata No. 2. He was particularly insistent about working on a Beethoven sonata with me, especially the slow movement.

"This is the ultimate test," he warned me. "It's where you can see if someone is capable of really entering into

dialogue with the composer. In a certain way, the slow movements in Haydn, Mozart, and Schubert are simpler: they're more melodic, more immediate. Beethoven is more modern, more abstract, and his music is made up of small units. It's when I can tell if a student has something to *say*."

He was right. Even today, I find that a slow movement by Beethoven is the ultimate test. I have heard many superficial or dull interpretations, or worse, ones completely devoid of meaning. A slow Beethoven movement should be part of every qualifying round in international competitions.

For Professor Chodos, Schumann was different. He found my attack somewhat neutral, like flowing water. This might be an aesthetic reference for a Chinese audience, but not for a Western one.

"Like a great actress, you have to be able to play everything, not just the pieces you love. We are going to work on Schumann—the best composer for teaching you how to vary moods—the *Davidsbündlertänze*."

I ventured to say that I had always hoped to study Schumann's *Carnaval*.

"There's no comparison," he answered. "You'll see. For me, this is much more profound."

Once again, he was right. There was an entire world contained in the pages of the *Davidsbündlertänze*, one that reached far beyond the introspective Eusebius and the passionate Florestan. A world we took our time to explore—an hour's lesson for a line of music.

"When you play this work, everything must remain even," he said. "Avoid any obvious effects like changes in tempo, or excessive *fortissimi* and *pianissimi*. If you don't, the whole structure crumbles. Only your attack must vary. This

is the only technique you should use to express the piece's emotion."

Gabriel Chodos is a consummate interpreter and teacher, and—like all real musicians—a modest man. He stood humble before the music, which he considered sacred. When he gave a concert, he stopped giving classes a week in advance. The day before the performance, he would gather his forces, neither eating nor touching the piano. And when he played, he removed his watch and wedding ring. With his students he was self-effacing, as only true masters know how to be.

"Haydn? You know him better than I do," he said once when we were discussing the composer.

Of course, I didn't believe him: he just doesn't particularly like Haydn!

A few years later, the extreme modesty of this artist became fully apparent to me. I was living in Paris, and had thrown myself into a brief, nerve-racking career as a concert organizer. On the day Chodos arrived, he changed hotels three times. This one had no hot water, that one was too noisy, in the third the carpet was dirty. Finally, he agreed to stay with a friend of mine. To get to the concert hall, he refused to take either a taxi ("French taxi drivers are too unpleasant") or the metro ("too noisy").

"But Gabriel, how are we going to get there? I don't have a car."

"Ask a friend who has a car to take us there. But make sure that he or she doesn't say a word on the way!"

The night of the concert, we drove silently to the Sacem concert hall. When we got there, he gave me his final instructions:

"I don't want to see anyone at the intermission, and I don't want to hear any remarks after the concert."

That evening, however, what I found even more touching than his almost childlike vulnerability was the question he asked me at the end of the concert. He had just given a magnificent interpretation of Schubert's *Impromptus*, Opus 142, and Beethoven's Opus 111, which he considered to be the single greatest work in the entire piano repertoire.

"Do you really think that I have it in me to give concerts? Should I go on?"

I was moved by his doubt. I wanted to tell him that, in my opinion, the very finest pianists, like him, are vulnerable and fragile, even those who don't seem like it—Rachmaninoff, Schnabel, Serkin, Guilels, Lipatti, and Kempff, not to mention Chopin. Or I could have quoted Laozi, with whom I had become acquainted: "Therefore the stiff and unbending is the disciple of death. The gentle and yielding is the disciple of life." I was too moved, however, to say anything more than, "If you stop, you will be unhappy."

Of all of Gabriel Chodos's lessons, one in particular stands out. He believed that it is through exhaustive exploration of a single piece of music that you deepen your knowledge of both the piano and of music, rather than by studying a range of different works. Many renowned scholars know that the most important discoveries are the result of long and in-depth study of a very specific topic. By doing so, you develop a method that can be applied to any subject.

Discovering the universal in the particular, and striving to reach the infinite by patient exploration of the finite— these are lessons worthy of reflection.

18

With Oliver

No one listens to him,
No one notices him,
And the dogs growl
Around the old man.
(Franz Schubert, *Winterreise*,
set to poems by Wilhelm Müller)

I needed to find a place of my own in Boston. Mary Lou was extremely generous, but she was already putting up Like and Xiaohong, and I couldn't impose on her hospitality any longer. Fortunately, ever since the Boston Symphony Orchestra's tour in China, there was considerable interest in Chinese people. Dominique, an exceptionally talented flutist, offered to let me stay with her. She lived in a spacious nine-room house with her dog, Oliver.

The first night, I was jolted awake at two in the morning by shouting.

"No—no—that's still not right!"

Oliver was howling madly; I rushed from my room. There I found Dominique, flute in hand, out of sorts. Nothing was particularly wrong—she was just practicing.

This was a nightly occurrence: she never stopped working until she had achieved the result she wanted.

She also kept to a very strict diet: one small, midday meal, eaten at breaks during the orchestra's rehearsals; this was complemented with drugstore vitamins.

"Fasting allows one to conserve energy," she would say. Oliver's diet matched hers: during the day he wandered disconsolately through the house, looking for something to supplement his spartan regimen. One day, desperate, he flung himself at the refrigerator and managed to open it. Punishment was swift in coming; from then on, the holy citadel was put under lock and key. This hardly seemed necessary, as it was by and large empty.

Oliver was very handsome and intelligent—and, naturally, very thin. In China, it was rare to keep a dog as a pet. My first real experience with dogs was with Brown in Los Angeles, and it had been an unhappy one. At first, I was wary of Oliver, but later I got to know and appreciate him. I admired his loyalty, especially considering his draconian diet. Every night when we came home, he would greet Dominique first. But this was to be expected: Oliver barked in excitement as soon as he saw her, though not at me.

I didn't dare mention anything to Dominique, but I was also hungry. And neither Oliver nor I had the means to purchase vitamins. One day, I confided in Gabriel Chodos.

"This is the first time I've had a student who was starving to death," he chuckled. "You have to bring this up with her! Here in the US, we're pretty straightforward. When something's amiss, we speak up."

In China, this wasn't the case: one never asked for anything. Instead, you waited for others to realize what was happening.

That night, when I returned home, I screwed up my courage:

"Dominique, for the last few days I've been afraid to mention anything, but the truth is—I'm hungry."

"Why didn't you say something earlier? I'll go shopping immediately!"

She quickly returned.

"Here you go," she stated confidently. "This should do the trick."

She handed me a loaf of whole-wheat bread. When she went upstairs to practice, I seized the loaf and wolfed it down immediately. The following morning, when I came down to breakfast, I found Dominique greatly concerned:

"Is it really true—did you eat the whole loaf?"

I was so abashed I couldn't speak. She continued:

"You don't know it, but you're going to make yourself sick. Then you'll have to go to the doctor, and that costs a fortune, even if you have health insurance. I'm happy to buy bread, but you really shouldn't eat more than two slices a day."

That same day, a rumor began to make the rounds among the musicians at the BSO: contrary to popular belief, Chinese people don't like rice—they much prefer whole-wheat bread.

As for me, I made my way to church. There, at least, there was always something to nibble on after the service.

* * *

At church I made the acquaintance of a disabled person who was looking for a home-care assistant. It paid twenty-five dollars a week—with that kind of money, I could eat my fill! That same evening, I told Dominique about my plans to change apartments.

"I can give you thirty dollars a week, if you like. All you have to do is straighten things up a bit."

I was terribly embarrassed, and I blurted out:

"Fifteen dollars is fine, really."

And indeed, fifteen dollars was enough for a week's groceries. I bought eggs, rice, and carrots—which I shared with poor Oliver. It was more than enough, especially since my housekeeping skills at times left something to be desired.

One day, when her daughter was spending a couple of days at home, I heard Dominique say in a raised voice:

"My blouse! Xiao-Mei, what have you done? You've scorched my blouse—what can I wear for the concert?" She added, "You're going to have to reimburse me."

It was indeed my mistake; I had left the iron on the blouse too long. But her daughter came to my rescue:

"Mother, that's not fair! You're the one who should be apologizing to Xiao-Mei. You don't understand a thing; can't you see what you are putting her through?"

Dominique froze. The young woman continued in the same vein while I absented myself. A good half hour later, from my room, I heard Dominique's daughter shout:

"If that's the way it's going to be, I'm leaving! And don't expect me to ever come back!"

There was the sound of the door slamming shut. And then silence. I ventured downstairs and found Dominique standing in the middle of the living room, distraught.

"I'm sorry about what happened earlier; my daughter was right. Let me tell you a story: when I was young, I left home because I wanted my father to hand over his business to the employees, and he refused."

I didn't answer, but I knew what she was trying to say. When one is young, one is always too hard on one's parents—often due to some kind of idealism.

* * *

When Dominique had guests, she sometimes asked me to cook. The first time was a dinner she was giving in honor of a string quartet. She hinted at the possibility that they might invite me to one of their concerts; this was at a time in my life when a concert ticket was a real luxury. I threw myself into preparing a delicious meal, and I even served it. They seemed to enjoy it. At the end of the night, I told them that I was a musician, and I screwed up my courage to ask them if I could attend one of their concerts. The answer was categorical:

"If you want to come, you'll need to buy a ticket."

Luckily, not all dinners were like that. One time, Dominique had two friends over for the evening. They were a well-to-do older couple who lived outside of Boston, where they had established a school for disadvantaged children. I absorbed everything they said, captivated by their story; then I told them about growing up in China, and about those ten dark years when we were denied access to education. I explained to them how terrible that void was for my generation. I had to stop in the middle of my story—overwhelmed by painful memories that their account had brought up in me. Finally, I shared with them my vision of

one day founding a school in China. They listened attentively. Two days later, I received a letter from them. *If one day you decide to open your school,* they wrote, *we are prepared to give you all the support you need.*

* * *

My fifteen dollars a week hadn't solved all my problems, however. As it turned out, the scholarship I received from the New England Conservatory covered my tuition for the first semester, but it would be reduced by half for the second. I had to find some kind of real work, not just so I would be able to continue my studies, but also so I could live a bit.

In the US, everything, big and small, costs money. At the Conservatory, I had to pay, of course, for my piano lessons, and sometimes for carpooling. I also needed money for the students who assisted me in putting my assignments into correct English. My culture and my upbringing had led me to scorn money, and I felt embarrassed even taking money for the various minor tasks I did—this seemed like another world. At the same time, I understood: it was expensive to study at the Conservatory, and not every student received help from his or her family. They worked hard during the summer to earn enough to live on for the rest of the year. But that didn't prevent me from feeling ill at ease, like everyone does when they are thrust into an entirely new situation. In both the US and China, people had an unhealthy relationship to money. Either end of the spectrum is excessive.

The only solution to my problem was to get a job working as a waitress in a Chinese restaurant.

* * *

My waiting career began in a very luxurious restaurant, but it was short-lived. I received a first warning for arriving late to work. But the final straw came when I was serving a distinguished older Bostonian couple who were particularly put out by my accent. I was unable to stop myself from asking them if they wanted *soap* instead of *soup,* and this didn't go over well. The management had had enough; I was fired on the spot.

Other restaurant owners were more insightful: they immediately saw that my English wasn't strong enough, and they declined to hire me. One by one, I made the rounds of every Chinese restaurant in Boston, until I found work at a place in the red light district. There, at least, my English pronunciation was not a handicap. Before then, I had never laid eyes on either a prostitute or a sex shop, but this was quickly corrected! In that part of town, that's all there was, with drug addicts added to the mix.

The first few days weren't so bad. The prostitutes were generous customers; when they had had a good night, they left wonderfully large tips. And I feasted on leftovers. Some of the regulars were professional fishermen, and they scrupulously respected the old tradition according to which it was bad luck to eat the side of the fish that has touched the deck of a boat. They had a nickname for me: "the starving Chinese girl."

But the work was hard. I was on my feet for hours, and as the evening wore on, my feet would swell up—so much so that I had to buy a pair of shoes three sizes too large so I'd be comfortable at my shift's end. Drug addicts and

drunks who were regulars never failed to try to grab and make fun of me, or they would leave without paying. Late in the evening, around eleven o'clock, I would begin to worry. I thought about the distance that separated me from the nearest subway station; it cut through the worst section of the red light district. The first few days, I ran at breakneck speed. Then I told myself: *If you run, you'll show that you are afraid.* I forced myself to conquer my instincts, and I walked slowly, avoiding anyone's gaze. One night around midnight, as I was leaving the restaurant, I had the feeling I was being followed. I began to walk faster and glanced behind me: three men were on my heels. I couldn't help it—I broke into a run. But I could hear them: they were running, too. What could I do? I prayed. It didn't matter to whom—Jesus in this case. And this time, he answered:

"You're safe. Nothing will happen to you," he said in my ear.

He was right: I made it to the station. At last! Just in time for the last train. I collapsed into my seat. As I was catching my breath and pulling myself back together, I thought about the life I was leading. I was aware that things couldn't go on like this much longer. I had less and less desire to play the piano. My Bach and Beethoven scores smelled like soy sauce. If I didn't stop working there, I'd never find the proper style to play the music that I loved.

A few days later, a knife fight broke out in the kitchen: one of the two cooks' head was cut open, and there was blood everywhere. Enough was enough. The next day, I called my employers and told them I was quitting and that they should find another waitress. Once the feeling of relief subsided, however, I had to start looking for another job.

This time, I found work as an usher at the Boston Symphony Orchestra. This seemed nothing short of a miracle, except that I couldn't attend the concerts: as soon as the music began, I was to leave the hall. It was only at the end, during the encore, that I was able to slip back in as the first audience members were leaving.

I learned one day that Vladimir Horowitz was going to perform. This time, I couldn't make do with just the encore—the mere mention of his name sent chills down my spine. As soon as the box office opened, I bought myself a ticket for thirty dollars. I would gladly have paid three hundred! As the concert approached, my excitement grew. Suddenly, a few days before, I learned that I had to take a piano exam on the afternoon of the concert. I knew that students were called in alphabetical order for tests: this was very bad news. I decided to risk everything: the exam had not yet started, so I went and knocked on the door of the test room. The jury looked at me, astonished:

"It's not your turn. We'll call you when the time comes, but it probably won't be until the end of the afternoon."

"Please listen to me. I've spent all of my money on a ticket for the Horowitz concert tonight. I can't play later, I have to go hear him."

Sometimes it pays to be bold. Not only did the president of the jury, amused, let me play first, but I got the highest score in the entire Conservatory—which, on that occasion, had nothing to do with my playing! As for Horowitz, I was disappointed. But I must confess that I was on cloud nine that night, and I probably would have been critical of any other pianist on the planet.

* * *

It was around this time that Dominique decided my English was really becoming unbearable. She was at her wits' end with the chaos I created mixing up cleaning products. Gabriel Chodos felt the same way—he had to use a dictionary to give me lessons. And so, as summer approached, Dominique offered to pay for an intensive English course for me at one of the most exclusive establishments on the East Coast, the School for International Training in Vermont.

I bid farewell to Oliver, my partner in crime, who began barking madly when he saw me leaving the house. I would never forget him: we had been hungry together.

19

An Act of Love

I came here a stranger,
As a stranger I depart.
(Franz Schubert, *Winterreise*,
set to poems by Wilhelm Müller)

I think I must be the only pianist in the world who has gone to Brattleboro, Vermont—home to one of the world's most famous music festivals—with the goal of learning English.

Brattleboro is associated with Marlboro Music, a very special institution that was founded after World War Two by a number of renowned European musicians, including the pianist Rudolf Serkin, the violinist Adolf Busch, and the flutist Marcel Moyse. Each year young musicians have the opportunity to mingle with celebrated artists during unforgettable master classes and chamber music sessions. Between daytime practice sessions and evening concerts, the atmosphere at the Marlboro Festival is entirely unique.

During the evening concerts, sitting in the last row, I noticed a tall, quiet, somewhat bald gentleman wearing thin-framed, round glasses. He closed his eyes when he listened to the music.

"How can you not know who that is?" I was told when I asked about him. "That's Rudolf Serkin. Come tomorrow night; he's going to play a Haydn trio."

Rudolf Serkin, the legendary pianist, was listening to his younger colleagues as if they were his teachers. When I returned the next night, the musician was on stage, playing Haydn with the playfulness of a child and the demeanor of a man who had lived through everything. I'd never heard anything like it. I attended his master classes, went to his concerts, listened to his recordings. This man embodied what I value most: integrity and humility before music. I observed him discuss the *Hammerklavier* and Opus 111:

"You are cheating Beethoven," he said to a student who had altered a difficult passage to make it easier to play. "But you are also cheating yourself—and God!"

I was astounded by how he brought the great Beethovenian form to life from the inside, infusing it with a fire and an emotion that I had never heard before—musical architecture combined with passion. He forbade any changes in Beethoven's scores to make them easier to perform. I set myself the goal of studying with Serkin, but I didn't dare approach him. My friends encouraged me:

"You're mistaken; he never refuses to listen to anyone. What he doesn't like are pianists who are affected. He listens to them politely, like all the rest, but then lets them know, with a big smile, that it won't go any further. You don't have a thing to worry about."

The more I was told how kind and generous Rudolf Serkin was, the less I wanted to impose on him. The summer ended, and I still hadn't gotten up the courage to approach him.

* * *

When I returned from Marlboro, Gabriel Chodos found that my playing had undergone a transformation. How could it have changed so much in so short a time? The only official courses I had taken were in English, but something had "clicked" for me at Marlboro. By listening to Rudolf Serkin and those around him, I understood how I could add a decisive element to my playing—the pleasure of communicating, of "transmitting" the music.

The academic year passed without incident, and I was granted my diploma from the New England Conservatory. At the age of thirty-three, I had earned the diploma I should have received when I was twenty! Once again, I thought back to the lost years, to my stolen youth. I thought about the education that had been denied me, an education I had been forced to look for here, in far-flung Boston, my path fraught with obstacles and humiliations. But finally, with this diploma, I had cleared another hurdle. Had Jesus heard my prayers? I couldn't be sure, but I thanked him with all my heart, just in case.

* * *

The first few days of summer in Boston were beautiful. Squirrels scampered in crowded parks. I was strolling through the city's streets, when suddenly I thought I should buy myself a present as a reward for my efforts. There was something that I had always dreamed of having, but I had been denied it when I was at the right age. Afterwards, I never purchased one because they were always

too expensive—compared to a bag of rice or a pound of carrots. A friend sent me to a discount store.

"You can find one there for four dollars," she told me.

I decided that the occasion of receiving my degree was worth at least four dollars. At the discount store in question, I did indeed find what I was looking for, and wonderful ones at that. I looked at them for a long time. Then I chose one.

The first doll of my life.

* * *

With my diploma in hand, I would finally be able to earn a living from my real profession. In Brattleboro, my reputation as a pianist had been established during the summer, when I had given a benefit concert for a student who had been diagnosed with cancer, and whose family didn't have the means to pay for treatment. Catherine, the director of the Brattleboro Music Center, was looking for an instructor and asked if I was interested. My first teaching assignment—of course I was interested! It was settled.

To help me with expenses, Catherine offered to put me up at her house. The little room was in the basement; it was dark and damp, but it was free. And Catherine had a beautiful grand piano that I could use to practice Bach and Liszt after work.

I quickly found that my salary wasn't enough to live on. My wages were based on how many students took my courses, and I never earned more than eighty dollars a month.

It was back to baby-sitting.

Then I learned that the Christian Science Church was looking for a Sunday organist. I was offered thirty dollars for each service: how could I refuse? That meant, however, that I had to master the pedalboard, a technique with which I wasn't familiar. My first few tries were traumatic for the congregation. Up in the organ loft, I was seized with stage fright: I dreaded every wrong note—the bass ones were particularly unbearable. I was afraid that the assembly would climb the stairs and strangle me, and for good reason! In a very gentle manner, the minister came to see me at the end of the service:

"We are going to find you an organ teacher."

This turned out to be an elderly organist, from whom I learned the art of playing the pedals.

* * *

It was around this time that I heard that a restaurant in Brattleboro was looking for a pianist. I headed over. This was still far from my dream career, but at least I would have the chance to play. The two owners, Thom and Gregg, welcomed me with open arms. They offered me five dollars an hour, which meant I would have to work two evenings to earn as much as I did on Sundays at the church. I started that very night, with pieces that would become my standard repertoire—Mendelssohn, Chopin, and Schubert.

As soon as I began playing, a waiter placed an empty glass on the piano. Why did he do that? What was he going to put in it? But he didn't fill it with anything, and the hours went by. Later, when the first customers got up and headed for the exit, they slipped a dollar or two in the glass as they

passed the piano. They couldn't possibly have known it, but for me, each bill was an insult. When the last customer had left, I went straight over to Thom and Gregg.

"This is impossible. I can't possibly continue to work under these conditions."

They were taken aback.

"Why bother to play if you don't accept tips?"

The next day, the glass disappeared. Thom and Gregg had decided to pay me ten dollars an hour instead.

* * *

Spring arrived. One day, I found my room flooded: the snow had melted, and water had seeped into the house's basement. My bed and all my belongings were afloat. I camped out at the music school, which ironically had its advantages: if I slept in a classroom, I could play the piano in the evening, undisturbed.

But it was just another in a series of temporary solutions. In a single year, I had changed my address no less than thirty-five times. My friends teased me about it:

"When you put Xiao-Mei's name in your address book, leave three blank pages for the addresses."

Shortly afterwards, I learned that I had been chosen for a permanent teaching position at the Brattleboro Music Center. It was a chance for me to get my green card, which is crucial for any foreigner who wants to work in the States on a long-term basis. As soon as I was hired for the job, I went to the local immigration office. The person behind the desk carefully inspected my file, then got up in order to check other documents. There was something wrong. He

left his office and I sat alone, waiting. He returned in a few minutes, which had seemed like an eternity.

"I'm sorry, but we've already reached our quota for Chinese immigrants for this year, and we can't issue you a green card. Try again next year; you can apply as of January."

Just as he was about to return my passport, he gave it one final glance.

"No, actually you can't. Your visa expires in three days. You have no other choice; you'll have to return to China."

Return to China? And explain to my family that I spent more time in the US cleaning houses and doing dishes than playing the piano?

I hurried back to Catherine's house to ask her advice. Straightaway, she called a senator, with whom she was acquainted through friends. The answer was unequivocal: nothing could be done in such a short period of time. She called a lawyer. The conversation went on for a while. I saw her nodding in agreement. She hung up the phone and turned to me:

"There's only one solution. You'll have to get married."

I stared at her, stunned.

"That's crazy!"

Under the circumstances, all I could do was accept the inevitable and go back to China. Before I did, I wanted to give a concert to thank everyone who had helped me. The next evening, the small hall where I was set to play was overflowing with people. News of my predicament had spread across town. At the end of the concert, my friends came to say good-bye, each one trying to think of a way to help me. Thom and Gregg were there as well, and they took me aside.

"Xiao-Mei, we've thought it over. If you want, you could marry one of us. It would be a marriage of convenience, but it would allow you to remain in the States. You just have to choose which one of us you prefer. Think it over and tell us what you want to do."

It took me a long time to decide. I was caught in a bind: on the one hand, there was China, my anxiety about the future, and the shame of having to confess my failure to my family. On the other hand, there was a marriage that was a lie, a farce, and the risk of throwing in my lot with someone I barely knew. Finally, fear and shame won out. I went to my friends' house and accepted their offer.

"All right, which one of us do you want to marry?"

What a question! How do you decide such a thing? My selection criteria were not those of other women. Since Gregg had a family name that I just couldn't seem to pronounce, by process of elimination, I set my heart on Thom. Neither of them complained.

"All right then," was all that Thom said. "Let's start immediately. There isn't a moment to lose."

He was right; for our marriage to seem credible in the eyes of the immigration authorities, we had to pay attention to every detail. Our first concern was about the minister who would be performing the ceremony. The simplest thing to do was to explain the situation to him. As he listened to us carefully, he looked at me—what was he thinking? As we were leaving, he drew me aside for a few seconds:

"I know what you must be feeling. But rest assured. In fact, what you two are doing is an act in support of free-

dom. For this reason, it will be the finest wedding I've ever presided over."

But neither he nor Thom could allay my fears. The night before the ceremony, I panicked, and it was terrible. All of a sudden, I saw myself as I really was: alone in a little American town, far from my family and my country, without a piano, without a visa, and about to take the name of a man with whom I would never start a family—all in order to deceive the authorities of a country that had taken me in. Beijing, Zhangjiakou, Hong Kong, Los Angeles—everything passed before my eyes. I was thirty-three years old with only a diploma from the New England Conservatory to my name. I had only ever given a few informal concerts. None of this made sense. The next morning, when Thom came to get me, I barely had the courage to go with him.

But there was a surprise waiting for me at the church. Thom's and Gregg's families were there, along with countless friends and total strangers who had heard about my situation. They had all turned out to "lie on my behalf," their arms full of gifts, which could be used as hard evidence of the legitimacy of our marriage. I was overwhelmed, but also galvanized.

We entered the church to the strains of Fauré's *Requiem,* which I had chosen for the occasion. As we approached the nave, I looked at the faces of those present: their eyes were wet with tears. During the ceremony, the minister chose the most tactful and apt words. Then he gave us his blessing before we exited the church to the sound of *In Paradisum,* also from Fauré's *Requiem.* The guests cried so much you'd

have thought it was a funeral! Thankfully, the evening that followed was a great deal more festive, thanks to several excellent bottles of wine and a huge wedding cake in the shape of a grand piano.

The first step had been completed, but the biggest challenge still lay ahead: the Immigration and Naturalization Service interview. Our union, it must be said, had all the signs of a marriage of convenience. The lawyer who was advising us gave us advance warning: the test was really tough. We would be placed in separate rooms, and we would have to answer the same questions in an identical way. I couldn't trip up on anything, including the brand of Thom's shirts! I prepared for the test, learning "the man of my life's" biography down to the last detail.

On the day of the interview, Thom was even more nervous than I was. I sensed that he, too, feared the worse. But he sailed through without a single error. In fact, it was on my side that we came close to disaster, and all because of one little mistake. The name of the Unitarian Church where we were married escaped me, and when the official asked me about it, I innocently told him that I had married Thom at the Vegetarian Church! But his interest in the Vegetarian Church didn't go much further than that; he jotted down my answer without much of a reaction.

We had made it through! I would be able to get my green card, stay in the US, and start my career. Little by little, I came up for air. After all, weren't marriages of convenience also a part of the story of human beings who sought

to rescue one another? Was it really so crazy? In its own way, wasn't it an act of love?

That was when I received a letter from my father.

20

The Power of Emptiness

Therefore, existence is what we have,
But non-existence is what we use.

(Laozi)

My mother and I exchanged letters every week, but my father had only written me once, a short time after my arrival in Los Angeles. I had been extremely touched by his letter. He told me that he regretted not having a son, but that, through what he had witnessed of my courage and my ability to withstand hardships—to him typically masculine qualities—it was as if he now indeed had one.

I wasn't hurt by the silence that followed. I knew that my father considered all correspondence to be needless. One should never, ever leave a trace.

I was thus very surprised one day to find in my mailbox a letter in his handwriting.

Xiao-Mei,

Since the last time I wrote, I have not felt the need to share my news with you. I understand from your regular correspondence with your mother that everything is going well. I also understand what "everything going well" means: I imagine that your life can't always

be easy. I can't completely know, here in Beijing, exactly what you are doing, but I have faith in you. I know you.

As for me, now that I am over sixty, I have begun to compre-hend the secret of the Tao.

Thanks to a friend who remembered my knowledge of ancient languages, I have had the chance to take part in a research group. This group is responsible for editing texts from sacred Tibetan Buddhist books, the Da zang jing. As soon as I began reading these texts, I felt that I had finally discovered my life's purpose. Until now, my life has been a disappointment. Although innocent, I've been subjected to many trials and humiliations.

Thanks to my work on these texts, I have understood many things. The need to rise above the day-to-day, to not become dis-tracted by worldly things and money, to not seek professional success or recognition. You must be yourself. And as one nears the secret of the Tao, one discovers the truth.

To reach it is part of one's destiny. If you have upheld what is good during the course of your life, it will be given to you. If this does not occur, it is because you have not suffered enough and you must continue searching. But my intention is not to try and convince you. One day, I am sure that you, too, will be given the chance to experience this truth.

Please know that I don't have any regrets and that I am now very contented.

Father.

I read the letter over a number of times, with a growing sense of confusion. The man who had written it bore little resemblance to the one I had known as a child—cold, strict, and often violent.

However, the more I read it, the more I sensed in it—over and above the mystery it represented for me personally—a

gentle invitation. An invitation to discover, during my exile, the wisdom of the great Chinese philosophers. To seek the truth in their reflections by deepening my knowledge of their writings. From far away, from across the ocean, my father was taking me by the hand. I wanted to follow him, in order to be with him for a moment. And also to discover this sense of serenity. If my father, the most pessimistic, resigned, and depressive of men, could find this inner peace—to such an extent that he wanted to write to me about it—there was no reason why I couldn't experience this grace as well.

From then on, I set aside time to meditate and to study the great seminal texts of Chinese philosophy. Little by little, without knowing it, I began to undergo a change. I experienced far more than a connection with my father, or a sense of reconciliation with someone whom I had hurt. I discovered that, in turn, I was calmer and more peaceful.

By constantly practicing, without casting about or forcing the matter, insight into life and how things worked emerged without my conscious awareness of it. This is the essence of Chinese philosophy: something that can be experienced without always needing to be explained. The Chinese path to understanding is quite different from that taken by Westerners. It is more intuitive, less strictly rational. The Chinese believe that many things do not need explanation because they are natural phenomena. Unlike their Western counterparts, who see understanding as a prerequisite to practice, Chinese people see practice as one way to achieve understanding. They are skeptical about any single-minded search for an ideal or a truth. The life of the great philosopher Shijiamoni offers a perfect example of this. For years, he sought the meaning of life, but in vain.

One day, he renounced his quest, and the meaning of life appeared to him in all its clarity.

I think about my experience with Western music. My limited language skills mean that I cannot discuss it as well as others. I often feel hindered by my nationality; I sense, in the gaze of others, unspoken doubts about my abilities as a foreigner to truly understand Bach and Beethoven. To be sure that I am on the right track, as soon as I begin to work on a piece, I make it a point to listen to every recording of it available. It would be unthinkable for me to play a Beethoven sonata without first checking how Kempff interpreted it, or take on a composition by Chopin without Rubinstein's imprimatur. Working with Gabriel Chodos only heightened this fear in me; for him, approaching a work structurally, through a process of analysis—or even dissection—was paramount. His approach to music was, like his idol, the writer Thomas Mann, fundamentally intellectual.

If, however, in Chinese philosophy, the truth can be attained as much through committed practice as through explanation, why should it be any different when dealing with the truth of music?

Unconsciously, these reflections brought about a change in how I approach a musical work. Once I have analyzed the entire piece, I play it evenly and attentively; I never force it or try to grasp its meaning too quickly. I do this until I experience love for each passage and note, until I reach a state of natural and intuitive understanding.

Using this method, you understand that the first layer of a work to be uncovered is the tempo. By living with a piece, by not attempting to impose yourself in any way, you begin to breathe with it. One day, completely naturally, a

tempo emerges, one that feels organically right. If you deviate from this revealed truth, you feel uncomfortable.

This largely has to do with the connections that exist between breathing and life, but also with those between tempo and thought.

If you have a great deal to say, in life or in music, you must take the time to express it. The beauties of a score must be brought out, they must be made to spring forth. The composer wrote them for that very reason: to be heard. And yet, there are limits. There is a risk that the audience will cease to pay attention, that they will become lost in the details without comprehending the whole—and all because the tempo is too slow for their thinking process. The reason is clear: the right tempo is not merely the one with which you breathe naturally, it is also the pace that allows thought to encompass both the forest and the trees.

But this is only the initial stage, the elemental stage of grasping a work. The hardest part—the search for meaning—is yet to come. When you have the meaning, you have the solution to every problem involving technique. The search for the meaning of a work is a quest for the essential. If a run of sixteenth notes needs to be played very quickly, obviously there are some notes that matter more than others. When you have identified them, you know how to play the run. Perhaps the word *thrust*—with its twin meanings of "line of reasoning" and "forward motion"—best conveys the concept I am attempting to describe.

It is increasingly clear to me that the thrust (line of reasoning or meaning) of a work is linked to its thrust (forward motion or direction). That the music—propelled forward and shaped by the life-giving bass notes—advances horizontally,

and that this horizontality ultimately takes precedence over its verticality. This is not to say that we should reject the critical element of verticality and harmony when approaching a piece. But it is the bass that forms the pulse of the work. No, what I find even more striking is the need to look beyond the bar-lines in one's quest for the musical line, the work's progression. Gabriel Chodos made me work for months on musical phrasing. Over time, these phrases, these lines, are overlaid with concepts of progression, flow, movement, and transformation—ideas that find an echo in Chinese philosophy.

I also learned, during this same period, not to struggle with my piano. It is an eternal friend, regardless of external events and the day's fugitive moods. This in turn allows me to better explore its infinite resources, to get closer to the attack and the sonority that I am seeking. A story by Zhuangzi, "The Dexterous Butcher," really opened my eyes in this regard. In the story, Prince Wen Hui is admiring the skill with which a butcher is carving up an ox. The prince inquires about his technique, and the butcher answers:

"What I have wished for is Tao, far superior to technique. When I first dissected oxen, what I saw was nothing less than the whole ox. After three years, I no longer saw the whole ox. And now, I let my intuition, not my eyesight, lead the way [...]. A good butcher changes his knife every year; he uses it to cut muscles. An ordinary butcher changes his knife every month; he uses it to cut bones. I have used the same knife for nineteen years."

* * *

Now I can enter into music with greater ease. Many wise men retreat to the silence of the mountains, away from

everything, in order to meditate. Before playing a work, I have discovered I need to take the same approach: to be peaceful, to empty my mind.

The Chinese are well acquainted with this way of seeing things; they often use the image of water to illustrate it. To see down to the bottom of a lake, the water must be calm and still. The calmer the water, the farther down one can see. The exact same thing is true for the mind—the more tranquil and detached one is, the greater the depths one can plumb.

Increasingly, I understand that it is precisely by following this path of self-effacement and emptiness that one attains the truth of a musical work. Without attempting to impose one's will, without forcing something on the listener. Without struggling with the self. By disappearing behind the composer.

In meditating on the words of Laozi, I began to understand how he was able to express the essential nature of emptiness better than anyone, particularly in this passage, to which I endlessly return:

Thirty spokes join together at one hub,
But it is the hole in the center
That makes it operable.

Clay is molded into a pot,
But it is the emptiness inside
That makes it useful.

Doors and windows are cut
To make a room,
It is the empty spaces that we use.
Therefore, existence is what we have,
But non-existence is what we use.

Little by little, without even being aware of it, I began to apply this method to every musical work that I approached and to works that I took up anew. Each day, I would experience two great moments of happiness. The first was during my daily meditation session. The second was during what I will call my "piano meditation." According to Chinese philosophy, work—even work without purpose—is one of the greatest virtues, and this was exactly what I was seeking when I was seated at the piano. I worked, and worked tirelessly, with no other goal than the truth of the music. Since I was unable to build a career at that time, I had no professional obligations—no programs to prepare for upcoming concerts, no problematic dates in my agenda. I worked in the way I wanted, and for as long as I wanted, and this piano meditation brought me the same sense of fullness as my morning meditation sessions.

Looking back, I now see that those years of so much hardship were, in fact, a period of great privilege. How many pianists, once they are over thirty and often involved in a career, still have the time to work at their piano, strictly for their own pleasure, with no particular goal in mind? How many have the opportunity to seek the essence of a work that they would never consider playing in public? As I see it, in life it is important to know how to work, without any thought of recompense. During my meditations at the piano, I never imagined that I would perform real concerts before a real audience, or that I would make real recordings. Sometimes in life, work for work's sake can reap the greatest benefit.

21

Dreaming of Paris

One day two bandits entered the Summer Palace.
One plundered, the other burned.
Victory can be a thief, or so it seems.

(Victor Hugo)

I began to think about Paris.

In Brattleboro, despite all my different jobs, I simply wasn't able to make ends meet. Thom and Gregg were wonderful, yet I sensed that I was a burden on them. And then there was the fact that, even though I was surrounded by friends, I felt unchallenged.

I was drawn to Paris; I was linked to it by a very old memory. By a connection that was at once tenuous and sustained, one that had been forged long before I was born, when my family lived near Fuxing Park, in the French Quarter of Shanghai. When I was a child, my mother often talked to me about the Louvre, which she considered the most beautiful museum in the world. I could still remember the scent of the little perfume bottle that she had kept for so long, and that the Red Guards had poured onto the floor of our Beijing apartment. And then there was Rodin's *Art*, for which I had traded two years of free piano lessons.

Now that I live in France and I have read Lin Yutang, I have a better understanding of what connects the French and the Chinese. Lin Yutang, the great Chinese author—and bridger of cultures—studied at Saint John's University in Shanghai and subsequently in the US and in Leipzig, the city forever associated with the name of Bach. He then divided his time between the East and the West. In *The Importance of Living*, Lin sets out what China and France have in common: a sense of humor, depth of feeling, and a genuinely artistic way of approaching life.

And, of course, how could I not want to discover the country of the French Revolution—the revolution that inspired so many others.

I shared my plan with my friends, who thought it was unrealistic: if I couldn't establish a career for myself in Brattleboro, the idea that I was somehow going to be able to do so in Paris was simply crazy. When one friend—a former student of Yves Nat at the Paris Conservatory—heard that I was thinking of going to France, he was horrified:

"Don't do it. It's the worst place on earth for pianists. The critics are merciless there." He then told a story about a great living pianist who shall remain nameless: "After one of his concerts, the French critics wrote: 'He gave a concert of music by Chopin. One wonders why.' That was it. It's a frightful country; all people care about is being clever. Don't go."

No doubt there was truth in what he said.

Sue Fleisher was the one person who offered encouragement. I had met Sue at the School for International Training—where she was working when I studied in Brattleboro—and we had hit it off immediately. She

had lived under terrible conditions in France during the Occupation because she was Jewish. Nevertheless, she still considered it the most beautiful country in the world.

I still remember her words when, one day, I asked her about Judaism:

"Let's not talk about it. Religion is what sets people against each other."

She was convinced that France would welcome me, and she promised to attend my first concert. The likelihood seemed so improbable that she and I had a good laugh about it together.

* * *

As my departure plans took shape, I began wondering why former colonial powers, like France, can hold an unhealthy fascination for populations that were once subjugated by them at an earlier point in their history.

In China's case, the subjugation took place without any real resistance on the part of the Chinese people. Nevertheless, it was carried out with brutality, as attested to by the sack of the Summer Palace. When I was in Beijing, I would often walk through its grounds. All that remained were a few ruins, hidden in the foliage, faint reminders of what had once been a splendid monument.

In one of his letters, Victor Hugo responds to this dramatic event and describes it very aptly. I don't believe the text of the letter is well known in France, but it is famous in China. In Mao's time, schoolchildren read it in class as an illustration of the crimes committed by the imperial powers. In it, Hugo is responding to a certain Captain Butler,

who wrote to him while he was in exile, and asked for his assessment of the event.

Hauteville House, November 25, 1861

You ask my opinion, Sir, about the China expedition. You consider this expedition to be honourable and glorious, and you have the kindness to attach some consideration to my feelings; according to you, the China expedition, carried out jointly under the flags of Queen Victoria and the Emperor Napoleon, is a glory to be shared between France and England, and you wish to know how much approval I feel I can give to this English and French victory.

Since you wish to know my opinion, here it is:

There was, in a corner of the world, a wonder of the world; this wonder was called the Summer Palace. Art has two principles, the Idea, which produces European art, and the Chimera, which produces oriental art. The Summer Palace was to chimerical art what the Parthenon is to ideal art. All that can be begotten of the imagination of an almost extra-human people was there. It was not a single, unique work like the Parthenon. It was a kind of enormous model of the chimera, if the chimera can have a model. Imagine some inexpressible construction, something like a lunar structure, and you will have the Summer Palace. Build a dream with marble, jade, bronze, and porcelain, frame it with cedar wood, cover it with precious stones, drape it with silk, make it here a sanctuary, there a harem, elsewhere a citadel, put gods there, and monsters, varnish it, enamel it, gild it, paint it, have architects who are poets build the thousand and one dreams of the thousand and one nights, add gardens, basins, gushing water and foam, swans, ibis, peacocks, suppose in a word a sort of dazzling cavern of human fantasy with the face of a temple and palace, such was this building. The slow work of generations had been necessary to create it. This edifice,

as enormous as a city, had been built by the centuries, for whom?
For the peoples. For the work of time belongs to man. Artists, poets,
and philosophers knew the Summer Palace; Voltaire talks of it.
People spoke of the Parthenon in Greece, the pyramids in Egypt,
the Coliseum in Rome, Notre-Dame in Paris, the Summer Palace in
the Orient. If people did not see it they imagined it. It was a kind
of tremendous unknown masterpiece, glimpsed from the distance in
a kind of twilight, like a silhouette of the civilization of Asia on the
horizon of the civilization of Europe.

This wonder has disappeared.

One day two bandits entered the Summer Palace. One plundered,
the other burned. Victory can be a thief, or so it seems. The devasta-
tion of the Summer Palace was accomplished by the two victors acting
jointly. Mixed up in all this is the name of Elgin, which inevitably calls
to mind the Parthenon. What was done to the Parthenon was done to
the Summer Palace, more thoroughly and better, so that nothing of it
should be left. All the treasures of all our cathedrals put together could
not equal this formidable and splendid museum of the Orient. It con-
tained not only masterpieces of art, but masses of jewelry. What a great
exploit, what a windfall! One of the two victors filled his pockets; when
the other saw this he filled his coffers. And back they came to Europe,
arm in arm, laughing away. Such is the story of the two bandits.

We Europeans are the civilized ones, and for us the Chinese are
the barbarians. This is what civilization has done to barbarism.

Before history, one of the two bandits will be called France; the
other will be called England. But I protest, and I thank you for giving
me the opportunity! The crimes of those who lead are not the fault of
those who are led; Governments are sometimes bandits, peoples never.

The French empire has pocketed half of this victory, and today
with a kind of proprietorial naivety it displays the splendid bric-a-
brac of the Summer Palace.

I hope that a day will come when France, delivered and cleansed,
will return this booty to despoiled China.
Meanwhile, there is a theft and two thieves.
I take note.
This, Sir, is how much approval I give to the China expedition.

<div align="right">

Victor Hugo

</div>

I was impressed by the nobility of spirit in Victor Hugo's letter. To admit one's errors, isn't that a reflection of real courage in a man, or a country? A strength of character that Mao never possessed.

But the French and the English were not the only ones to attack China's cultural heritage. As I reflected on Hugo's account, I thought about the unimaginable acts that were committed during the Cultural Revolution, acts that resulted in the destruction of entire swaths of China's history. Without anyone having had the courage to step forward and make amends.

Hugo, in his text, shows where the real strength of the soul resides. He also alludes to how culture and education must serve as bulwarks against crimes of all sorts. I was powerfully drawn to a country that could produce such writers.

My mind was made up.

I wrote to my friend Xiaoqin; she had settled in France after having been granted permission to marry her French boyfriend. She had given up on a career in publishing and was dedicating herself to writing instead. Her husband had gone to work in China, and she was expecting her second child. She would be thrilled to put me up.

And so it was that, in December 1984, I flew to Paris.

22

Starting Over

I'm used to going astray,
And every way leads to the goal.
(Franz Schubert, *Winterreise*,
set to poems by Wilhelm Müller)

In France, I didn't know a soul other than Xiaoqin. And, of course, I didn't speak a word of French. I was staying in her apartment in Issy-les-Moulineaux, yet I didn't dare go out because I was afraid of getting lost. Thus, for some time, Paris for me was reduced to a few streets in the suburbs.

Xiaoqin took very good care of me. She spent days on the telephone telling my story to her friends and asking them for help. As a writer, she knew many of the Chinese intellectuals and artists who had immigrated to France. Despite their willingness to help, however, they were perplexed about my situation. Was I American or Chinese? Was I a pianist, a house cleaner, a baby-sitter, a cook—what exactly did I want? Zhao Wuji, the renowned Chinese painter who had come to France in the aftermath of the Second World War, was looking for a caretaker for his house. Xiaoqin suggested me to his son, but Zhao Wuji couldn't imagine that a pianist would want to work as a caretaker, and nothing

came of it. It was only much later that I met him. He came to my first concert, and generously invited me to choose one of his works to use for the cover of my first CD.

After a few days, it became plain as day—my diploma from the New England Conservatory didn't mean anything to anyone in France. If my goal was to play and give concerts, I would have to make myself known to some influential musicians, and to do that, the best thing would be to go and study with them. Before leaving Brattleboro, I'd finally gotten up the courage to write Rudolf Serkin, who personally responded—like the gentleman that he was—inviting me to come see him. I told myself that I had missed the opportunity of a lifetime, that it had been a crazy idea to move to France, but it was too late to turn back.

Xiaoqin made some inquiries. I had already passed the age limit for the Conservatory, but the École Normale de Musique didn't have the same restrictions; I could go there and study. She advised me to contact Marian Rybicki. He spoke English and I would be able to explain my situation to him.

The very next morning I telephoned him.

"I am a Chinese pianist, and I have just arrived in France from the US, where I was studying. Would it be possible to play something for you?"

"Of course!"

He was so welcoming that I immediately followed up with:

"When might I come?"

I heard him page through his datebook.

"The earliest I can manage is the day after tomorrow. Would that suit you?"

That meant I only had a single day to prepare! Xiaoqin didn't have a piano at her house, and I hadn't played in a good two weeks. We hurried over to Daudé, the well-known piano showroom on Avenue de Wagram, where there are magnificent Steinway pianos. They were out of my price range: I just had enough to rent the least expensive, smallest upright piano, which was berthed at the back of the store. But that was good enough for me to work on my beloved *Davidsbündlertänze*. I didn't have much time.

When the day came, I went to see Marian Rybicki. I asked about his rates: four hundred francs an hour. Since this represented a large part of my savings, I gave myself one hour, and no more, to convince him.

Marian Rybicki was as warm in person as he had been on the telephone. I described my personal and professional history to him in a few sentences, all the while keeping an eye on my watch. He was incredibly kind and asked me question after question. Meanwhile, I was preoccupied with my savings, dwindling as we spoke. I was impatient but did my very best not to let it show. When was he going to ask me to sit down at the piano? Finally, after a half hour had passed, he said:

"Wonderful. Now I'm very anxious to listen to you. What are you going to play for me?"

"Schumann. The *Davidsbündlertänze.*"

I placed my watch on the piano, and not merely because I was following Gabriel Chodos's example. The *Davidsbündlertänze* take approximately thirty-seven minutes to play. Even if I sped up the tempo, I wouldn't be able to

play them in the remaining half hour: I was going to have to stop before the end. My watch would let me know when.

Even today, Marian Rybicki loves to tell the story of what happened next. I was in the process of playing the penultimate *Davidsbündlertänze* piece, one of the most beautiful in the series. At that moment, the alarm on my watch went off; the time was up. I didn't have the means to pay for anything more. I abruptly stopped playing.

Marian Rybicki leaped out of his seat.

"What's the matter?"

"I only have four hundred francs. I have just enough for an hour with you."

"You're out of your mind! I've never heard Schumann played like that before, and you stopped right in the middle! Obviously, I am not going to ask you to pay. Instead, let me know how I can assist you."

It wasn't difficult to know how to respond: he could help with so many things. I quickly explained my situation: I dreamed of settling in Paris; this meant obtaining a long-term visa as well as a scholarship. He listened to me very seriously, not saying a word, and then promised he would get back to me.

In less than two days, he had made good on his promise. During this time he had found a scholarship, a maid's room on the seventh floor of a building on Avenue de Suffren, and he had seven students standing by, ready to let me play their pianos, one for each day of the week. It was nothing short of a miracle. What I had heard was true: France really was a land of welcome!

* * *

I left Xiaoqin's apartment for my new home. The room was empty; furnishing it would have to wait for better days. But it didn't matter—I'd sleep on the floor. What was important now was not settling in, but getting down to work. Working to get myself known, once again, at thirty-six years old, an age when most concert pianists already have a long career behind them. I never ceased to pay for those long years of education-less "re-education."

Happily, the students Marian Rybicki introduced me to were a great support, and many of them became close friends. Like me, most of them had also left their native counties; together, we formed a bulwark against adversity. Despite my miraculous encounter with Marian Rybicki, I learned how hard Paris can be for foreigners. We stuck together and accompanied each other though the inevitable administrative obstacles, without which France would not be France.

The most flamboyant of my friends was called Braz. He was from Brazil, and he turned out to be an unbelievably sensitive pianist. Born into an upper-class family from Rio de Janeiro, he lived the high life in Paris—at least for the first two weeks of the month. The rest of the time, having gone through the monthly allowance he received from his parents, he didn't even have enough money to eat. I met him during one of these periods. For some time now, I had been a master of making delicious Chinese food with just a little rice, a few eggs, a bit of carrot, and some peas. This was how he made it through to the end of the month.

Braz's working method was the exact opposite of mine: he got down to work in his own good time.

"You practice too much," he would always say.

One day, I told him about the shock I had experienced coming up out of the Pont Neuf metro station: before then, I was completely unaware that Paris was so beautiful. I admitted that, since my arrival, all I had seen of the city was the inside of the metro. Braz shot me a dismayed look:

"Clearly, I'm going to have to step in, or you'll never stop working."

And thanks to him, I came up from underground. He became my first Paris tour guide.

Later, after Braz had gotten acquainted with my maid's room—which didn't take long—he suggested that when I practiced the piano at his place, I might also take advantage of his more comfortable bathroom facilities. I readily agreed. One Sunday morning, however, I couldn't open the door of his apartment with the key he had given me. I repeatedly tried the lock, but nothing helped. I was still at it when suddenly the door opened and Braz stood on the threshold, grumpy and half-asleep.

"Xiao-Mei, what's going on?"

"I came to practice the piano—I'm sorry, I didn't know you were here."

"Not only am I here, but I'm not alone. And it's Sunday morning! Don't you know anything about life?"

* * *

Nasi also became my friend. She was an Iranian princess—beautiful, elegant, and discreet in a quintessentially Middle Eastern way. She was also my first French teacher. With her, Braz, and a few other friends, including Lin, a Chinese woman married to a reverend, we often did things together.

Even if we didn't have a cent, we attended concerts, visited Paris, read books out loud, and led a wonderful bohemian life, always busy, always laughing.

* * *

Another of Marian Rybicki's students would also come to play an important role in my life: Madame Aalam. She was over eighty but looked twenty years younger, and her life was like something out of a novel. She was the daughter of one of the Shah's physicians. At twenty, a bit like my mother, she had left her family to run off with a Russian violinist with whom she had fallen head over heels in love. Later, in Iran, she opened one of the first institutions dedicated to the education of young girls, before fleeing the country when the Pahlavi dynasty fell.

The first time we met, she told me the story of how, one day, when she was in charge of the Iran House at the Cité Universitaire in Paris, a group of young Maoists had heatedly criticized her for her past. She invited them to her house to talk it over. By the end of the evening, they had all become friends. I quickly saw that she had a quality that I will never possess: she was fearless!

When she found out about the modest nature of my accommodations, she invited me to stay in her magnificent Paris apartment and take advantage of her Steinway. The morning after I moved in, I made the same offer that I had made to my other hosts: to do a little housework in exchange for a place to live. Her black eyes fixed on me:

"Absolutely not! Do you hear me? Never! On the contrary, my cleaning woman will take care of *you*. I want you to practice the piano without a thought of anything else."

It was the first time anyone had ever spoken to me like that.

She took me to the Louvre. In the Denon wing, she pointed out a statue to me, which stood at the top of a wide staircase.

"You see, when you go on stage, I would like you to be like her: victorious and masterful, but light and graceful at the same time."

I admired the masterpiece that rose in front of me: the Winged Victory of Samothrace.

"I understand what you have been through," she told me another time. "What you need now is to have confidence in yourself."

She had a very oriental way of affirming and promoting me. When we took the bus, she would announce to the conductor that he had the good fortune to be chauffeuring a great pianist. When we went to buy medicine, she would inform the pharmacist that he was waiting on an important artist. In those moments, I didn't know which way to look, but what could you say to someone who one day declared, in all seriousness:

"If I knew that it would allow me to play *Kinderszenen* the way you do, I'd be ready to leave immediately for ten years in camp at Zhangjiakou!"

* * *

A few months had gone by when Marian Rybicki announced that he had organized a series of concerts in Poland for me. My first tour! Six concerts!

The first event was held in the house where Chopin was born, in Żelazowa Wola. At the end of the concert, I was congratulated. The audience had enjoyed how I had played the Mazurkas, which I had worked on with Marian Rybicki. I was reminded that my fellow countryman, Fu Cong, had received the Mazurka Prize for his interpretation of the same pieces at the 1955 Chopin Competition in Warsaw. Then, seeking an answer to a question that intrigued them, they asked: "Is there a particular Chinese aesthetic for the interpretation of these short works?"

I love Poland and its audiences, which are so sensitive to music. I felt a particular sympathy for this people, who, like the Chinese, were not yet free. I understood them, and shared their frustration.

I received a princely sum for the six concerts—the equivalent of two years' salary for a Polish worker. Unfortunately, the złoty was not convertible at that time, and I wouldn't be able to take the money out of Poland. I then had the idea of contacting the Chinese ambassador to Poland. I explained to him who I was and the nature of my call. I wanted to entrust him with my concert wages so that he could purchase scores of Chopin's music for the Beijing Conservatory. The ambassador was at first suspicious, then aggressive, and then subjected me to a veritable interrogation before hanging up on me. Another tie with my country was broken. When I think that Teng Wenji advised me not to leave China! Instead, I donated the money to Solidarity, which at that time was a symbol of hope for so many Polish people.

* * *

Back in Paris, I was faced with a new and quite difficult challenge: my student visa was about to expire, and I had to go and plead my case at the immigration office at the Prefecture of Police. On my first visit, I waited eight hours, and I finally reached the window just as the office was closing. The next day, I got up at five a.m. in order to be first in line. I didn't fare any better; after four hours, I was rudely turned away without being able to offer a word in my defense. I went back again—and again. I got a glimpse of a very different side of France: bureaucratic, indifferent, hostile. The only clear information I was able to obtain was that it would be easier for me to apply for French nationality with an American passport than a Chinese one. I would have to return to the States and wait a year and a half for my official papers to come through.

Everything had been going so well. In Paris I was happy, I had made wonderful friends, and I was starting to have a concert career. And now, due to the visa predicament, I had to turn around and go back. I felt bitter and discouraged. Would I ever find a permanent home?

I didn't have much choice. I made some calls to friends in America, hoping to find a place to land. Janet, a musicologist living in Boston, agreed to take me in.

I filled my bags with my few items of clothing and all my scores and flew to Boston. Janet owned two beautiful Blüthner pianos. I consoled myself with the fact that, at least, I'd be able to practice.

Unfortunately, it can sometimes happen that professional musicians have difficulty listening to the repertoire of others. Except for one musical work...

23

The *Goldberg Variations*

> *Returning is the movement of the Tao.*
>
> (Laozi)

There was simply nothing to be done about it. Following my arrival in Boston, I had to face facts: I couldn't impose my playing on Janet. I understood her reasons all too well—between working on her thesis in musicology and giving piano lessons, she was up to her ears in music. There was only one solution: I'd have to practice when she wasn't at home.

One day, when I was glancing through her extensive music library looking for a piece to sight-read, I fell upon a thick score by Bach, the *Goldberg Variations*. The work was composed late in Bach's life, and the story of how it came to be written is a curious one. Count Hermann Carl von Keyserlingk, the Russian ambassador to Dresden, suffered from insomnia. He commissioned Bach to write a work that his young harpsichordist, Goldberg, could play for him at night while he was waiting to fall asleep. It is one of the rare works that Bach—who never imagined a posthumous legacy—had printed.

I had never before attempted the *Goldberg Variations*, and I thought to myself that there was enough material to keep me occupied for a while.

I placed the score on the music rest.

The opening aria—what a gentle beginning! Here was music that took its time, that welcomed the listener. I went on to the first variation, and then the second. An hour and a half later, I was back to the initial aria, which concludes the work's thirty variations.

While I was practicing, I was unaware that Janet had returned home. This time, however, she didn't interrupt me. It wasn't until I had finished the last note that she came up to me.

"You can play the *Goldberg Variations* as often as you like," she said. "You have no idea how much good that did me. I could listen to them forever."

I was only too willing to oblige. For several weeks, I worked on the *Goldberg Variations*, sometimes up to eight hours a day, and Janet never complained. I became Goldberg to her Countess Keyserlingk. As soon as the opening notes of the aria sounded, she felt well again. As a sign of encouragement, she even presented me with a copy of Frederick Neumann's *Ornamentation in Baroque and Post-Baroque Music*. I, however, curiously enough, was not yet entirely won over by the piece: to be truthful, its overriding virtue was that it allowed me to play.

* * *

When Janet was just about to defend her thesis, I decided—in spite of the restorative virtues of the *Goldberg*

Variations—to find another place to live, so that she could work in peace. The first friend I asked to take me in replied, in all seriousness:

"It's out of the question. My husband isn't working. He is at home all day, and I can't leave the two of you alone together."

I couldn't get over it. First, that she could have had such a thought, and second, that she would dare to express it to me. *Remember,* I told myself, *you're not in China anymore*—a response like hers would have been considered a serious offense there.

Things went better with the second call: Mary and Ryan agreed to put me up. Mary taught ceramics at an art school, and Ryan was an insurance salesman. They lived outside of Brattleboro, where I had met them, in Saxon River, a village that had only a supermarket, a bakery, a post office, and a church.

At the same time, I applied for a job at the music school where I had previously taught. The answer was unequivocal:

"I'm sorry, but you left. That's it. This is not a hotel."

Next, I tried my luck at Smith College, one of the area's most prestigious institutions. I will never forget the compliments the Dean paid me following my interpretation of a mazurka by Chopin. I had played it for her to demonstrate my abilities. She promised to do her best to create a position for me, but there was nothing she could offer me at the present time.

I sent out fifty resumes; no responses. My friends suggested that I look for a position in Washington. I put all I had into a plane ticket, but to no avail.

Desperate, I tried my luck at the bakery in Saxon River. The owner, doubtful, asked me if I was ready to get up at

four a.m. every day. I explained to him that I had done that for years, in a labor camp. He stared at me, and then looked at my hands.

"They're too small; you'll never be able to knead the dough."

I thought of Professor Pan, who had once said: "Try to draw energy from the keyboard, not just transmit energy to it. Imagine you are kneading dough. You'll see, this will entirely change your relationship to the instrument." There was no point in arguing with the baker; he didn't think I was right for the job.

Things were not looking good. I had neither work nor any prospects. Thankfully, Mary and Ryan were there to support me. When, at the end of the first month I stayed with them, I tried to give them a hundred dollars to help out, Ryan refused. He was interested in everything, and not a day went by without him asking me about China or the Cultural Revolution. He went all out to keep me busy; on weekends he took me skating and on motorbike outings. I wasn't sure how I felt about the motorbike excursions, but I reassured him that they were great fun.

Meanwhile, Mary understood what I needed most— to have quiet time for myself. She was also an artist, and she understood the value of silence. If I was practicing when she returned home from work, she would slip silently into the living room to listen, gesturing for me to keep playing. When her friends came to visit, she told them not to disturb me. When she organized a party, she apologized. She showed me great respect, and I returned it in kind.

There was only one thing that Mary and Ryan couldn't understand: why I practiced so much. Mary would say to me gently:

"You don't have a job or any upcoming concerts. Where do you find the energy to keep up such discipline? Where does that come from in you?"

I didn't know how to respond.

* * *

But what I did know was that I had just had the musical encounter of my life. The *Goldberg Variations* completely took over my existence. This music contained everything: it had all one needed to live. The first variation gave me courage. I smiled when I rehearsed the tenth, which is playful; I sang to the thirteenth, whose musical line soothes me like no other work. The polonaise rhythm of the twenty-fourth had me dancing, and I meditated during the fifteenth and twenty-fifth, two of the three variations in minor keys: they moved me to tears.

Then there is the thirtieth, the famous Quodlibet that I understand as a sort of hymn to the glory of the world. The more I practiced it, the more it amazed me. By blending two popular songs from the period in the bass line that provides the backbone of the variations, Bach is at the height of his powers; the profane gives birth to the sacred, the most learned counterpoint gives way to the greatest simplicity. One day, I discovered the name of one of the two melodies that he used for this particular variation: "Cabbages and turnips drove me away—had my mother cooked meat I'd have chosen to stay." What were cabbages doing in this

sublime variation? At the same time, how was it not possible to recall the cabbages that we had been forced to harvest in the fields of Zhangjiakou, the same cabbages that turned up each day in my mess tin? It was a sign of fate. Even today, when I reach this final variation, I see the gloomy, arid hills of Zhangjiakou.

Finally, the initial aria returns, for me the most moving passage of all. Throughout the thirty variations, the tension mounts. Bach has drawn upon every possible human emotion. Then, suddenly, all that remains is a serene, comforting music, the exact opposite of the great crescendos that end so many classical works. Gently, the aria sinks into oblivion: a void that is not an expression of want, or death, but rather of well-being and light. As the music subsides, the spirit ascends.

* * *

I took my new working methods and tried to apply them to the *Goldberg Variations*, pushing them to the extreme. It was a difficult challenge, and only rarely was I successful.

First, I emptied my mind before playing. Then came the search for a tempo that simultaneously allowed the piece to breathe, brought out all of the splendors of the score, and also allowed thought to develop as naturally as possible. Incidentally, the search for a proper tempo is not confined to the world of music—one must seek it in life as well. Then I tried to uncover the thrust and the truth of the score. Finally, I disappeared behind the music, as though my study of Laozi and Zhuangzi had finally showed me that the best

pianists—like the best rulers—are those of whom one is barely aware, and that this was a worthy goal.

It was not as though I had found the key or discovered an explanation or a response to a question. I didn't consciously alter my manner of playing. Instead, each day, through practice, this new approach became more natural.

The more I worked on the *Goldberg Variations*, the more it seemed to me that Bach provides a perfect illustration of this horizontal thrust in music, of the line and movement that had become increasingly precious to me. Whether in the *Variations* or elsewhere, there are very few rests in Bach. The music is more about flow, with lines continually overlapping in the composer's learned counterpoint, even in the most prominent articulations in the discourse. As I see it, this is what makes Bach's music so soothing for its listeners. With few exceptions—such as in the two *Passions*—it is never dramatic or halting, but rather serene and sustained.

And yet, the *Goldberg Variations* provides an unsurpassed example of how this horizontal motion needs to be underpinned by the throbbing pulse of the bass—isn't the theme of the variations made up of the bass notes of the thirty-two measures of the initial theme? In the *Goldberg Variations*, it is the bass that is the giver of life.

I was astounded to find the most basic elements of Chinese culture in the *Variations*, as though Bach had had a premonition or was the reincarnation of a great Chinese sage. In my opinion, Bach surpassed his calling as a Lutheran who placed his art in the service of God. He is universal.

The intertwining musical lines of Bach's counterpoint reminds me of calligraphy, a typical Chinese art form that is

primarily the art of breathing and meditation. When I practice, I think of the great masters of Chinese calligraphy who withdrew into the silence of the mountains. They watched and contemplated, refraining from any action, until one day they found they were ready. Under the Ming Dynasty, the eighteen-year-old prince Zhu Da was forced to flee the Manchu invasions and become a monk in a mountain monastery. He lived there, poor and unknown, spending most of his life in contemplation. Finally, he painted a few rare masterpieces and achieved fame at an advanced age. Zheng Banqiao, a prodigious painter of bamboo trees, spent forty years of his solitary life contemplating and painting his subject. He wrote:

> *When you think you are descending,*
> *you are climbing, but you do not know it.*
> *When you think you are climbing,*
> *in reality you are descending.*
> *Keep working and one day, without expecting it,*
> *you will achieve your desire.*

I took heart from the stories of the lives of Zhu Da and Zheng Banqiao. Instead of being destroyed by the poverty, the anonymity, and the scorn that they both suffered—they grew stronger.

My attempts to withdraw in my thoughts to the mountains, as they had done, helped me to achieve a long-sought goal: to disappear behind the composer. In doing so, I feel as though I no longer exist, and therefore cannot willfully place myself between the composer and the music. All I can do is show the composer's genius.

The range of musical climates and moods in the *Goldberg Variations* reminds me of the concept of the "golden mean," which Professor Pan first told me about. Through this work, I think I now understand what he meant. The point is not to take a middle path that is a type of compromise resulting from a refusal to choose extremes. Rather, it is about finding a point of equilibrium that allows one to bring out every dimension of the work. What is special about the *Goldberg Variations* is that it calls on every human emotion, every feeling. This is what makes it one of humanity's greatest masterpieces, and why it speaks volumes to an audience. In this work, Bach has put life itself to music—life in all of its infinite variety.

Buddhists always depict Buddha smiling. There are always two aspects to everything, to every being. There is no single truth—everything depends on the way in which one wants to see reality. That is life, and that is the *Goldberg Variations*. Through it, I also now understand why polyphony, Bach's in particular, affects me more deeply than any other type of music. By means of its various voices, it alone is capable of *simultaneously* expressing multiple and contradictory emotions, without one necessarily taking precedence over another.

And then, of course, there is the mystery of the aria that introduces and closes the *Variations*. Western musical masterpieces that employ such a structure are rare indeed. And none of them are as essentially Taoist as Bach's composition. It reminds me of what Laozi said about the Tao, that endless, universal movement infused with the breath of life: "Returning is the movement of the Tao."

The water of the initial aria gives birth to the river of variations; it flows, evaporates, and returns as a shower of

fine rain. Water is present in Bach's very name—*Bach* in German means "brook." The water of the closing aria is that of the opening aria, and yet it is not the same. We are witness not to an eternal return, but to a transformation.

The end has joined the beginning, but it is different.

24

A Haven

To breathe Paris preserves the soul.

(Victor Hugo, *Les Misérables*)

When I had received my US passport, I was finally able to leave the United States for Paris. I bid farewell to Mary and Ryan.

Madame Aalam welcomed me like her own daughter.

"Now we can look after you properly," she told me.

And indeed, my second stay in Paris would be characterized by the occurrence of one miracle after another. I met extraordinary friends, I became acquainted with France and the rest of Europe, and I discovered what respect for artists means.

To begin with, I finally started to explore the city. I love the weather in Paris, the colors of the sky, always a bit overcast and melancholy. I wandered along the banks of the Seine and through the streets, enchanted by the beauty of places I stumbled upon—the Place Dauphine, the Place de Furstenberg, and the Place des Vosges, where the memory of Victor Hugo still lingers. There are many churches that offer a glimpse of heaven as soon as you enter them: Saint-Julien-le-Pauvre, Saint-Germain-des-Prés. I discovered a

former residence of Marie Curie—a role model for me—as well as places where Chopin, Picasso, and others had once stayed. With every step I felt that my life was becoming linked with humanity's guiding lights. I went to the Père-Lachaise cemetery to see the Communards' Wall, imagining the final battles of the Commune. I visited museums and exhibitions—where else in the world do people stand in such long lines waiting to get into shows? I lingered in cafés; I liked watching the people who work in them, the swift, elegant waiters moving like actors on stage. Paris seemed marvelously beautiful to me. The only thing that shocked me was the way Parisians can lock themselves up in loneliness, the indifference they often display, the haughtiness of certain shopkeepers. But take it all around: is it possible to imagine a better place to drop anchor?

* * *

Madam Aalam put me in contact with a couple she knew—Jean-Luc Chalumeau and his wife, Estelle—whom I had met at her place before my departure. They both sensed my secret desire to finally have a place of my own, and it was Jean-Luc who helped me find my first real apartment. It was just a little studio on the second floor, and gave onto a fairly dark courtyard, but it was in a building on the Quai de Conti where he and his wife lived, and the rent was affordable. I moved there in the early fall of 1988. It was my own home. Something I'd never had before.

However, if I were to settle in, I had one final task: I had to buy a piano. A real one, a grand piano. Not a Steinway, certainly—that was beyond my means—but a solid instrument

on which I could practice in a professional manner. Then came the delivery day for the piano. I couldn't help thinking about that *other* piano, the one that had been delivered to my parents' house when I was three years old. What had become of it, the Robinson, my faithful companion at Zhangjiakou? For the first time in my life, I was deliberately unfaithful to it. I had replaced it. Would it be upset with me when I confessed what I had done?

My neighbors soon became friends. Estelle found me my first students. Josette Devin, a member of the French Resistance in World War Two, was a great source of moral support. I learned from her that it is possible to have "known the smell of fear" and still live happily. The American painter Marion Pike, who painted stupendous portraits of André Malraux, Coco Chanel, and others, gave me several of her paintings—in time, she suggested that I sell them to pay my rent, which of course I refused to do. Laurence Rousselot, my first student, not only suggested that I join her in the south of France but also offered me a train ticket to get there. Thanks to her kindness, I took the first vacation of my life.

Anna Kamp was drawn to my apartment by the music she heard coming through the thin walls that separated our two flats; she insisted on introducing me to her painter friend Gérard Fromanger, a well-known figure on the French cultural scene. Thanks to him, I met the cellist Alain Meunier. Alain spontaneously suggested that I play with him at the Accademia Musicale Chigiana in Sienna. One of the works that we interpreted together was Beethoven's Sonata No. 5 in D Major for Cello and Piano. The score had not been on my music rest since my chamber music sessions at Zhangjiakou

with Like. I started to play it: D–F sharp–E–D, D. On my old Robinson, the string for high D was among those that I had replaced with wire; this was the first time I was able to hear the note as it should sound! A few months later, he invited me to perform with him at the Paris Conservatory. Alain's wife was Annick Goutal, the well-known perfume creator. She was very beautiful, the embodiment of French sophistication. Her elegance was matched only by her generosity: a good example of this was how she invited the street person who lived outside her building to come wash up in her bathroom when he needed. He thanked her with bouquets he put together using flowers salvaged from a nearby florist. Since her death in 1999, I've never stopped thinking about her. I often pass by her house. The street person is also no longer there.

During my first stay in Paris, my intimate circle consisted mainly of foreigners. This time I also had French friends— and what friends they were!

Each individual filled me with courage, and this allowed me to believe in myself. One day I asked Estelle if she wouldn't mind helping me organize my first real concert in Paris. I intuitively thought of my two favorite churches, Saint-Germain-des-Prés and Saint-Julien-le-Pauvre. In the end, it would be the latter. My choice of program was already clear to me: the *Goldberg Variations*. After all the years, I sensed the moment was right: I felt ready.

Saint-Julien-le-Pauvre is in the center of Paris, but it feels like a country church, with its lingering Romanesque touches, its heavy buttresses, and its small, round chapels. The intimate atmosphere it creates reminds me of Chinese architecture, a contemplative space that perfectly matches Bach's music.

Sue Fleisher kept her promise and was there for my first concert in France. Even though she was battling terminal cancer, she wanted to be present with me one last time, in the country of her childhood. She arranged for a program to be printed in which she explained the history of the church and the legend of Julian the Poor as told by Flaubert in his *Three Tales*. Flaubert—the bourgeois writer whom I had been forced to denounce during my self-criticism at the Conservatory. I thought back to the second of the *Three Tales*, "The Legend of Saint Julian the Hospitalier," which is another name for Saint Julian the Poor. I remembered the scene in which Julian slaughters an entire herd of deer, and is cursed by a great stag who intones: "Accurst! accurst! accurst! one day, ferocious heart, thou shalt murder thy father and thy mother!" Julian's two parents wander in search of him, and finally arrive at his castle, "an old man and an old woman, bent and dust-covered, wearing coarse linen garments, each leaning on a stick." I thought of my mother and father, whom I had not seen in nearly a decade, and I wished they could have been present.

I spent some time visiting the church in order to connect with its spirit; I felt entirely at ease there. Preparing for the concert seemed superfluous. This time I trusted myself.

* * *

The following Wednesday, the weather was a bit brisk as I headed over to Saint-Julien-le-Pauvre. The church was full. All the seats in the nave and the aisles were occupied, and the audience was starting to sit on the floor, up against the platform that my building's caretaker had insisted on putting

up himself, out of friendship. My friends had gone to great lengths to help; without either a poster or any kind of advertisement, word of mouth had brought everyone together. Yet another miracle. Estelle informed me that the parish priests had prayed that my concert would be successful.

It was after nine thirty when I was told that I could begin the concert. I sat down at the piano and began the aria. Everything was so simple, natural, and easy. After everything I had been through, the time had come. The silence that reigned in the church let me know that I was in communion with the audience. I played the final notes of the closing aria as if transported.

My first real public success. At forty years old.

Ever since that evening, Saint-Julien-le-Pauvre has remained for me a place of solace, contemplation, and protection. Whenever I feel my spirits flag, or before a concert, I go there to pray or meditate: whatever word one uses, the act is universal. You don't have to be a Christian to experience the special atmosphere of this little church. I prefer it to its larger neighbor, Notre Dame, which is magnificent, but much less intimate.

* * *

The concert was my salvation. I began to plan projects, and I was regularly asked to give concerts. However, I still needed to take on French citizenship. Once again, my friends did their utmost, taking turns helping and accompanying me through the process. Nasi often got up with me at five a.m. when I had to wait in line for six hours. Another friend, Blandine Gravereau, helped to prepare my citizenship

application with so much care that it became a model file within the Prefecture. Madame Aalam took the matter in hand in her typical Middle Eastern fashion, thanking the government employees in charge of my application with Gucci bags!

And finally, one friend from this small circle helped me to buy the Steinway piano I had always hoped for.

When the piano tuner made his first call to my little studio, he said straight out:

"I'm sorry, but this will be my only visit. It makes me heartsick to see your piano installed here. Look, it's right next to the radiator; that's going to damage it."

He was barely out the door when I switched off the heat. I had a cold most of the winter, but the Steinway stayed in tiptop shape. Another piano tuner, Helmut Klemm, took care of it. This simple, unassuming man, who tunes pianos for renowned musicians, agreed to do the same for me. During our first meeting, when our conversation turned to the *Goldberg Variations*, he took from his briefcase a photocopy of the twenty-first variation: he carried it along with him everywhere he went. With only a few words, a friendship was born.

* * *

In 1990, yet another miracle occurred. A small record label offered to put out my first CD, a recording of the *Goldberg Variations*. My friends encouraged me: "Accept the offer," they said. "Without the publicity that a CD offers, it's going to be hard to give concerts." However, I wavered: "Don't leave any traces on the earth." I recalled with a smile the

story about Laozi that my American seatmate had told me on the flight to Los Angeles. Laozi, who all his life had refused to write anything down, and had done so only under duress, right before he vanished forever. At the risk of overstatement, I enjoyed the parallel: I would record the *Goldberg Variations* and then I, too, could disappear. I would leave behind the thing that was, for me, the most important.

The recording went well. Then, just as the CD was about to be released, I received a call from the publisher: due to financial difficulties, he had to drop the project, he could no longer afford to put it out. But, he added, there was always the possibility that I could underwrite the CD myself. The cost would be about fifty thousand francs. To fail so close to completion seemed crazy, and I really liked the recording. I talked with friends and then made a decision: I would borrow the money necessary for the project. The CD needed to find its audience. I paid the fifty thousand francs to the editor. And nothing happened. He had filed for bankruptcy.

Panic ensued. I had only one person to turn to, Antoine Tchekhoff, the guardian angel of musicians. Antoine is a lawyer and a music-lover—so much so that, for pianists, he often waives his fees. I think, on this point, there is a real difference between France and the US. In the States, when I told people that I was a pianist, they were nonplussed.

Antoine's assessment of the situation was clear: there was very little chance that I would be able to recover the money, and the best I could hope for was a supply of CDs. Thus, I found myself with a fifty-thousand-franc loan to be repaid. Once I had taken care of my monthly installments for the recording and the Steinway and had purchased my

subway pass, I didn't have much left for living expenses. But I had three hundred CDs.

Happily, despite an extremely limited distribution, the recording received very positive reviews in the press. Antoine, like many of my wonderful friends, took on the role of impresario and decided to organize a second concert for me in Paris. It was still too soon to imagine playing in one of the prestigious venues, and so it took place in the auditorium of the Sacem.

This second concert would have had only a small circle of admirers if Estelle hadn't managed to convince the music critic from *Le Monde* to come and hear me—the occasion for yet another miracle. Contrary to all expectations, an article about me appeared in the paper the following day, entitled "The inner strength of Zhu Xiao-Mei." I read and reread the article, wracked with anxiety: I couldn't grasp the nuances of the French, and I was worried that each turn of phrase was actually criticism.

I saw that the critic had compared me to Artur Schnabel and Clara Haskil, two pianists whom I hold in high esteem. But in which sense had he made the comparison? My friends reassured me that the article was indeed positive.

* * *

I had recorded my first CD and given my first concerts. Thanks to Alain Meunier, I had a position teaching at the Paris Conservatory. Now I could return to China. I could see my parents without feeling ashamed.

My parents, my friends—I wondered if they would recognize me, how they would greet me. It had been twelve

years since we had seen each other! I couldn't run the risk of surprising my mother, but if I let her know too far in advance, she would make herself sick waiting. I held off until the last minute before I wrote to her: she would have to wait a week, that wasn't too long.

Then it was time to think about gifts. I didn't have the means to buy presents for everyone, but I had to bring perfume for my mother—a real bottle of Dior from Paris. It would replace the one she had saved as a souvenir of happier times in Shanghai, the bottle that the Red Guards had smashed in front of her. And a book about Zhao Wuji, whose work fascinated my Chinese friends.

The Christmas holidays arrived. It was time to leave.

25

The Tree of Mama Zheng

*Acknowledge diversity
and you will achieve unity.*
(Rabindranath Tagore)

Beijing Airport. My plane from Paris had just touched down. For years I had waited for this moment, but now, I suddenly felt awkward, like a stranger. There they were, standing in front of me: my father, my four sisters and their husbands, as well as nieces and nephews whom I had never met. They had all turned out, except for my mother. As I had feared, the announcement of my arrival had made her ill.

I gazed at my father, unable to believe my eyes. Everything about him seemed smaller—his height, his face, his eyes. I didn't dare touch him, or address him as "Papa." We were overwhelmed with emotion, and everyone was impatient to ask me questions, but tradition won out. We exchanged a few pleasantries: they thought my voice sounded lower, and I learned that they had been waiting there for two hours, for fear of missing me. But we had to hurry—the reunion dinner was waiting.

* * *

264 | ZHU XIAO-MEI

My parents had moved since I had left China. They now lived in a 270-square-foot apartment on the fourth floor with no elevator. To get there, one had to climb an untidy, narrow flight of stairs, cluttered with neighbors' garbage pails on the landings. The windows faced a dark courtyard, and there was no bathroom. At their age, this is what my parents had been reduced to: an apartment that was even more miserable than our original family home, and much worse than I could have imagined. The apartment itself was impeccable, proof of how much time they had spent making it presentable—they no doubt imagined that I lived a life of luxury, and were afraid that I would find their apartment unacceptable.

I was overwhelmed by tremendous feelings of guilt; despite twelve years in exile, their daughter still didn't earn enough money to help them. They, on the other hand, had continued to keep my piano in their tiny living quarters.

My mother did what she could to welcome me, but she became dizzy if she kept her eyes open too long. Seeing me literally made her ill. I don't know why, but I handed her the bottle of Dior perfume I had purchased for her, in the naive hope that it would soothe her. But of course, it did the opposite. Both the scent and the memories it invoked made her nauseous.

A sumptuous meal had been laid out on the apartment's only table.

"Do you remember?" she asked me. "When you left for Hong Kong, it was just before the New Year, and you couldn't celebrate it with us. Well, here's the dinner that we couldn't have together."

I looked at the dishes that she had lovingly prepared. Every kind of dumpling, and my favorite dessert, *Tangerduo,* or "sugared ears." As the evening wore on and we ate, talked, and laughed together, I saw my mother slowly come back to life.

* * *

The party broke up late in the evening. I lay down in a corner of the hallway, the only place in the apartment where there was enough space for me to stretch out. When I awoke, about six the next morning, I could see three little candles flickering on the table. My mother was drawing. I didn't move a muscle, pretending to be asleep so as not to disturb her, while I observed her through half-closed eyes. The sky grew light. My mother put away the candles and her materials. She was waiting for me to wake up.

As we were eating breakfast, my father told me a piece of news:

"You're not aware of this, but your mother is a celebrity now. She was on television the other day. The journalists wanted to finally learn who had composed the well-known children's song 'Let's Go to School'—it was your mother. She wrote it forty years ago."

"Why are you telling her that? If children like my song, that's fine, but it is unimportant."

My mother hadn't changed a bit. I thought my father seemed less calm, but gentler. He was no longer the same man who had sent me the letter that had meant so much to me. He managed a photocopy shop for its two young owners. This was a more interesting job than it seemed;

photocopies had recently made their appearance in China, and were being used to spread ideas quickly and discreetly.

My father also mentioned that my mother took painting lessons every day, that she had recently been in a group show in Shanghai, and that she had met with a certain degree of success. Since she was feeling well enough to go out, I suggested that I accompany her to her class. At the age of seventy-five, she still had the desire to learn: I admired her for that, and at the same time, I understood what it meant. During the long, dark night of the Cultural Revolution, art—and painting in particular—had been her salvation, just as music had been mine.

After our return, while I was helping her to prepare lunch, she let slip that the piano had been tuned in preparation for my arrival. She didn't ask me outright, as was her custom, but I guessed that she was very anxious to hear me play. But I couldn't, not just yet anyway. It was too soon. I still had the sound of the Steinway in my ears.

* * *

My mother's artistic activities made her an exception in China. As the days went by, I was amazed to see just how materialistic the Chinese had become. All they seemed to want was a larger apartment, a television, a refrigerator. I didn't recognize my country anymore. But I understood why it was happening.

My American passport gave me access to special stores, and I was able to buy appliances to make life easier for both my parents and my friends. I spent whole days going shopping with, as usual, mixed emotions. On the one hand, I

felt extraordinarily happy to be able to help my family, yet I also experienced a sort of sadness. There we were, standing in line to buy a refrigerator instead of sharing our experiences, or expressing everything that we hadn't been able to say for so long. Nevertheless, once the purchases were made, I felt free. Free to become reacquainted with my very oldest friend.

* * *

There it stood, just like on the first day, despite its yellowed keys. Faithful, discreet, humble, and kind. The one I had plastered with an ignominious *Dazibao*, the one that had crossed China in a coal car, the one whose strings I had patched up with wire. The one I had almost sold to buy a plane ticket, the one I had thrown over for a Steinway. It was generous and courageous—two of the three qualities of an ideal husband.

I could hear it sighing: "I'm old now, you see. I've done all I can for you, and I'm tired. I never said anything, but if you only realized how cold I was in Zhangjiakou. Leave me in peace. I'm useless: I'm no longer enough for you. I'm aware that you've been unfaithful to me. Everyone knows that Paris is the land of temptations…"

It also had the third quality of an ideal husband: a sense of humor. I told it that, contrary to popular belief, the French are not unfaithful—at least not in friendship.

And I played it for my mother: Schumann's *Reverie*. Just as she had played it for me when I was three years old. My first piece of music.

* * *

It was time to visit Professor Pan. I knew that he was now considered one of the very greatest teachers in China. He had no telephone, so I couldn't call in advance, and the Conservatory, where he still resided, was more than an hour away from where my parents lived. But I had to try. When I got there, around five in the afternoon, the buildings resounded with music. Everywhere, students were in the process of practicing. I stopped to listen for a moment—they had no idea that the pieces they were playing had been forbidden three decades earlier. That students had been packed off to camps to be "re-educated." That scores had been burned. That professors had been driven to suicide.

I rang the doorbell at Professor Pan's apartment.

"Zhu Xiao-Mei! I can't believe it!"

There he stood, looking at me with a big smile.

"You haven't changed one bit!" He called to his wife, "Look who's here! We must buy something for dinner tonight."

We spent the evening together, talking over the dozen years that had passed since my departure, about their son, who was a member of the Singapore Symphony Orchestra, and about the hordes of young people who were now studying the piano. Professor Pan knew all of the great Western pianists, either through their records or from having attended their concerts in Beijing. I asked him who was his favorite.

"Murray Perahia," he answered. He went on: "There are now many great foreign pianists who come and perform or give master classes in China. I also listen a lot to their recordings. Oddly enough, I don't take that much away. After so many years, I think I have arrived at similar results.

And it also seems to me that there's always something lacking in their playing."

I couldn't resist a smile when I heard his words. No doubt there were Westerners who thought that Chinese people were incapable of understanding Beethoven; but here one of the greatest Chinese masters was saying that Westerners didn't understand him either, or at least not fully. There was a gap on both sides. When interpreting music, the hardest thing is not merely to express something, but to express it to another culture.

I talked to him about how cultures overlap. About I.M. Pei's pyramid at the Louvre. About the magic I heard Seiji Ozawa bring out of the Boston Symphony Orchestra. A unique sound, as if a single musician were playing—and yet, what a mosaic the orchestra was! Germans in the string section, French woodwind players, and a Japanese man at the podium. The result surpassed anything you could imagine: the very best from every school had been selected. They were all listened to and respected, and produced something unique and new—a form of perfection. As the great Indian author Rabindranath Tagore once remarked: "Acknowledge diversity and you will achieve unity."

"I would have loved to see and hear all that," he answered. "How fortunate you are."

We then talked about Beethoven's Opus 111. He asked me if I had played it. When I told him I hadn't, he urged me to tackle it immediately.

"These days," he said, "I spend hours with the second movement. I feel so well when I play it. I want time to stop, for it to never end. Do you remember what our dear Romain

Rolland said about it? 'A nearly impassive smile of Buddha.' That's beautiful, isn't it?"

Much later, standing at the door, he confided in me:

"This is no doubt the last time that we will see each other in Beijing. I want to live a normal life. Here, we are endlessly wondering what the future will bring."

And in fact, shortly after my visit, he and his wife left China to join their son in Singapore, where I still go to see him from time to time.

* * *

After I left Professor's Pan's apartment, I lingered for a moment on the Conservatory grounds. The school was being expanded, and there was a lot of new construction. Night had fallen and all was still. Unbidden, images rose to the surface—of broken lives, victims, the dead.

I found myself in front of the infirmary. Here, too, the bulldozers had done their work. The tree from which Mama Zheng had hung himself was gone. He had no family to honor his memory, and there had been no funeral service after his suicide. Now there was nothing left of him, not even his tree.

It's time that I paid him tribute.

Mama Zheng, you were a great man. You gave up wealth and honors to take care of us children. I learned later that you were related to Sukarno, the Indonesian president, as well as to Zhang Ji, a minister to Chiang Kai-shek. You could have chosen an easier path.

"Mama Zheng"? No. Huabin Zheng was your name, and it's high time that it be given back to you.

We return it to you, Huabin Zheng, we, your children. In the name of all of the students of the Conservatory, I want to say thank you. Thank you for everything you did for us. And let me proclaim the truth that no one dared to utter at the time: you were innocent. Your life—and the lives of the other victims of injustice—gives meaning and purpose to this book.

Farewell, Huabin Zheng.

26

Life Starts at Forty

At fifteen my heart was set on learning;
at thirty I stood firm;
at forty I had no more doubts;
at fifty I knew the mandate of heaven;
at sixty my ear was obedient;
at seventy I could follow my heart's desire
without transgressing the norm.

(Confucius)

The Chinese believe that life begins at forty. It always amuses me to think about this, because that's exactly how old I was when my career really started to gain momentum.

After my return from China, I began to receive a number of offers to perform. My network of friends continued to help make things happen. I couldn't get over it: were there many other people whose professional debuts began so late in life?

At the same time, these projects threw me into turmoil. I wasn't used to playing so often or so many different programs in such a variety of venues. A feeling of anxiety began to slowly surface in me. This was not my pace, this was not how I wanted to live. But I had no choice—if I turned the

offers down, I soon wouldn't receive any at all. This is the harsh reality of the performing artist's world.

My friends told me not to worry. Their network was functioning admirably. At the Conservatory, I became acquainted with the musicologist Rémy Stricker, an extremely cultivated man with an in-depth understanding of both music and musicians. He treated his students like his own children. Before every concert, I liked to play for him. I trusted him implicitly. Then, a young impresario joined our circle. He was twenty-three years old at the time and looked like Saint-Exupéry's Little Prince. He was both sensitive and intelligent, and played French music from Rameau to Ravel like no one else. He had everything he needed to succeed, and had already started on the path to a brilliant career. But Alexandre Tharaud—that's who I am referring to—is also extremely generous, and he began to keep an eye out for me. After hearing my recording of the *Goldberg Variations*, he bought dozens of copies without telling me and handed them out to concert organizers, saying:

"She's the great pianist, not me. She's the one you should invite."

This was not true, of course, but very moving. It was, however, the start of a long musical friendship that would lead us to play piano four hands together often.

* * *

The first major Parisian venue to take a chance on me was the Théâtre de la Ville, a concert hall that is still very dear to my heart. This is in large part due to the personality of Georges Gara, its musical advisor. I initially met him

through a common acquaintance, Benoît Choquet, who was a supporter from the very beginning. Georges had fled Hungary, and had been a publisher before coming to work at the Théâtre de la Ville. As fellow emigrés, we hit it off immediately. One day, in the course of a conversation, he asked:

"If you could give a concert here, what would you play?"

There was only one possibility. The *Goldberg Variations*.

A few days later, he called me:

"You're on the program for next season."

That was in 1994, and the time had come for my official Parisian debut. The hall was completely full. But in spite of how successful the concert was, it made me ill for months, both before and after the actual performance.

I felt incapable of attaining the perfection that I desired. I was, like so many musicians, devastated by my powerlessness. Like Richter who, at the end of his life, stated, "I don't like myself." Undoubtedly, a wiser path would have been to admit that perfection did not exist. The Chinese understand this very well—in a piece of embroidery or calligraphy, they will deliberately introduce a fault, believing that the flaw renders their work even more beautiful. The Iranians do the same with their carpets to show that only God is capable of perfection.

Yes, the smarter thing to do would have been to admit this. To model myself after the *Winged Victory of Samothrace*, in all its powerful, mutilated beauty. Instead, I chose to not even walk in front of the Théâtre de la Ville, which was right around the corner from where I lived. I finally managed to quell my anxiety and stood in front of the theater, only to break down in tears at the sound of an organ grinder

playing a nostalgic melody of exile. A passerby came up to me:

"Excuse me, madam, was it you who played the *Goldberg Variations* the other night?"

I held back my tears.

"Yes, that was me."

"It was magnificent. Thanks to you, I've started to listen to Bach. But I see that you're upset, and I won't bother you any further. Thank you so much."

* * *

That first concert at the Théâtre de la Ville was followed by several others. A year later, I played Scarlatti, Mozart, and Schumann—my beloved *Kinderszenen*, with its *Reverie*. The *Goldberg Variations* had placed me in the category of "serious pianist"—as it does for every pianist who takes it on, heaven knows why—and the audience perceived this new program as strangely light and childlike, as if childhood could not be at the same time an age of great maturity.

Then there was a Haydn and Beethoven concert.

A few days before the performance, I felt so discouraged that I called Georges and told him that I was not going to be able to play. He came to my house that very evening.

"What's wrong?"

"I'm not happy with what I'm doing."

"If you want to cancel the concert, we'll cancel it. And we won't call in a substitute. But before we do that, I want you to know one thing. Although neither of us are churchgoers, I can tell you that when you play, a feeling of spirituality

fills the hall. People stay on after the concert; they just can't seem to leave."

What could I say? Georges had convinced me: the concert took place. He had found a way to describe the connection that links a performer and the audience.

During a recent trip to Beijing, I visited Teng Wenji, and we talked about his latest films. At one point in the discussion, he said:

"When I first walk onto a film set, I say a prayer before filming."

I asked why, although I already anticipated the answer.

"Because we're disturbing the spirits. We make noise and cause a commotion. No one asked us to come; we have to apologize for our presence."

We both smiled. Since then, to tell the truth, I have adopted the same ritual. When I arrive, I pay honor to the place, because it is always sacred. I like to breathe in its atmosphere well before the audience begins to file in. I walk around the entire building, touching the walls, the seats, the boxes. They speak to me, and I absorb their history.

My most successful concerts have always occurred in theaters and churches, venues where I can sense something.

Take the Théâtre de la Ville. It's been a favorite ever since my first concert when, before going on stage, I rehearsed on a small upright piano on the top floor, beneath a portrait of Sarah Bernhardt. I'm known by everyone there. When I call the switchboard, the operator says to me:

"Hello, Xiao-Mei. I recognized your voice."

I feel very much at home.

Other places include the little Chapelle Sainte-Cécile near Tours, the church at Lourmarin—one of the main

venues of the La Roque-d'Anthéron festival—the Martinu Hall in Prague, and the Teatro Bibiena in Mantua, where Mozart once played and which Richter loved so much. And then there's the Teatro Colón in Buenos Aires, a place I especially like, even though I also almost canceled my first concert there.

* * *

I had just arrived in Argentina. Roadwork was underway near the hotel where I was staying, and my room was incredibly noisy. Since I didn't speak a single word of Spanish, I was unable to make the people at the reception desk understand that I needed a quieter room. The concert was fast approaching, and I could neither meditate nor concentrate.

Early in the afternoon, I called the organizer to tell him I was going to cancel. He came over immediately. He was insistent, repeating that everything was planned for the concert and that he couldn't cancel it. Then he added:

"Visit the theater, and we'll talk afterwards. Come along, I'll take you there."

A few minutes later, I walked into the Teatro Colón.

"Look around; go wherever you like. I'll wait for you here."

I entered the hall. It was enormous, but at the same time, it was permeated by a strange feeling of intimacy, of warmth. I visited the boxes, each one unique. I admired the curtains, the ceiling, the chandeliers. Here, the greatest artists had performed, and the audience knew one another, you could feel it. I went downstairs. The gilded silence of the hall gave way to the bustling activity of a veritable small

city, where several hundred people were busy with costumes and sets. I watched them working away intensely, as if their lives depended on it. Women smiled at me and stopped what they were doing to speak with me. We didn't get very far because of my lack of Spanish, but I was extremely moved by them. Of course I would play that evening.

A few hours later, when I walked on stage, I felt very well. Under my feet I imagined the activity of the small city; I recalled the faces of the women I had glimpsed that afternoon. I greeted the audience: many of them had the score of the *Goldberg Variations* on their laps. I hadn't been mistaken: this was indeed a unique place.

After the concert, a music critic sought me out.

"I must be Chinese," he told me. "Everything you played has convinced me it's true."

He was exaggerating, of course. But what better proof of music's universality that a Chinese woman was able to win over a South American man while performing a European composer?

* * *

Of the many moving places I have visited, for me the most stirring of all is the Thomaskirche in Leipzig, where Bach worked from 1723 until his death, in 1750. It was during this period that he composed his greatest works. I had always wanted to visit Leipzig, and a concert in former East Germany finally gave me the chance. The French Cultural Institute had organized a performance in Hoyerswerda, a town where, ten years earlier, a group of skinheads had carried out attacks on Vietnamese street vendors and other

foreigners with the tacit approval of the local population. Even today, people still refer to "Hoyerswerda Syndrome." I decided to play the *Goldberg Variations* in memory of these immigrants, who were victims of racial violence. When I walked onstage, the atmosphere was chilly, so chilly in fact that I—a Chinese woman who dared to play Bach in his native land—could readily identify with the Vietnamese who had been beaten. As the *Variations* unfolded, however, a sense of community began to set in, and by the end, the applause was such that I had to take several curtain calls. The audience didn't want to leave. I asked for silence, then offered these few words:

"After Bach, one can play nothing else."

The entire audience rose to its feet. They had given me their blessing.

I had never before been so close to Leipzig. The next day, buoyed by the previous night's reception, I shared my desire with the cultural attaché, a friend, who had arranged the concert. She warned me that the Thomaskirche had been restored on several occasions, that certain parts were new and that the building's authenticity was debatable. I told her that it didn't bother me. She telephoned the church to see if we might be able to visit. Unfortunately, it was closed for repairs. It didn't matter. I still wanted to go; it would be enough to breathe the air of Leipzig. My friend Marion offered to accompany me. As we drove along the roads of Saxony in her car, I began to feel emotional, and then tearful. Happily, Marion didn't see. I felt so ridiculous crying over such a little thing. How could I explain what this trip meant to me? How could I tell her that right then, as we neared the city, I suddenly became aware that Bach had

really existed, that I might have met him, gotten to know him, seen him play?

I recalled another pilgrimage that I had made a very long time ago, to Shaoshan, Mao's native village. This pilgrimage was the genuine one, but would Bach find fault with me for comparing the two journeys? I asked for his forgiveness: *Master, I apologize for this thought—please know that this pilgrimage is sincere. After everything I have been through, allow me to say that, thanks to you, I once again became a human being. That I learned about life, and about myself.*

We arrived in front of the Thomaskirche and—miraculously—it was open. Wherever he was, Johann Sebastian Bach was looking out for me. I asked Marion if I could have a few moments alone, and I entered the nave. There was Bach's tomb beneath my feet, bearing this inscription that overwhelmed me with its simplicity:

<div align="center">JOHANN SEBASTIAN BACH</div>

Nothing else. No dates, no titles. Only what was essential—just like his music—not a single extra note.

For quite a while I stood there in silence by his tomb. Then I explored the Thomaskirche from top to bottom, sure that I would find some trace of Bach. I climbed the bell tower, touched the stones and breathed the air. On the way out, I said to Marion:

"Now I can die. I have no regrets."

A few years later, at the end of my appearance on the cultural television program *Double Je*, Bernard Pivot asked me the famous Proust Questionnaire, which I love.

"If God exists," he asked me, "what would you like him to say to you?"

"You've been courageous enough. Come, I'll introduce you to Bach."

27

A Wounded Life

One who is skillful in using men puts himself below them.

(Laozi)

The Cultural Revolution scarred me for life. Each morning when I get up, I wonder how I can go on living, how I can find peace after what I have experienced. The legacy of that period has left me with a severe psychological handicap.

The sessions of collective denunciation I endured rendered me perpetually afraid of criticism, unable to trust either myself or anyone else. When one has lived through such a regime, when one has been forced at twelve years old—at an age when one *cannot be guilty*—to criticize oneself, then what is a friend or a family member but someone who will denounce you tomorrow, and that you will in turn criticize?

Whenever I walk onstage, there is always a moment when I wonder why the audience has come to hear me. I am tremendously grateful, but at the same time I want to give them their money back; I do not deserve their presence. Doubts begin to set in: the audience is actually there to criticize me, to judge me, just as if it were a self-criticism ses-

sion. Only my faith in music gives me the strength to carry through to the end.

* * *

I also fear being manipulated, as I was so often in China. I try to tell myself that I was young at the time of the Cultural Revolution, and therefore susceptible to all forms of propaganda. This was the case and is why I have always felt an aversion to student demonstrations. But it wasn't just students who were involved. Hundreds of millions of Chinese—people who were older and more experienced than us—allowed themselves to be indoctrinated. Age didn't make any difference, either in China or in any other country that experienced totalitarianism. I try to understand how the Communists' noble ideas could have led to such a catastrophe, or how, for years on end, I couldn't see anything or didn't want to believe what I saw. I try, but I simply don't understand.

The Cultural Revolution was debasing; it turned me into a perpetrator. At one point, it even extinguished in me all sense of a moral life. I criticized my fellow human beings, accused them of grave misdeeds, investigated their pasts. I took an active part in a process of collective destruction. How can I ever be free of such things?

Five years ago in Paris, I met Shaohua again.

Shaohua, on whom I had willingly informed. She came to give a concert one Sunday, as part of a string quartet. At the end of the performance, I went backstage to congratulate her. I felt relief just seeing her again.

"I hurt you so much. It still causes me pain, and I can't bear it. Is there something I can do? Can you ever forgive me?"

Shaohua gave me a tender smile:

"You've already been forgiven a thousand times over. We were so young. We are all victims of the Revolution."

During the conversation that followed, I learned that she had been window-shopping in Paris and a coat had caught her eye. The next day, I dashed over to the shop, but it was closed. The following day Shaohua returned to China—without the coat. It was better that way: I was naive to think that a piece of clothing could close a wound, or right a wrong with its attendant feelings of guilt.

I felt the same inability to redress the past when it came to my grandmother. Shortly after Shaohua's visit, my family undertook to finally provide my grandmother with a decent headstone, and we all contributed towards its purchase. I was moved by this idea. She had done so much for me, and she was such a role model. I felt as though I were reunited with her—or better yet—honoring her. Once again, a futile solution. How could money possibly make up for all those years when I believed it more important to be a zealous revolutionary than to write to her?

* * *

Friends gave me passages from Hannah Arendt to read. I found her description of one of the governing principles of totalitarian regimes very accurate: the "arbitrary selection of victims," the first step in the process of total domination. Arendt elaborates:

The next decisive step in the preparation of living corpses is the murder of the moral person in man. [...] Through the creation of conditions under which conscience ceases to be adequate and to do good becomes utterly impossible, the consciously organized complicity of all men in the crimes of totalitarian regimes is extended to the victims and thus made really total.

When I read this passage, I relived my own experience. At thirteen years old, I was definitely an "innocent victim," selected through a process far greater than myself. I had been branded a *Chushen bu hao*, a person with a bad family background. Then came the second step: the Cultural Revolution took away my status of innocent victim and made me an active participant in its crimes.

I am continually haunted by this part of my past. In a certain sense, I was released from prison only to become a prisoner of myself.

I often wonder whether I should hate Mao Zedong for what he did to me. On a purely theoretical level, his analyses were not incorrect. The Chinese people did need to be liberated. How could I forget the documentary they screened for us at school, which showed the sign the English erected at the entrance to Waitan Park. On it was clearly written: "Dogs and Chinese Not Admitted." Nor could I forget the peasants who were so cruelly exploited, or the old woman I met during my first session of *Yi ku si tian*. Despite these things, and the spirit of hope he kindled, Mao was a criminal. He was responsible for killing tens of millions of people, and for the moral deaths of hundreds of millions more. Therefore, yes, I hate him. And every passing day deepens

my hatred of this man who, since he lacked the courage to admit his mistakes, carried out a cynical headlong rush into the future. "One who is skillful in using men puts himself below them," as Laozi said. Mao kept himself above men, even if it meant killing them to remain there. During the thirty years that I have lived in fear, in despair of ever finding inner peace, I have had time to understand this.

* * *

After the Cultural Revolution, there were no important trials, except one for the Gang of Four. Nothing at all like the Nuremberg trials organized in the West in the wake of World War Two.

No doubt this is because the truth of Mao's disastrous reign has yet to be precisely established, due to a lack of well-researched historical studies. How many deaths were caused by the Cultural Revolution? By the Great Leap Forward? The full extent of the catastrophe remains unknown, as well as the real reasons why it happened. The time has not yet come for an objective assessment of what occurred.

It is understandable that the Chinese people wish to turn the page on those dark times and finally lead normal lives. I think, however, there is a deeper source for this attitude, which is their concept of life. It can be found in the first great book of Chinese philosophical thought, the *I Ching*. Its title—known in English as *The Book of Changes*—says it all. Life is a continual process of transformation, and it is this process of change that we should honor, rather than a return to the past. Criminal acts are not forgotten, but a sort of natural justice that only the passage of time can

bring about eventually supplants human justice. Chinese philosophers have an expression for this: *bu de liao*—knowing when to leave the past behind, instead of endlessly seeking revenge.

On the other hand, the absence of criminal justice is evidence of a profound weakness. The trials that followed World War Two immensely buttressed the West's resolve: by enshrining the principle of "Never again!" Western nations encouraged a sense of vigilance. They strengthened universal moral standards and forged new ones, all of them designed to prevent, now and forever, the return of the Hydra.

28

Music, Water, and Life

Great sound is silent.
[...]
The Tao is hidden and nameless;
Yet it alone knows how to
render help and to fulfill.
(Laozi)

In 2003, I was seated in Dr. Krishna Clough's office at the Institut Curie. My tests had come back positive, and his diagnosis left no room for doubt. I thought about my mother, who had refused chemotherapy. Like her, I was scared to undergo this type of treatment, not so much because of the suffering involved but because I feared it would destroy my energy. I asked the doctor how long I would have if I did nothing. He hesitated a moment. Three years, at the most.

For the first time, I was confronted with the truth that we all try to hide from: one day, we all pass away. Oddly, this thought, which could have plunged me into despair, relieved my anxiety. After all, three years is a long time. I had led a very rich and varied life.

I had experienced everything—except for happiness and peace—but I didn't think that they were within my reach.

I was still sitting in Dr. Clough's office when I became aware of what I still desired to do. I wanted to play the entire piano repertoire, to record as much as possible. The final sonatas of Beethoven and Schubert, to understand what those towering figures were attempting to say as death approached. The complete *Well-Tempered Clavier*, my constant companion since Zhangjiakou. For the longest time, I had thought it was easier to play than to listen to, but I now glimpsed the possibility of communicating it to a wider audience.

What I wanted to do was to play music, to record masterpieces, to not leave this earth regretting that I hadn't done that. I wondered if three years was too short to fully accomplish it. No, it should be possible.

And yet, when I returned home, I fell apart, overwhelmed. Just as I was beginning to become successful, everything came crashing down, one more time. It didn't make any sense.

My friends urged me to follow Dr. Clough's recommendations and undergo treatment. Finally, Josette, the friend who had introduced me to this eminently sensible doctor, found the right thing to say:

"Be reasonable. Here, you are surrounded by family—your family of friends. Your illness has been detected early, don't waste any time. Take matters in hand."

I was tempted to seek the solitude of the mountains in China, where I thought I could regain my health in the

290 | ZHU XIAO-MEI

silence of nature. But I couldn't play or record there. It was then that I decided to follow my friends' advice.

I was extremely touched by the expressions of friendship that poured in. While I was still in the hospital, I received invitations to perform. One difficult month followed another until, one day, I returned home and was reunited with my beloved Steinway. That day I found myself as emotional as when I had come across that worn-out accordion in the courtyard at Yaozhanpu, or when my piano arrived at the Zhangjiakou train station. I played the *Goldberg Variations*. And I was reborn.

Once again, I was saved by music.

* * *

While I was still a child, I lost everything, but music helped me to survive.

Then, at the Conservatory, ideology got the upper hand. It convinced me that books and musical scores should be burned, that *The Little Red Book* was enough. When I arrived at Zhangjiakou, I had been reduced to a brainwashed wild child. During my first year there, I don't remember having felt a single emotion. Like my companions, my mind was empty. We had all been turned into puppets, into machines programmed to blindly obey the regime's every command. Music became something of minor interest; my revolutionary activities were so much more important!

Mao had always understood the power that art—and music in particular—had over the people. He knew that artists were dangerous individuals, constantly questioning reality, always demanding more freedom. For this reason

he attacked them, and allowed his wife to appropriate art through her *Yangbanxi*. Mao actually considered knowledge itself to be dangerous—his organized, systematic, and extremist obscurantism is proof of that.

But the power of music is such that it inexplicably thrust its way back into my life. The weakness and gullibility of "Thousand-Drops" played a role in this rediscovery. Far less intelligent than Mao, he had no idea of the domino effect he was setting in motion by not banning our concert. He was unlike any of the other commanders of artists' camps, where it was strictly forbidden to touch an instrument.

Like my companions, I also sensed that the regime, in all its madness, had pushed us to the brink of total dehumanization. So far, in fact, that we couldn't go any further. The Cultural Revolution was on the verge of stripping us of our humanity completely, and this was impossible. Just as we were about to be transformed into beasts, some sort of instinct saved us. Deep inside us, there remained a spark of humanity. At their peril, totalitarian regimes—which underestimate a human being's resources—always forget this fact. Music blew on this spark and revived it.

* * *

Our reawakening to music, and to art in general, changed everything—both for me, and for my camp companions. Music gave us back our humanity. It offered us a glimpse, far off in a corner of the sky, of the possibility of spirituality. It

taught us how to love again, including in the most concrete sense of the word: five couples were formed at Zhangjiakou.

It was in camp that I understood music's power, and how fortunate I was to be a musician.

Music brings people together, in ways that politics or religion cannot. It instills a powerful love of humanity that allows you to overcome every hardship. When you play music, you give of yourself unconditionally—and this is my definition of love.

Only now I am able to understand the extent to which my experience of the Cultural Revolution taught me to never use music's power to impose anything on my audience. I suffered too much under the yoke of servitude, and I prefer to speak rather than to compel. Perhaps this is what moves certain listeners. I often think back to my seat companion on the flight to Los Angeles, who quoted Laozi:

> *The best man is like water.*
> *Water is good; it benefits all things*
> *and does not compete with them.*
> *It dwells in lowly places that all disdain.*
> *This is why it is so near to Tao.*

I can now better comprehend what Laozi was saying. Water is useful, it serves. It descends and does not rise. It nestles in the unloved hollows, not in the heights where everyone dreams of world domination. It competes with no one, and yet it overcomes rock—the hardest substance in the world. Without water, life would not exist.

* * *

This is one reason why, since I have lived in France, I have tried to bring music into prisons, retirement homes, hospitals—places of despair.

I remember one concert I gave in a prison in Bergerac. It was under the auspices of Musique Espérance, an association created by the Argentine pianist Miguel Ángel Estrella. Before the concert, I gave a great deal of thought to the program, hesitating between light, accessible works and more serious pieces. In the end, I once again chose the *Goldberg Variations*. I shared my plans with a few friends: they were skeptical, they thought the work was too long and not right for the "general public." They instilled enough doubt in me that I finally decided to perform only a few of the variations.

Before I started to play, I said a few words to the hundred inmates who had decided to come to the concert:

"I don't know why all of you are here, in this prison. But I can tell you that I was also once in prison: I spent several years in a labor camp in China. There, at one time, it was believed that people who liked the music I'm going to play for you needed to be 're-educated.' It was composed by Bach, and is entitled the *Goldberg Variations*. Since it's quite long, I'm only going to play ten of its thirty variations."

The prisoners didn't want me to stop, and one hour later I had played the entire piece. The small upright piano on which I performed was totally out of tune, but I gave it everything I had. Then, an older prisoner spoke up:

"Could you play some Beethoven for us?"

I obliged with the *Waldstein* Sonata, which I often interpreted at that time. He came up to me at the end of the concert:

"I know who you are. I recorded one of your concerts that was broadcast by France Musique. You played the *Waldstein* then as well. I listen to that cassette every single day."

As I was leaving, I asked one of the guards why the man was in prison.

"A crime of passion," I was told.

* * *

After everything I have experienced, I cannot take an intellectual approach to music. When I play, I try to speak to people, to tell them something, to show them the beauty of a work, to move them. Having an audience is crucial for me. Some of my fellow artists assert that they play for themselves rather than for an audience. I take the exact opposite approach: my goal is to share with others.

Humanity is the truth of music. What is important to me is that, this evening, I may be able to reach one person, someone who is not a musician. That I might be able to reveal a part of his or her humanity, of our shared humanity, of which he or she may be unaware. And one day, who knows, perhaps this may help that person to speak out when what is essential is threatened.

29

Wisdom and Non-Being

He who conquers himself is truly strong.

(Laozi)

These days, when I get together with my former classmates from the Beijing Conservatory, they always bring up the same topic:

"Xiao-Mei, you don't have any safety net. Who's going to take care of you if you're ill?"

What this means is, *You haven't really achieved success because you aren't able to assure a comfortable lifestyle for yourself.* But since we are really old friends, they add:

"Don't worry. We'll take care of you when you're old."

For many of them, the impact of the Cultural Revolution had been too overwhelming; they gave up on their artistic careers, thinking that it was too late to start again. One became a real estate agent, another is an acupuncturist, others work in piano import-export. Even those who became musicians invested their money, and nearly all of them have become wealthy. The Cultural Revolution destroyed their idealism. But, by an odd twist of fate, it turned them into capitalists instead of communists!

* * *

My friends are not wrong, of course. After I recovered from my illness, I thought a great deal about how uncertain my situation was; I worried how I would earn a living if a relapse put an end to my musical career. That said, material success is the exact opposite of what I am seeking, of the feeling of accomplishment I am after.

And I have come close to this feeling. I experience it each time I think I'm ready to interpret a work after many years of practice. The first time this happened was when I performed the *Goldberg Variations* in Paris. It seemed that nothing bad could happen, and that I knew—as strange as it seemed for someone who lives in a perpetual state of doubt—exactly what had to be done.

Yes, those moments—which one hopes for all of one's life—are blessed moments of clarity. But they are rare and pass too quickly. The Chinese word for happiness, *kuai le*, says it all—it literally means: "fleeting happiness." For Chinese people, there are moments of bliss, in a day or in a lifetime, but they never last.

Also, it often seems that when people finally fulfill their dreams, it is too late. This is something with which I have often been confronted.

In 2001, when I was finally granted French citizenship, I asked my parents if they would like to come visit me in Paris. My father refused, which I was half expecting. As a good Chinese philosopher, he saw travel as superficial and useless.

"What good would it do?" he asked. "How can you discover a country in just a few days? Don't hold it against me, but to me traveling seems pointless."

My mother, on the other hand, accepted with pleasure. She had longed for such a trip since she was a child. She came with one of my sisters and her husband.

When I met her at the airport, she was in a wheelchair. Several years ago she had begun to suffer from Alzheimer's disease, but I immediately saw that her condition was now considerably worse. My sister explained how hard it had been to get through customs—our mother had forgotten everything, even her own name.

I took her to all of Paris's great museums: the Musée d'Orsay, the Picasso Museum, the Musée d'Art Moderne, and of course, her beloved Louvre, where we went nearly every day. I wheeled her through the painting galleries, where she talked about each work of art. She already knew many of them from art books, or from having copied some of them. I felt that she was happy. But once we had left the Louvre, she almost immediately forgot that we had spent the entire afternoon there.

A friend took her on a tour of Paris in her car. We drove past the Théâtre de la Ville:

"That's where Xiao-Mei performs," she said.

My mother looked at her:

"But what does Xiao-Mei do for a living?"

My mother had always hoped to see me play in a great concert hall, but she never imagined that it would happen in Paris—Paris! And now her dream had come true; her daughter was a "success" in her understanding of the word, and now this was something she could no longer grasp.

Success in itself is nothing. Once you have achieved it, the most difficult task still lies ahead—mastering yourself.

Some people are helped by religion. Others, like my mother, don't seem to need it. They draw instead on a sort of natural strength—an inner power, fate—or simply life itself. In any case, it is something spontaneous and unconscious. I admire such people. There exists a life force in spontaneity and the unconscious that is often underestimated. This can be seen in Zhuangzi's story of Hui and the Centipede. One day, Hui asked the Centipede:

"I walk by bouncing on one foot. I can't imagine doing as you do. How do you use so many feet?"

And the Centipede answered:

"I do it naturally, without knowing either how or why."

A baby cries but never harms its voice. Drunks, like sleepwalkers, rarely hurt themselves.

In order to play, one must avoid thinking too much, so as to rediscover one's spontaneity and the power of the unconscious. Because it is in those moments that receptivity to others and to the world's vital, spiritual energies come together—and inspiration may descend.

* * *

Wisdom dwells within us, it seems to me, but finding that wisdom requires efforts that are often painful. All my life, I have defined myself by my relationship to what is exterior: people's opinions of me and the various forces to which I have been subjected. For a very long time, the endless sessions of self-criticism and denunciation—which I find so difficult to forget—kept me from being myself.

Now I am beginning to understand: for the truly wise, the exterior is unimportant. Their strength is inside them.

Even when they are imprisoned, rejected, and reviled, they understand that liberation lies within.

The piece that expresses this best for me is Beethoven's final sonata, Opus 111. It was the favorite piece of both of my masters, though one lived in the East and the other in the West. Its second movement consists of variations. Once again it seems that, in order to express the inexpressible, one must speak of a process of *transformation*, parallel to that found in Chinese philosophy. A simple, unadorned theme, close in its essence to the aria of the *Goldberg Variations*.

The theme of the arietta in Opus 111 leads us forward in the same gentle way as the *Variations*' aria. An initial variation followed by a second, in *fugato*, heightens the tension. The third variation then arrives; many pianists play it as if it were a furiously paced piece of virtuoso jazz, although I feel that it is imbued with nobility. We are nearing the renunciation. The fourth variation lifts us into another world; with the rising *pianissimo*, we break the bonds of earth, we climb into a resplendently colored sky, piercing the banks of clouds that encircle the planet. We are elsewhere. The fifth variation summons both the piano's highest and lowest notes, the ones I loved to hear when I was first learning to play. Here, Beethoven throws open the instrument to the whole world, both the yin and the yang. The original theme then reappears, like a hymn to the glory of the world, before disintegrating and sinking into a sort of nothingness, which, in itself, is a sort of deliverance.

We have reached a place of supreme wisdom.

* * *

It is perhaps clear by now that, of all the great Chinese philosophers, it is with Laozi that I feel the closest affinity.

To demonstrate the difference between Confucianists, Buddhists, and Taoists—who are disciples of Laozi—the Chinese like to invoke the allegory of the glass of water. The Confucianist says: "This glass of water must be shared. Give your parents the first sip." For the followers of Confucius, the greatest virtue is the social order, how society is organized. The Buddhist says: "Must I drink?" because, for him, the most important thing is mastering emotion and desire. Finally, the Taoist looks at the glass and says: "Water does not exist."

30

Return

When the storms still raged,
I was not so miserable.
(Franz Schubert, *Winterreise*,
set to poems by Wilhelm Müller)

It is 2006. This January 27th marks the 250th anniversary of the birth of Mozart. Is there another great artist—musician, writer, painter—whose exact birthday we celebrate in such a manner? Leonardo da Vinci? Shakespeare? Dante? Who would do such a thing? "Happy Birthday" is what we wish to children, and Mozart is a child—but one who experienced everything, and thus was a child who possessed the wisdom of an elderly sage. Laozi prefigured Mozart when he wrote:

He who is in harmony with the Tao
is like a newborn child.

Finally, I found the strength to seek out my old camp companions. For more than two decades I had stayed away: seeing them would have filled me with despair.

I took advantage of several concerts in Tokyo to search for Cunzhi, my bassoonist classmate. It was Cunzhi who was beaten before the entire Conservatory on that summer night in 1966, the memory of which still haunts me. I knew that he

had given up his career and moved to Japan, where he opened a Chinese restaurant. A white-haired man approached me— Cunzhi! We hadn't seen each other in over thirty years. Although we didn't shed tears, we were overwhelmed with emotion. He told me how, several times a year, he transforms his tiny restaurant into a musical salon. He invites artists to perform, and plays himself from time to time. In all, he has organized more than two hundred musical events.

We talked over what had happened during that long-ago summer: the summary executions, the bodies stacked up in the Conservatory's annex.

"I was lucky," Cunzhi simply remarked.

The fate of this talented musician—who had everything he needed for a career as a great soloist—was intensely moving, but he did not speak about it. The moment came to say good-bye. I tried to find the right words:

"You are the real hero of our class. You endured everything—ostracism, fear, violence, and solitude. But you have remained true to yourself, an idealist, just like I remembered you."

* * *

I received news of Huang Anlun. I knew—we all did— that after leaving China, he first went to Yale and then to Canada, and that he had become one of the greatest contemporary Chinese composers. I learned that he had converted to Christianity. But music inspired by Christianity was only permitted to be played in churches.

Were Christian works banned from public performances simply because freedom of expression is limited in

China? Or was the authorities' decision also a defensive reaction against religious proselytism—a word that is not easily translatable into Chinese—which is viewed as a form of aggression? Since the West continues to adopt the same viewpoint for every culture other than its own, such proselytizing is not only religious, but also, in a more general sense, cultural in nature.

Christianity—which means a great deal to me—suffers from this flaw of wanting to convert others, to extend its influence. The very concept is foreign to the Chinese. Buddhists, Taoists, and Confucianists all practice religions that are more akin to philosophies. China never experienced anything like religious warfare, and the idea that one single religion can encapsulate truth is incomprehensible.

* * *

2006. Return to Beijing.

My mother asked me to play the *Piano Music Masterpieces* from my childhood for her. The doll I purchased in Boston kept watch near the piano; through it, I remain close to my mother's side. My mother remembered each piece in the collection, and hummed them along with me. One day, she asked:

"Could you teach me how to play?"

I helped her to sit at the keyboard, but she was unable to attempt anything. I played Schumann's *Reverie* for her. She looked at me:

"How is it that you play so well?"

* * *

For once my father, who hardly says a word, had a favor to ask of me. He wanted to pay a visit to the grave of his friend Lao Xue, the president of the university where my father worked for so long; it was also thanks to Lao Xue that I was able to find employment after my return from Zhangjiakou. This man was so important to my father that, as the end of Lao Xue's life approached, my father visited him every day.

We called his son to ask about the exact location of his father's grave. It was off in the countryside, not far from the Great Wall. We had trouble finding it, and only the presence of a large pine tree finally showed us the way.

My father spoke to his friend:

"Lao Xue, I have come to see you." Then he turned to me: "Xiao-Mei, we have forgotten to bring wine for Lao Xue."

I went in search of some water.

"It's all right," he told me. "Laozi preferred water to wine."

We each drank a mouthful and then, in accordance with Chinese tradition, my father poured out the rest onto his friend's burial place.

He stayed and talked to Lao Xue for two hours, while I waited at a distance. I owe you my thanks as well, Uncle Xue.

It was time to leave. In the car that took us to Beijing, my father was lost in thought, not uttering a word. Then, suddenly, he told me:

"I also want to be buried there, when the time comes." After a moment, he added, "Lao Xue was the only person who trusted me during the Cultural Revolution."

It chilled me to hear him say this, but it was true. We, his family, did not stand by him during his ordeal. As children,

my sisters and I thought he was harsh with us. Later, the regime taught us to mistrust him, to withhold our love.

As we drove into Beijing, my father had something else to tell me. Ever since I moved to Paris, every afternoon at five thirty p.m., he listens to a daily program broadcast on Chinese radio devoted to France. If he has to go out, even to visit friends, he brings a transistor radio with him, so he doesn't miss this daily appointment.

"I have been by your side," he concluded simply.

* * *

I had another visit to make. I wanted to see Aizhen again, the friend who had, the day after my self-criticism session at the Beijing Conservatory, left something on my desk for me to eat. We hadn't seen each other in thirty-two years.

One night in Paris, she had appeared to me in a dream. I awoke with a start, unable to get back to sleep, tormented by the thought that I hadn't sufficiently thanked her. I got up and found pen and paper; I had to write to her. But she had never written back, and since then I couldn't stop thinking about her.

How the two of us had changed.

"I'm ashamed that I abandoned my career," she told me.

And yet, Aizhen had been a very fine musician. After the Cultural Revolution, she had been sent to a job in Dalian, an intellectual and cultural wasteland. There, she had poured her heart out giving piano lessons to apathetic students, and had married a university professor. He was diagnosed with throat cancer the same year her daughter was born.

"After something like that, you realize you can withstand anything," she concluded.

Her husband was there, by her side. He had been ill again when Aizhen got my letter, and this was why she hadn't answered. I turned to him.

"I have to tell you—you married a very fine woman."

He smiled.

During our talk, I learned that her parents had always been Christians. Is that why she extended a helping hand when I was shunned by everyone else?

As we took our leave of each other, I felt a great rush of well-being. I had finally been able to thank my friend.

* * *

The time had come to return to Zhangjiakou.

A friend of mine from Beijing had convinced me to travel there with her. After arriving at the station, we began talking with the person who had come to pick us up. We wanted to try and visit Dayu. But it had been thirty years since I had been there, and after driving for some time we couldn't locate it. Finally we arrived at a large, modern prison with a high exterior wall—nothing like the damp, filthy buildings where I had been held. We were welcomed by the prison director, a pleasant man. I told him who I was, and he offered to give us a tour. We declined—the new prison had nothing to do with my experience. Nevertheless, as we were leaving, I asked him: were there political prisoners here? He smiled. No, not here, elsewhere. I decided that he could be trusted.

After we left, we walked around the town, which had completely changed. All around the new prison, neat rows of

two-story houses stood on either side of wide, well-maintained streets. What progress. No, clearly, all my points of reference had disappeared—except for the howling wind.

My friend took my arm. She wanted to show me the churches that had been built in the area. The nearest one was a very large yellow and white building. Its steeple looked like a minaret, so much so that I had to ask if it wasn't actually a mosque. But it clearly wasn't, as a service was being held at that very moment. We slipped inside and took our place among the congregation. There were hundreds of worshipers, most of them peasants, praying and singing hymns. I reflected on the church's interior, which was not completely successful. We had the same experience in Quijia-zhuang, near to my third place of imprisonment, where we secretly gave food to the starving peasants.

To think that people were praying in the same place where, thirty-five years earlier, we had been prisoners...I thought about the success of Christianity in this far-flung region of China. No doubt the local clergy had worked hard to make this happen. But the Christian faith also provided a community, that of Christians, which one could join. This stood in contrast to the great Chinese philosophers, who extolled the virtue of solitude and distance, of withdrawing from the world. Whatever the reason, the fact remains that many Chinese people who had once lived in misery, deprived of a future, had discovered hope.

As for me, I am more at home with Chinese philosophy— I prefer to be alone, face-to-face with myself, rather than in the company of others. Religion is too private a world to be shared. On the other hand, my life has been intimately bound up with a stalwart of the Christian faith—Bach. My

days and my nights have been devoted to his music. And Bach did not live like a sage in retreat from the world; he was always surrounded, always in demand, and he worked hard to make his music something through which one might glimpse the meaning of life. This idea of service is an important part of the Christian faith. Each person possesses a part of the truth, for those who can glimpse it.

* * *

As I left the last church, I once again thought about the project that had never been far from my thoughts: to create a school in China. Even though I left my country twenty years ago, I realized that I'd never given up the idea that I might someday return—despite my protestations to the contrary.

Before then, the idea of giving concerts in China didn't make a lot of sense to me. My generation—the lost generation—was mostly concerned with earning a comfortable living, which I can understand. For so long, they had been denied any sort of artistic education. But what about the new generation? Shouldn't we try to pass on to them some of our knowledge?

I began to have a dream.

I saw all of us together, myself, my former classmates, and a few others, in a school that we had founded, a school in which all the different arts were paramount. We would live with the students, talking and discussing things together. Classes would be free of charge. The money that each teacher had earned—in whatever varying degree—would be used to provide scholarships for the students. In today's

China, only very rich parents can afford to send their children to the Conservatories in Beijing and Shanghai.

The dream unfolds...I would do my best to share with my few students some of the truths I have glimpsed in my life as a pianist. I would try to convince them to serve only music, to turn a blind eye to materialism, to cultivate a spirit that is at once humble and passionate.

My friends and I would not only be able to pass on some of our experience but also rectify what was most painful for our generation. Even worse than our loss of freedom and the misery of our living conditions was that we were denied an education. The absence of books, scores, and even dictionaries—this was a torture far worse than the physical deprivation we endured: it creates a void capable of extinguishing the future and rendering death preferable to life. What good is an existence without the hope of growth—an existence that can only imagine before it the darkness of ignorance—and submission, which is ignorance's handmaiden? Yes, my friends and I are in agreement. The world needs to reflect on this lesson of the Cultural Revolution: to ensure peace and the future of the world, the absolute first priority is education.

In my dream, our school would be founded in Dayu, our former prison.

Aria

Alone, I walk through the streets of Zhangjiakou.

Often in my life I have chosen to return to the past to find the energy to go forward. I believe Zhangjiakou will give me this courage. It's true, life has brought me many things. But it has also broken me, left me unable to accept myself, forced me to subject myself to constant, unhealthy doubt.

The longer I live, the more I feel the presence of Bach and Laozi beside me. They have helped me to overcome past trials, and they will help me to face those to come, because the hardest trial lies ahead: to finally find inner freedom. I have the impression that I have not yet done anything with my life, and that I no longer have the strength to give it a sense of meaning.

* * *

The wind sweeps the streets of Zhangjiakou. The afternoon comes to an end. I look up at the sky. There are none of the red tonalities that led my grandmother to predict that my life would be a "resplendent tapestry," and yet, it is still the same sky. A somber sky of blues and grays, that of a cloudy spring day. But it is also a sky full of the subtleties and nuances that my painter friend, Fu, once shared with me here, in Zhangjiakou. Yes, now I can identify them all: shifting colors and mixed emotions. At night I question myself, I am afraid of others, of myself. I have an acute awareness of my impotence, my

inability to achieve perfection. But in the morning, I know that it is still there, in the next room, waiting for me. It always keeps its promise of fulfillment. My piano.

I contemplate the sky over Zhangjiakou. I hear the voice of my grandmother:

"The evening you were born, I looked out at the sky over Shanghai..."

Acknowledgments

With thanks to Dr. George Zhao of Skidmore College and Kristen Wanner of Harvard University Asia Center.

Sources

Arendt, Hannah. *The Origins of Totalitarianism.* Harcourt Brace, 1973.

Bach, Richard. *Jonathan Livingstone Seagull.* Scribner, 1970.

Chan, Wing-Tsit. *A Source Book in Chinese Philosophy.* Princeton University Press, 1969.

Dittmer, Lowell. *China's Continuous Revolution: The Post-Liberation Epoch, 1949–1981.* University of California Press, 1987.

Feng, Gia-Fu, and Jane English, trans. *Tao Te Ching, 25th-Anniversary Edition.* Vintage, 1997.

Flaubert, Gustave. *Three Tales.* Arthur McDowall, trans. Alfred Knopf, 1924.

Fox, Matthew, and John R. Mabry. *God as Nature Sees God: A Christian Reading of the Tao Te Ching.* Element Books, 1995.

Hugo, Victor. *Les Misérables.* Isabel F. Hapgood, trans. 1887.

Hugo, Victor. "The Sack of the Summer Palace." Reproduced courtesy of *The UNESCO Courier,* November 1985, 11.

Lang, Ye, Zhenggang Fei and Tianyou Wang, eds. *China: Fire Thousand Years of History and Civilization.* City University of Hong Kong Press, Kowloon, 1997.

Mao, Tse-tung. "Report on an Investigation of the Peasant Movement in Hunan" (March 1927). In *Selected Works of Mao Tse-tung,* Vol. I.

———. "Talks at the Yenan Forum on Literature and Art." In *Selected Works of Mao Tse-tung,* Vol. III.

Mitchell, Stephen, trans. *Tao Teh Ching.* Harper Perennial, 1992.

Naydler, Jeremy, ed. *Goethe On Science: An Anthology of Goethe's Scientific Writings.* Floris Books, 1996.

Rodin, Auguste. *Art: Conversations with Paul Gsell.* Jacques de Caso and Patricia B. Sanders, trans. University of California Press, 2007.

Urban, Louise McClelland, trans. *Schubert's Winterreise: A Winter Journey in Poetry, Image & Song.* University of Wisconsin Press, 2003.

Wang, Wei, Tony Barnstone, Willis Barnstone, and Haixin Xu. *Laughing Lost in the Mountains: Poems of Wang Wei.* University Press of New England, 1991.

Wu, Chung. *The Wisdom of Zhuang Zi on Daoism.* Peter Lang Publishing, 2008.

Wu, John C.H., trans. *Tao Teh Ching.* St. John's University Press, 1961.

Xing, Lu, *Rhetoric of the Chinese Cultural Revolution: The Impact on Chinese Thought, Culture, and Communication.* University of South Carolina Press, 2004.

About the Author

Zhu Xiao-Mei was born in Shanghai. She began studying piano in early childhood with her mother and by the age of eight had already played for Peking radio and television stations.

At the age of eleven she entered the Beijing Conservatory, where her studies were interrupted by the Cultural Revolution. She spent five years in a labor camp in Inner Mongolia. Despite the difficult conditions, she managed to continue to study the piano in secret. When she finally made it back to Beijing, she completed her studies at the Conservatory and left China, first for the United States and then for Paris, where she has lived since 1984.

Since then, Zhu Xiao-Mei's career, although late and without any media support, has been expanding rapidly. She has given concerts throughout France, Europe, North Africa, Russia, South America, Asia, and Australia, in search of the public in venues that speak to her and where

she enjoys playing, performing demanding works that she's nurtured for years, such as Bach's *Goldberg Variations*.

The Secret Piano was originally published by Editions Robert Laffont in October 2007 and received the Grand Prix des Muses in March 2008. This is its first publication in English.

Zhu Xiao also teaches at the Conservatoire National Supérieur de Musique in Paris.

About the Translator

Ellen Hinsey was born in Boston, Massachusetts, in 1960 and has lived and traveled widely in Europe for two decades, working on projects related to democracy.

She has been the recipient of a number of literary awards and prizes including a Berlin Prize Fellowship from the American Academy in Berlin and a Lannan Foundation Award. She is the author of *Update on the Descent* (2009), *The White Fire of Time* (2002), and *Cities of Memory* (1995), which received the Yale University Series Award. She has also edited and co-translated from Lithuanian *The Junction: Selected Poems of Tomas Venclova* (2008). Her recent translations of contemporary French fiction include *Someone I Loved* by Anna Gavalda and Hélène Grimaud's memoir, *Wild Variations*. Her poetry, essays, nonfiction, and translations have appeared widely in publications such as the *New York Times*, the *New Yorker*, and the *Irish Times*. She currently teaches at Skidmore College's Paris program.

Made in the USA
Las Vegas, NV
04 June 2022

49799425R00194